T. R. R E I D

Confucius Lives Next Door

T. R. Reid is *The Washington Post*'s London bureau chief. He has appeared on *Nightline* and *Meet the Press,* and has weekly commentaries on National Public Radio. Reid graduated from Princeton University and had several careers–Latin teacher, Naval officer, lawyer–before joining *The Washington Post* in 1977. He covered Congress and three presidential campaigns before taking over the Tokyo Bureau in 1990, and has written for numerous magazines, including *National Geographic.* T. R. Reid lives in London.

Confucius
Lives Next
Door

T. R. REID

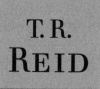

Confucius Lives Next Door

WHAT LIVING IN THE EAST

TEACHES US ABOUT

LIVING IN THE WEST

Vintage
Books

A DIVISION OF

RANDOM HOUSE, INC.

NEW YORK

FIRST VINTAGE BOOKS EDITION, MARCH 2000

The Library of Congress has cataloged the Random House edition as follows:
Reid, T. R.
Confucius lives next door / T. R. Reid.
p.   cm.
Includes index.
ISBN 0-679-45624-4
1. Japan–Social life and customs–1945– I. Title.
DS822.5.R43   1999
952.04–dc21   98-36438

Vintage ISBN: 0-679-77760-1

Author photograph by Katayoma Kishin

www.vintagebooks.com

Printed in the United States of America
10 9 8 7 6 5 4

To my oldest Asian friend,

Yoshida Makiko

Contents

Confucius
Lives Next
Door

The Other Miracle

WE TOOK A JET PLANE TO THE NEXT CENTURY.

When our thoroughly American family of five moved from the wide-open spaces of Castle Rock, Colorado (population 7,600), to the noise, rush, and crush of teeming Tokyo (population 27,600,000), we knew that we were in for a long journey, in more ways than one. The trip itself seemed endless–it took two taxis, four buses, two airplanes, one train, one subway, and more of those assembly-line meals on little plastic trays than I care to remember. Our flight to Tokyo took off in July and didn't land until August. While this was actually just a quirk that came from crossing the International Date Line, we all felt as if we'd been traveling for a month or more when the jet finally came to a stop at Narita International Airport. Still, we didn't realize how far we had come until we got settled in Asia and began to look around.

For a family that had previously considered it fairly exotic just to cross a county line, the prospect of moving to a vastly different culture had an element of adventure to it. Ever since my bosses at *The*

Washington Post had asked me, a few months earlier, to take over the paper's Tokyo bureau, we had been eagerly studying the life skills that we would need in our new home: eating soup with chopsticks, washing at the public bath, greeting people with a polite bow, taking a child's temperature in Centigrade, and so forth. But on that August afternoon when we finally landed at Narita and took our bearings, we felt deflated. The place looked depressingly ordinary. It was an airport, after all, a vast sea of concrete with planes from United and Northwest and British Airways tooling around and people with big orange fans in each hand guiding the planes to their parking spots. In the terminal, there were crowds of travelers and lots of signs, primarily in English, leading us to Customs, Baggage Claim, and the like. The PA system was broadcasting announcements in English as well. For this we packed up all our belongings and traveled halfway around the planet? We've been here, we thought. We've done this.

Fairly quickly, though, it became clear that this wasn't just another airport—or at least, not an airport like the ones we knew back home. Those workers out on the tarmac, guiding the planes, pumping fuel, unloading luggage, weren't dressed in the standard jeans and T-shirts; they wore neatly pressed gray uniforms, maroon neckties, and white gloves. And when our jet successfully steered up to the landing gate and came to a stop, the entire uniformed crew lined up on the tarmac beside the plane to give us a deep, respectful bow of welcome. As for the signs and PA announcements in the terminal, they were in English, but not the sort of English we knew back home. The first poster we spotted, just inside the door at International Arrivals, said, "Welcome to Here!" We found this friendly, if a little strange. When we boarded the shuttle bus to get to the train station, a chipper tape-recorded voice welcomed us again, in English, and said, "We hope you enjoy your life on our bus." Friendly, but a little strange. My favorite sign, on the wall of the Narita Airport train station, had a delicious ambiguity to it: "We are glad you could come in Tokyo," it said. Was this just a mistaken English preposition, or something more suggestive?

Over the next few weeks, as we adjusted to life in the new land, we found many more indications that Asia really was the distant and different place we had imagined. The countryside really was marked by patch after square patch of pale green rice shoots rising from the paddy fields beside bamboo groves swaying gracefully in the breeze. A couple of times I saw farmers in round-brimmed straw hats bending over the rice crop, knee-deep in mud—an image straight out of my junior high world geography text, circa 1960.

As we settled in Tokyo, and began traveling to Osaka, Seoul, Singapore, and the other major cities of East Asia, we relished the sights and smells and flavors that seemed to match our expectations for a place called The Orient. We bought fried octopus and roasted ginkgo nuts on the street. We rode that notorious commuter train out of Tokyo's Shinjuku station—our kids called it the pancake train—where polite conductors with white gloves really do push you onto the train, jamming three hundred riders into a car built to seat fifty. In almost every big city we found impossibly crowded, noisy, bustling, fragrant, and delicious Asian bazaars—tightly jammed collections of tiny shops, stands, or handcarts stacked with goods, with runners in rice-straw hats weaving through the crowds, pushing wagons filled with fresh fish or bunches of bananas or color TV sets or cases of sunglasses or massive burlap sacks full of rubber bands.

These places were incredibly fun and colorful—and great shopping as well. On Petaling Street in the old Chinese section of Kuala Lumpur, I bought not one but two solid gold watches for a total price of $8. Genuine Rolex, too—the salesman told me so. In the marvelous Nandaemun Market in Seoul, where youthful waitresses slithered through the crowded alleys with five lunches, on five separate trays, stacked neatly on their heads, some guy sold me a brand-new pair of Nike Airs—a $180 pair of running shoes—for $13. As he pocketed my money, the salesman decided to come clean. "Actually, they're not really brand-new," he told me, in a half whisper. "Actually, they're not really Nike, either."

BUT FOR ALL THE SIGHTS and sounds that came straight out of the textbooks and the travel guides, we also found something, in East Asian countries in the 1990s, that we hadn't expected. We found ourselves smack in the middle of a fundamental shift in world history—a basic realignment of global stature and political power that will change the way the world has worked for the past five hundred years or so. To use a phrase we heard time and again, we found ourselves in the Asian century.

Anyone who spends some time in Shanghai or Singapore, in Taipei or Tokyo, can see and feel the new era emerging. Whether we like it or not, the familiar world order we have all grown up with, a world dominated and controlled by the nations of Western Europe and the United States, has come to an end. Today, the countries of East Asia consider themselves just as important as the traditional Western powers. They think they have just as much right as Americans and Europeans to run the United Nations, the World Bank, the Red Cross, the Olympics, and all the other international organizations that have always been the preserve of white Westerners. After centuries of indoctrination from Christian missionaries and education in Western universities, the Asians now argue that they have valuable lessons to teach the rest of the world.

And they're right.

By the simplest measures—size and wealth—the Asians already outrank the West. East Asian nations have more people than the West. They have more money, too; of the three richest countries on Earth, as measured by total output, or gross domestic product, two are in East Asia. (The United States has the highest GDP, followed in order by Japan and China, with Germany and other Western European democracies trailing behind.) The Western media paid enormous attention to the currency crises and economic disasters that hit some East Asian countries in the late 1990s. From reading this coverage, you'd almost think that Asia's economic growth was over, and that the Chinese, Japanese, Koreans, Malaysians, etc., were going to revert to their traditional role as water bearers and rickshaw pullers for rich whites. This is evidently an appealing notion to some people in the West—but it is wrong. Even after the series of crises that began in the summer of 1997, almost every East Asian country continued to record higher economic growth rates than the Western powers. Even after years of recession, Japan still has the largest foreign currency reserves in the world—which is an economist's way of saying that they are sitting on about $200 billion of our money. The world's second-biggest stash of foreign currency is in Taiwan.

The economic and political transformation that has turned East

Asia from a bystander to a major player in global economics and politics has been studied and chronicled and heralded under various grandiose titles: the "East Asian miracle," the "Asian renaissance," the "Asian ascent," the "Rising East." Not surprisingly, business and government leaders in East Asia like all these terms. But the one they seem to prefer for this reshaping of the globe is the "Asian century," embracing the belief that the twenty-first century will be the time when East Asian countries use their wealth, population, and power to stand equal–at least–to the Western nations that have run the global show for so long.

There's a certain logic to the claim that we are about to enter an Asian century. The timing is right, for one thing. The Asian "economic miracle" began in the closing decades of one century, and despite the setbacks of the late 1990s in some Asian nations, it will reach full flower in the first decades of the next one. For another, the end of the twentieth century marks the end of Western colonialism in Asia. On July 1, 1997, with less than three years remaining in the twentieth century, Great Britain returned Hong Kong to China. That left just one last sliver of Western colonial rule on the Asian continent. And on December 20, 1999, this last remaining colony–the enclave of Macao, across the Pearl River delta from Hong Kong–will revert from Portuguese to Chinese control. That means Asia will enter the twenty-first century free of foreign governors–for the first time in five centuries, Asia will be fully Asian.

The financial and political aspects of the Asian century–the story of the East Asian financial miracle and the ups and downs of Asian economies–have been the topics of many reports, studies, and books. This is not one of them.

This is a book about a different miracle. It's about another way of looking at the vaunted Asian century. For what my family and I noticed most as we traveled around this newly industrialized, modernized, and prosperous part of the world were social, not economic, indicators. We found a general state of civility, of stability, of public safety. We found, in short, what has been called East Asia's social miracle. This other miracle is probably more important, and certainly more instructive, than anything the Asians have achieved in the economic sphere.

By many of the standard measures of successful societies, the nations of East Asia have been extraordinarily successful: They have the safest streets, the strongest families, and the best schools in the world. To wit:

CRIME

The rates of murder, rape, kidnapping, assault, mugging, robbery, and theft in almost all Asian countries are vastly lower than the comparable rates in most of the rest of the world. In the late 1990s, the United States experienced a fairly remarkable drop in rates of violent and property crime; murders in the United States, for example, dropped from about 25,000 annually in 1993 to 19,600 in 1996. But even at these reduced levels, the per capita rates of violent crime in the United States are ten, twenty, in some cases one hundred times as high as those in the nations of East Asia.

There are murders, rapes, and robberies in Asian societies, but these events are much rarer than in the West. The "ordinary" precautions that have become part of daily life in the United States–bars on the windows, case-hardened locks, car alarms, staying inside after dark–aren't necessary in Asia.

In some cases–Singapore and China spring to mind–the Asian nations have achieved peace on the streets through draconian police measures: offenders may be beaten or locked away for years for minor offenses. But most of East Asia has managed to maintain admirably low crime rates without an overwhelming police presence. In Japan, Korea, Malaysia, Taiwan, and Indonesia, the ratio of police to private citizens is much lower than in the United States. Criminal sentences are generally more lenient. The number of people in prison, as a percentage of the total population, is much smaller. And yet the rate of crime is lower than in any Western nation.

DRUG USE

One of the reasons for the low crime rate in East Asian nations is the low rate of narcotic abuse. The percentage of addicts in the population is far lower than in Western nations, and thus the rate of drug-related crimes is lower as well.

Historically speaking, the crackdown on drugs is a fairly recent phenomenon. Asians have long been growers and users of opium and other narcotic plants. The traditional Chinese word for "drugs," in fact, is a compound of the character for "grass" and the character for "pleasure," suggesting that ancient China understood opium thousands of years ago. But today the old traditions of drug use persist only in a few areas, including the region on either side of the Thai-China border.

As with other forms of crime, the low rates of drug use result from heavy-handed police work in some Asian countries. Anybody who has flown into Singapore's airport will know this; as the plane nears touchdown, the flight attendant makes the arrival announcement: "We will soon be landing in Singapore. Please put your seat backs and tray tables in the full upright position, and please remember that anyone caught bringing drugs into Singapore will be sentenced to death."

But in most of East Asia, the main reason for low rates of drug use lies with the people, not the police. They have decided not to tolerate drugs, or drug users. We lived in Japan during the fervent "sa-kah boomu," or soccer boom, when the entire nation seemed to be crazy about the sport of soccer, and world-class soccer players were treated as matinee idols throughout the archipelago. (The American influence is so strong in Japan that the Japanese have adopted the American name, soccer, for a game that is called football in most of the world.) Perhaps the height of this fascination came when Japan qualified for the 1998 World Cup finals, and a series of practice matches was scheduled between Japanese teams and the veteran World Cup players from Argentina. When it was announced that the Argentine national team was coming to Japan, every ticket for every game sold out within minutes. Then, just days before the series was to begin, Japanese immigration authorities announced that the greatest Argentine soccer star, Diego Maradona, would not be granted an entry visa. He had been convicted of drug use a few years earlier, and nobody who has a record of drug convictions can be admitted to Japan—no matter how strong his crossing kick.

In a huff, the other Argentine players announced that none would play if Maradona was not admitted to the country. The Japanese stood firm; so did the Argentines. The long-awaited series was canceled.

The national sense of disappointment was palpable. And yet, the Japanese media and fans overwhelmingly supported their government. "I was really looking forward to that game," said the famous TV commentator Chikushi Tetsuya, holding up his now useless ticket on his evening news show. "But soccer games won't do us much good if we let ourselves become a society that tolerates illegal drug users."

FAMILY

Marriage: Once two people marry in Asian societies, they are a family. And family is a such a powerful concept that Asian couples are much more likely to stay married than couples in the Western democracies. Japan probably has the highest divorce rate of all the East Asian countries (I say "probably" because the official statistics on such matters are foggy in some parts of the region) but still ranks well below Western nations on this score. About 16 percent of marriages in Japan end in divorce; the figure is close to 50 percent in the United States and around 30 percent in most countries of Western Europe. In other East Asian countries that report family statistics, fewer than 10 percent of married couples seek divorce.

As with crime, this is a function more of social attitudes than of law. Divorce is legal in all the East Asian countries and is generally easy to achieve, if the husband agrees (a legacy of the traditional notion that a man should be free to leave the wife when he wants to but a woman is not free to leave her husband without his consent). But couples don't split up. This is not because every Asian marriage is made in heaven; rather, couples feel a responsibility to make a union work as well as possible. Maintaining a stable family is still considered something of a duty owed to the society as a whole.

Those who do get divorced tend to be ashamed of it, which is the key reason people don't do it. In Japan, a man or woman who is divorced is known as a *batsu-ichi*, which is to say, "a one-time failure." I've never met anybody in Japan who was divorced twice, but my unabridged Japanese dictionary says that such a person would be a *batsu-ni*, or "a two-time failure."

Millions of Americans had an opportunity to view the culture gap in attitudes toward marriage one evening on the Larry King show. It was "Japan Week" on *Larry King Live!;* the talk show host and his wife had traveled to Tokyo to focus on America's most important Asian ally. On his first show from Japan, Larry's guest was a highly respected Japanese newscaster, Tamaru Mizuzu. Tamaru-san had been invited on the show to discuss recent developments in Japanese politics. As is his custom, King did almost no research before the taping, about either the topic or the guest (he told me later that this no-preparation rule makes him a better surrogate for the audience when the tape is rolling).

For that reason, King was visibly stunned when the Japanese political analyst walked onto his set, just seconds before shooting was to start. Tamaru Mizuzu is a gorgeous woman, partial to elegant designer suits cut well above the knee so as to favor her long, perfect legs. Larry King took one look at this beautiful woman and her beautiful legs and forgot all about Japanese politics. "Well, Tamaru, uh, how's the social life here in Japan?" he asked. "A woman like you, must have a busy social life."

Now it was Tamaru-san's turn to be stunned. She has reasonably good English, and had in fact practiced a few English sentences–about the political situation in Japan–before coming to the show. But this totally unexpected turn of events threw her completely off kilter. "Well, I, ummmm, uh, ummm, I . . ?" she stammered, groping for something, anything, to say in response to this off-the-wall question.

King tried to help out. "Oh, I'm sorry, Tamaru," he said graciously. "You must be married, right?" This question threw the Japanese newscaster into deeper despair. "I was umm, umm, umm, uh–" was the only answer she could produce. "Oh, Tamaru, I get it," King went on in his peppy, casual way, slipping a thumb under his suspenders. "You're divorced, right?" This was clearly the worst question of all from Tamaru-san's point of view. She flashed red with undisguised anger, and spat out a reply that essentially ended the interview: "I'm not talking about that." King quickly turned to another guest and asked about U.S.-Japan trade friction.

I joined Larry King and his production team at a restaurant after the taping, and it was clear that this veteran interviewer was concerned about the painful glitch in the interview he had just conducted. "What happened with Tamaru?" he kept asking. "I mean, hey,

I really didn't mean to set her off like that." I explained that Tamaru-san was in fact divorced, that she had been criticized for selfishness in the fan magazines when she broke up with her husband, that this was considered a serious detriment to her broadcasting career, and that it was embarrassing for a Japanese person to talk about such a thing. "That's so strange," King replied. "Why would she make such a big deal out of a divorce?"

King then introduced me to his wife, Sherry, noting that they had only recently wed. I learned later that she was Mrs. Larry King number six. Larry and Sherry were divorced shortly after the visit to Japan.

Children: If marriage is deemed to involve fundamental responsibilities, parenthood is considered even more important. In East Asian countries, virtually every child is raised in a family with two parents; grandparents, aunts and uncles, and other relatives are frequently living in the same home, although that pattern is changing somewhat as populations become more mobile. But the conviction that every child deserves a mother and a father at home remains solid.

This, too, is borne out in statistics. There are few broken homes in Asian societies, and almost no births out of wedlock. In the United States, somewhere between 30 and 35 percent of all babies are born to single mothers. In the countries of Western Europe, the figure ranges between 20 and 25 percent.

In East Asia, 1 percent (or less, in several countries) of the babies are born to single mothers. This is not to say that every Asian family is ideal. But just about every Asian family is a complete family. The social problems that seem to be connected to a high rate of broken homes—crime, social stress, and dire economic straits for single mothers—are not problems for Asian societies.

EDUCATION

It's not easy to say whether one school or one education system is better than another in every academic area. But some fields of learning are fairly universal. When it comes to math, science, and geography, children are being taught essentially the same facts and formulas in every country on Earth. And in the areas of education that can be compared, the public schools in East Asia almost always turn out to be the best on Earth.

A joint study by the national departments of education in twenty-six nations in 1996 compared schoolchildren's performance on standardized tests of math and science. Here are excerpts from the results:

Fourth Grade Math		Fourth Grade Science	
1. Singapore	625	1. South Korea	597
2. South Korea	611	2. Japan	574
3. Japan	597	3. United States	565
4. Hong Kong	587	4. Czech Republic	557
5. Czech Republic	567	5. England	551
6. Ireland	550	6. Canada	549
8. United States	545	7. Singapore	547
AVERAGE	529	AVERAGE	524
12. England	513	14. Israel	505
17. Thailand	490	19. Thailand	473

Eighth Grade Math		Eighth Grade Science	
1. Singapore	643	1. Singapore	607
2. South Korea	607	2. Czech Republic	574
3. Japan	605	3. Japan	571
4. Hong Kong	588	4. South Korea	565
5. United States	500	5. United States	534
AVERAGE	513	AVERAGE	516

Source: U.S. Department of Education, "Pursuing Excellence" report

EQUALITY OF WEALTH

The traditional image of Asian countries—and the one I held before we moved there—was of overwhelmingly poor societies: city dwellers starving in the streets and farmers slaving to raise barely enough rice to feed a family, while a tiny clique of well-connected magnates lived behind barbed-wire fences in ornate mansions. Today, those scenes can still be found in parts of East Asia. But for the most part, the Asian countries are building a huge middle class, in which most people have about as much as everybody else.

Japan has been the model; when Japan became a rich country, it did so in ways that spread the wealth broadly and evenly. In opinion polls today, more than 90 percent of the Japanese people describe themselves as "middle class." In the other "high-performing Asian economies" the economic boom has also been broadly distributed. "The HPAEs are the only economies in the world that have sustained high rates of growth while simultaneously reducing the gap between rich and poor," a World Bank report says. (In Chapter 7 of this book, we'll see some of the ways this has been achieved.)

You can legitimately question whether equal distribution of a nation's wealth is a sign of social success. The American dream, in economic terms, at least, has generally been the dream of enormous success—not of making as much money as everybody else but rather of getting really rich. And that dream has been one of the key reasons for the dynamism and resiliency of the United States over the decades. On the other hand, the egalitarian distribution of wealth, and the resulting sense that everybody is getting a relatively fair shake, is surely one of the reasons that Asian countries have civil and stable societies.

THIS, THEN, IS EAST ASIA'S SOCIAL MIRACLE: the world's lowest rates of violent crime, theft, and drug use; strong, stable families with low rates of divorce, and virtually no single parents; public education that tests out as the best in the world; a broad sense of equality that gives almost everybody a stake in the society and thus helps assure, for the most part, safe and peaceful living conditions. To me, it's a miracle that is more important than the economic miracle, and one that seems less susceptible to cyclical ups and downs. Even as the region has become modernized, industrialized, Westernized—as rock 'n' roll, L. L. Bean, Starbucks, and Schwarzenegger have become part of daily life in the East—that fundamental social stability has not wavered.

During the years of rapid economic growth in East Asia, crime and divorce rates held steady—a fairly predictable result, from a Western point of view, because our own experience generally holds that social tensions decrease when the economy is strong. What is interesting in the Asian experience, though, is that even in bad economic years, crime and divorce remain low. To the extent you can judge from government statistics, South Korea, Malaysia, and Japan saw virtually no increase in crime rates or in the number of broken homes during that tough period in 1997–98 when they underwent serious economic trouble.

In December of 1997, six months after the first wave of currency crises hit East Asia, I went to Japan with a film crew from the Arts and Entertainment Network to make a documentary about Asian financial troubles. (It's called *The Story of Money* and is coming soon to a TV set near you.) Because time and funds were in short supply, A&E had decided to restrict its filming to one country; Japan was picked because it had experienced both economic boom and bust (and because the members of the film crew were dying to travel to Tokyo to get their hands on the latest video equipment, which hits the market in Japan about six months before it comes to New York). What I remember from that trip is the poor producer pulling his hair out every morning because it was so hard to find any sign of the economic disaster that Asia was supposed to be suffering. Everywhere we looked in Japan, we saw calm and order. We saw well-dressed people in late-model cars moving through their normal lives, going to work, shopping, strolling hand in hand through the parks. "Where's the recession?" the producer kept asking me. "Where are all the homeless? Where's the social breakdown?"

I used to wonder about those questions myself when I lived in Japan. In the mid 1990s, when the country was already in the depths of a long, severe recession, I arranged an interview with the director general of Japan's national police agency—in effect, the national chief of police, the boss of every patrolman and precinct captain in the whole country. I sat on a cracked vinyl sofa in this serious gentleman's small, unpretentious office, while an "office lady" in a blue uniform brought a small pot of green tea. As the police chief and I sipped our lukewarm tea, I asked him whether crime rates had increased in the wake of the economic downturn. The answer, in a word, was "No." "We've seen a gradual decline in crime over the past twenty years or so, and during the past two years this decline has continued," the chief told me. He was eminently polite, as Japanese social custom demands, but he was obviously astonished that anyone could ask such an ignorant question as mine. I grew defensive. "Well, see, in our country," I said, trying to explain, "we generally find that crime goes up when the economy turns sour." The chief seemed generally perplexed by this. "Ah, yes, I see," he said, but I could tell he really didn't.

The conversation was equally perplexing to me. That a recession leads to increased crime, divorce, and social disorder seemed elementary. But this Japanese crime fighter was telling me that crime and other social problems were not a function of economic conditions. As far as he was concerned, there was some other factor driving Japan's admirable social statistics. And as I traveled around East Asia and asked similar questions of police chiefs, government officials, scholars, and taxi drivers in other countries, I found that they all agreed with the Japanese police chief. There was a reason for Asia's social miracle, but it wasn't the economic miracle. Rather, the explanation lay in something deeper and more permanent than a spurt in gross national product.

These Asians told me that it all came down to two words: moral values.

All over East Asia, people told me that there is a set of shared beliefs, sometimes called the Asian spirit or Asian values, passed down over the millennia in Oriental societies and still assiduously taught and promoted today. What are these values? You could devote volumes to that question, and in fact much of this volume will attempt to identify "Asian values"—what they are, where they come from, and how they are transmitted in modern times. For the time being, though, we'll rely on the comments of some Asian experts:

Ogura Kazuo, a senior diplomat in Japan's Foreign Service: "The Asian spirit involves discipline, loyalty, hard work rather than inheritance as the key to entitlement, long-term investment, a focus on education, esteem for the family, concern for the collective harmony of the group, and control over one's desires."

Fei Ching-han, head of a Taiwanese think tank: "The strong points of [Asian] civilization lie in diligence, emphasis on education, and a philosophy of life that stresses self-improvement and self-reliance."

Kishore Mahbubani, a Singaporean diplomat who has spent a good deal of time in America: "East Asian societies are by no means universally harmonious. They have their share of family and social breakdowns. But, relative to most societies in the world, they are disciplined and cohesive. Social order prevails. The deep value placed on family in Asian societies is not easily erased.

"Family cohesiveness is not always an unmitigated blessing. It breeds nepotism. But it does generate, relatively speaking, greater social harmony. . . . the fundamental lesson that Asia can provide to the United States here is that societies can be better off when some boundaries of individual freedom are limited rather than broadened. The resultant increase in social and communal harmony in turn can be liberating for the individual."

NOT ONLY DO the East Asians tend to agree on their core values, they also agree, for the most part, on where these values come from. The Asian spirit is commonly traced back to a series of ancient books known collectively as the Chinese classics, or the Confucian classics.

It's an audacious argument: East Asians act the way they do at the dawn of the twenty-first century because of a few basic precepts laid down by a Chinese sage who lived at the end of the fifth century B.C. Kung Fu-tzu was a minor government official in the province of Lu— and also happened to be one of the great moral teachers of all human history. He was a thinker and philosopher so important that the Jesuit missionaries who traveled to the Orient in the sixteenth century honored him with a Latin name: Confucius.

There's something almost hopelessly romantic, hopelessly Oriental, about this notion of a purely Asian culture that dates back to an influential teacher 2,500 years ago and survives to this day essentially intact. A lot of Western experts on Asia laugh at the concept. In fact, though, there's nothing exclusively Asian about the idea. Other cultures around the world share the belief that ancient truths can have contemporary impact. The Western tradition that is said to underlie our modern democratic, individualistic, free-market societies stems from the teachings of Socrates (a figure similar in many ways to Confucius) and from the Judaeo-Christian Bible, some parts of which date back just as far as the old Chinese classics. If Solomon, Socrates, and Saint Paul still hold sway in the Western cultural sphere, it doesn't seem so far-fetched to suggest that the Eastern world draws its core lessons from a teacher who walked the dusty streets of rural China two millennia ago.

The idea that ancient Confucian teachings directly affect modern Asia has been employed by many analysts, both Asian and Western, who have attempted to explain East Asia's striking economic success in the last twenty years of the twentieth century. Among several explanations offered for the East Asian economic miracle, one of the more common was the suggestion that the secret to Asia's new wealth lies in Confucianism—or what is sometimes known as Confucian capitalism.

This line of analysis has been influenced by the work of the famous German sociologist Max Weber. Weber set out, around the dawn of the twentieth century, to understand why it was that the countries of northern Europe—England, France, Germany, Holland—had led the world in industrialization and acquired global colonial empires, while their neighbors in southern Europe lagged behind. Weber's answer was to become one of the most important ideas in the history of sociology: the Protestant Ethic. He argued—and here I will seriously simplify a dense and often obscure essay—that the ethical principles of the northern European Protestant faith spawned capitalism, and with it industrialism, which provided both the need and the wherewithal for the creation of global empires. It was not location, or weather, or racial characteristics, or simply good luck that made the difference for northern Europe, Weber theorized. It was culture.

Contemporary scholars trying to figure out why the world's most recent economic miracle took place in East Asia—and not, say, central Africa or South America—sometimes suggest that the answer in this case, too, is culture. The argument is that a sort of Confucian ethic helped breed Asia's late-twentieth-century transformation from ragged to rich. (There's a delicious irony to this theory, because Max Weber, in his last major book, *The Religions of the East,* argued that

Daoism and Confucianism would prevent the development of capitalism in Asia.) This idea has been argued in several recent books, and it will not be reargued in this one. But just to give the flavor, let me quote from one of the most persuasive advocates of the Confucian ethic theory, the Princeton historian Gilbert Rozman:

> "This-worldly" in its orientation, Confucianism teaches individuals of both high and low birth to strive for success in their lifetime and in the long-term interests of their direct descendants. One need not reconcile oneself to one's current lot in life, it says. . . . Education is for everyone. Moral cultivation can be expected to pay rich dividends.
>
> In this environment, families could anticipate that hard work, savings, study, and attention to market opportunities would improve their standing in society. Such circumstances fostered a competitive and, within understandable premodern limitations, an entrepreneurial spirit.

In much the same way, the ancient teachings of Confucius have been cited time and again by East Asians to explain the region's low rates of crime and family breakdown and relatively high level of economic equality and social civility. That is, a "Confucian ethic" in these societies has helped them escape some of the intractable social problems that have plagued the developed countries of the West. If this theory is true, it could be of enormous importance to Western countries; if they would embrace these Confucian values themselves, problems like crime and family breakdown might be ameliorated.

If this theory is true . . . But is it?

The argument that ancient Confucian teachings have contributed to a sort of Pan-Asian value system that explains East Asia's current economic and social success is an intriguing one. It's tempting, too. It takes all the complexities involved in a fundamental shift of global power—a shift that is certain to take place as we enter the Asian century—and reduces them to a bumper sticker: "Confucius Did It!" The stark simplicity of this theory is particularly appealing to an author who, like me, hopes to explain East Asia's social miracle to Western readers. ("Well, Mr. Reid, we have thirty seconds left before the commercial break, so just tell me quickly what your book is about.") But like many other neat little sound bites, the theory has many flaws—so many that it's going to take a whole chapter of this book (Chapter 9) to discuss them all.

I'VE SPENT A LOT OF TIME over the past few years trying to figure out why the East Asian countries have such admirable social statistics. But when we first arrived and settled in, we didn't have much time for these deep questions. The only thing that mattered was that this social miracle touched us—it influenced our daily life, for the better.

Although we were living in the heart of one of the largest cities in the world, we learned to live without fear. Or perhaps I should say that, over time, we forgot to be afraid. We forgot to worry about what might happen if a strange person started walking behind us on an unknown street after dark. We forgot to keep a constant eye on our luggage when we set it down in the airport or bus station. When we went bike riding, we forgot to carry that big, heavy Kryptonite lock we always used back home. We acquired a basic confidence that the members of our family, even the smallest ones, could go anywhere in a massive city without worrying about crime. And this made a fundamental difference in the way we led our lives.

I used to think of this almost like one of those good news–bad news jokes. The good news was, our American family had found a teeming inner-city neighborhood where our kids could walk the streets, day or night, without fear—a place that was virtually free of violence, theft, drugs, even graffiti. The kids left their expensive mountain bikes out in front of the house every night, unlocked, and we never lost one. (Actually, one did disappear for a while after our middle daughter left it unlocked at school; as it turned out, the local policeman picked it up, looked up our registration number, and called us to come get it.) In our city neighborhood, we were never once awakened at night by the scream of somebody's car alarm. There weren't any car alarms in our neighborhood. No need for them.

That was the good news. The bad news was, to find this idyllic city neighborhood we had to move across the across the Pacific and take up residence in Japan.

To state the obvious, I think it is fundamentally wrong that an American has to travel overseas to get that feeling of safety. We should have been able to find a safe city neighborhood in our own country. I now feel that we have a basic right as human beings to live without fear: to walk down a street or jog through a park at night without the cautious glance over the shoulder, to leave a mountain bike–or a car, for that matter–on the street outside the house and know for sure that it will still be there the next morning. In some inchoate way, I may have felt this basic right to live without fear before we moved to Asia. But now, having come back home from an almost completely safe society, I feel it more strongly.

To know that crime might happen at any time, to take reasonable precautions against it, to warn our children over and over that they shouldn't trust strangers–all that is part and parcel of our daily life back home, as I believe it is for most Americans. But now I know it need not be.

I can almost pinpoint the moment when I realized that standard American city precautions need no longer be part of our daily life. It was a Tuesday night, not long after we had arrived in Tokyo. At the dinner table, our fourth-grader, Kate, announced happily that next Saturday she was going to Tokyo Disneyland with her new pal Watanabe Mariko. "Just the two of us," she said proudly.

Katie was so excited at the idea that it was impossible for a parent to do anything but smile and say "Sounds great!" But my wife and I exchanged one of those meaningful glances that asks "Are we going to let her do this?" After dinner, we started thinking it over.

Just the two of them? To Tokyo Disneyland? But that's a ninety-minute trip one way, we thought. The girls would have to ride three different trains to get there, three more coming home, and stand around in all those big stations waiting to change trains. And they were ten years old.

Trying to conceal my concern, I called Mariko's mother.

"Oh, yes, how nice to talk to you," she said. "I understand our girls are going to Tokyo Disneyland together." "Are you going with them, Watanabe-san?" I asked. "Why, no," the mother said, with a tone in her voice that mingled surprise and confusion. "Okay," I responded. "Then I'll ride out there with them on the trains, and bring them back." Mrs. Watanabe was clearly puzzled. "You'll ride with them?" she asked. "Why?"

WHY? I wanted to shout at this dense woman. Why? Because they're two ten-year-old girls, that's why! Because you're going to have them travel ninety minutes each way, through a teeming urban center of 27 million strangers, and they won't come home until after dark, and they have to change trains at three different crowded stations, and who knows how many strange men might be hanging around in those stations, and theymightgetrobbedormuggedorraped- orsomething!

But then I started thinking about her question. Why? Why should I have to ride on the train with my ten-year-old? As long as the girls knew which trains to take–and Mariko was evidently a veteran of trips to Tokyo Disneyland–there was nothing to be afraid of. This was a society where you did not have to live with the fear of crime, where you did not have to worry when two ten-year-olds set off to travel all day around a city of 27 million people. So yes, in the context of daily life for the Watanabe family–and for every other family in Tokyo– Mrs. Watanabe's question was perfectly sensible. Why would I need to ride the train with these two girls?

After that I began to take a closer look at the society we had moved to. It wasn't a perfectly safe haven from crime and violence. But it was close.

There is crime in Japan. If you can believe the police figures, Japan's version of the Mafia, known as the *yakuza,* has far more members than organized crime in the United States (or in Italy, for that matter). People get murdered in Japan every year, although a good share of them seem to be *yakuza* members knocked off by members of rival gangs. Women get raped in Japan as well, and children have been kidnapped. Every twenty years or so, Japan has been confronted with violent terrorists. While our family was living in Japan, a crazed religious cult murdered seven people by releasing poison gas on the Tokyo subway. This would have been shocking and terrifying in any country. To make things worse, the Japanese police were warned in advance that this poison attack was coming but botched the effort to stop it. Even after this frightening event, it took the police six weeks to round up the perpetrators and shut down the cult. During that six weeks, we were afraid.

But in statistical terms, these serious crimes are rare events, compared with what happens in the rest of the world. There are about 7.5 murders each year for every 100,000 Americans. England's murder rate is roughly 5.5 murders per 100,000 people. Germany has 4.3 per 100,000, France has 4.1. In Japan, the murder rate is below 1.0 per 100,000.

Here's a comparison of the frequency of major crimes in the United States and Japan in 1996. This table shows the number of crimes per 100,000 people:

	United States	Japan
Murder	7.53	0.97
Robbery	255.8	1.75
Rape	37	1.5
Arson	46	1
Aggravated Assault	440	5.4
Burglary	1,099	187

Source: United States: FBI; Japan: Ministry of Justice.

Most of the murders in America take place in large cities, and it is the conventional wisdom that crowded inner-city neighborhoods are hotbeds of crime. But Japan's inner cities are more crowded, and they are hotbeds of public safety. New York City, a crowded (24,000 people per square mile) urban center of 7.3 million people, had 767 murders in 1997—a figure the mayor announced at a triumphant press conference, because it was so much lower than the number of murders the year before. Tokyo, a far more crowded (38,000 people per square mile) urban center with a population half again as large as New York's, had 133 murders the same year. On a per capita basis, that's about 10.5 murders per 100,000 people in New York, and 1.2 per 100,000 in Tokyo.

The most striking difference is in the rates of property crimes—

arson, burglary, robbery, car theft, etc. According to the American criminologist David Bailey, the United States has about 140 times as many robberies per year as Japan does. In Tokyo, there are about 500 robberies per year—a little more than one per day. New York City has about 215 reported robberies every day. The reason people don't use car alarms in Japan—even though most cars are left out on the street at night—is that auto theft is not a problem there. Neither is car-jacking, as I learned one day when I got a call from a reporter at one of the big Tokyo newspapers. He was writing about a sad case in Los Angeles, in which two Japanese foreign exchange students had been murdered by a car-jacker. The reporter's question to me was, "Reido-san, what is this word 'car-jacking'?" I racked my brain trying to think of the Japanese word for "car-jacking." In fact, there is no Japanese word for "car-jacking" because there has never been a reported case of car-jacking anywhere in the country. So I did my best to explain this phenomenon to a Japanese: "Well, you know, it's when you stop your car at a red light, and some guy comes up with a gun and steals your car and drives away," I said. "That happens?" the reporter replied.

Like the mass media everywhere else, Japanese newspapers and TV news shows are full of crime stories. It's just that in Japan the big crime story is frequently less frightening than the ones you see or read in the United States. One December evening when I tuned in the evening news on NHK, Japan's public TV network, the anchor announced with a somber face that he had to report two separate stories about serious crimes on commuter trains. First there was a dispatch from America about the horrendous events that day on the Long Island Rail Road. An angry man with a loaded revolver started firing randomly at passengers, leaving nearly three dozen commuters dead or badly wounded. Next, the newscaster moved on to a report from Tokyo's Chuo line. A gang of pickpockets had been working the Chuo line trains during rush hour, the reporter noted in worried tones, and nearly two dozen passengers had lost their wallets in the past two weeks.

If the NHK newscasters noticed any disproportion between these two crime stories, it was not evident in their voices or demeanor. The pickpockets were treated just as seriously as the mass murderer. There seemed to be no question that the theft of twenty-four wallets was indeed a significant national concern for the people of Japan. I remember thinking how lucky the Japanese were that their idea of a crime wave ran to lost wallets rather than to dead bodies on the afternoon train.

But of course Japan's high level of social civility and corresponding low levels of crime and violence are not a matter of luck. The pervasive sense of safety on the nation's streets doesn't just happen. Rather, the whole nation works hard to maintain it.

We came to discover that the other nations of East Asia are also remarkably safe, by the standards of Western countries. Almost everywhere we went in Asia, we had that same sense of freedom as we walked down the street, even late at night, without fear. If a shadowy figure approached to borrow a match or ask the time, it really was a person who needed a light or wanted to know the time.

The result is that almost everywhere in East Asia you can do things that evoke, for Americans, an earlier, simpler time that is now long gone. You can check into most hotels without giving the clerk a credit card, because the place trusts its customers to pay their bills when they leave. When you check in, the desk clerk hands you a room key that has the room number on it; that kind of key is rare in Western countries now because of the fear that a robber may obtain the key and use it to ransack the room. You can rent a bike or a fishing boat or skis without leaving your driver's license behind as security. You can get change when you board a city bus. You can step up to a row of public phones and find that every one works—and that the hotel listings have not been ripped out of the yellow pages. If you lose a purse or wallet with a wad of cash in it, the odds are quite good that you'll get a call from the police saying your purse has been found—and the money will still be there.

Most important, you can forget to be afraid.

As a husband and a father, as a reporter whose job often put him on the streets of some unknown city well after midnight, I felt great about the sense of security we found in East Asia. As a resident of Japan, I felt a real sense of gratitude toward the Japanese people and police for building a free, prosperous society where my wife and children could live in safety. And yet, for all my gratitude and admiration, I was perplexed. How did they do it?

I don't think of the Japanese as more honest or more decent people than Americans, Italians, Australians, or anybody else. White-collar crime seems to be far worse in Japan than in most other countries. In my career as a political reporter, I have covered both the U.S. Congress and the Japanese Diet, or parliament. I found that basic, everyday politics in Japan is vastly more corrupt, more dishonest, than anything I saw in Washington. (In other Asian countries, notably China, South Korea, and Singapore, the situation is arguably even worse.)

In the business world, the stories of bribes, payoffs, hush money, and laundered cash that show up routinely in the Japanese media would make the most hardened Wall Streeters cringe. In Tokyo, some of the world's most prestigious industrial and finance firms routinely pay protection money to *yakuza* gangsters. Every few years the police crack down on this practice, and a few Japanese CEOs are forced to resign in disgrace. But this doesn't seem to stop the payoffs, which are considered a cost of business in Japan.

And yet this ethos of dishonesty in the suites is not replicated in the streets.

The Japanese have ensured their domestic tranquility without police-state tactics. Compared with the United States, in fact, Japan seems scandalously unprepared to battle crime: the nation has one-third as many police per capita, one-fifth as many judges, one-twentieth as many jail cells. Japan's criminal sentences are so mild they would draw scorn from law-and-order politicians in the United States. The country has about 37 inmates for every 100,000 citizens; the United States has 519 for every 100,000. For about one-third of those convicted of property crimes—theft, arson, etc.—the criminal "sentence" is a requirement to pay back the victim for the loss, and to write a letter of apology. The goal in Japan is not to isolate the criminal from society, but precisely the opposite. A convict is sent back to his neighborhood, family, and job so that the social pressure to fit in and the pain of being shamed before the group will lead him to go straight.

Those who are sent to jail normally get much shorter terms than they would get for the same crime in America. Prison is a harsh and lonely experience in Japan; almost every inmate is kept in a tiny, individual room with no books, no television, and no contact with any other prisoner. The situation is so bleak that Western human rights organizations routinely complain to the Ministry of Justice about prison conditions. These appeals are just as routinely rejected, usually with some official statement comparing America's twenty-, forty-, and fifty-year prison terms with the two or three years most convicts serve in Japan.

In America nowadays, our periodic outbursts of "war on crime" generally involve hiring more police and building more prisons. The Japanese are convinced that this approach is precisely backward–that once you need police and jails, it is already too late. To build a safe and civil society marked by respect for people and their property, you have to start long before the police get involved.

BUT WHERE DO YOU START? How did the Asians do it? It would take a long time before we started to figure out what Asia was doing to make this social miracle come true. Initially, we saw the social miracle in small ways, in the context of daily family life, like that trip to Tokyo Disneyland (which the girls made, by the way, just the two of them, with no complications whatsoever). Gradually, I began to realize that these small family experiences reflected some much bigger truths about the way Asian society–and, for that matter, our own society–tends to work.

In this book I'm going to approach the issue by looking at the daily experience of our American family in Tokyo, and then drawing back to think about how those small epiphanies revealed the bigger picture of a safe, civil, and harmonious society. As it happened, my search for the larger truth pulled me back into ancient China and deep into the cultural heart of contemporary East Asia. But the journey began in a simpler way. We got our first real taste of Eastern flavor at the fast-food stand.

Eastern flavor

BEFORE WE MOVED TO ASIA, we warned our kids that they would no doubt run into some weird stuff to eat over there—pickled eggplant, fried octopus, barbecued eel, raw horse meat coated with green horse-radish, that sort of thing. But don't worry, we said. American fast food is ubiquitous these days. If it all gets to be too much, you can always find a McDonald's, a Mr. Donut, or a Pizza Hut for a taste of home.

Accordingly, it was no surprise when our family arrived in Japan and found all sorts of exotic Oriental flavors in restaurants. The surprising thing was that we found a lot of these alien entrées in places like McDonald's, Mr. Donut, and Pizza Hut. East is East and West is West, but anybody who still thinks the twain shall never meet has never been to Baskin-Robbins or Burger King on the far side of the Pacific. What we found in Tokyo, Seoul, Beijing, Singapore, Kuala Lumpur, was that local outlets of the U.S. fast-food chains have brought consummate ingenuity to the task of adding an Eastern twist to the basic Western staples. Living in Japan, we had our share (some of my children would say more than our share) of sushi, sukiyaki, sea urchin, and the like. But we also found ourselves eating–and even en-joying–such modern Asian delicacies as the squid pizza, the curry doughnut, the bean-paste Danish, the rice burger, the kim-chee burger, the tempura hot dog, the green tea milkshake, the sashimi submarine, and the ever-popular BST (that's bacon, seaweed, and tomato) sandwich.

We began to appreciate this culinary East-West alliance on our first night in Tokyo. Blitzed and bleary-eyed after our fourteen hours on the airplane, we took a friend's advice (rotten advice, as it turned out) and rode downtown from Narita Airport by taxicab. This ordeal added another three hours' travel to the day; by the time the driver, in her perfect uniform, blue cap, and white gloves, pulled into the im-possibly narrow street where our impossibly small rental house stood, we were far too hot, tired, and testy to think about any kind of dinner, Asian or American. At least, we adults were too tired. Our three children were thinking about dinner, or at least dessert. They wanted ice cream.

On one of those muggy and miserable evenings that mark late August in Tokyo, this did sound like a good idea. But where to find ice cream? We were hauling suitcases, briefcases, and backpacks into our little home and contemplating this question when I noticed a dis-tinguished figure–a short, kindly-faced, white-haired gentleman in a handsome blue suit, with a dark tie knotted perfectly against the starched collar of his white shirt and a crisp white handkerchief folded into three perfect peaks in his breast pocket–standing in front of our house. Actually, he was standing in front of the house next door, but it is hard to know that in a Tokyo neighborhood, where the houses are narrow and separated from the place next door only by an inch or two of bare concrete.

This nicely dressed gentleman was, in fact, our next-door neigh-bor, although we weren't to know that right away. Japanese people–and particularly those of a certain age, like our neighbor–feel it is essential to maintain a degree of reserve, to keep some distance when dealing with others. There's a word for this in Japanese: *enryo,* which my dictionary defines as "restraint." To the Japanese, *enryo* is a form of courtesy, a practice that assures you don't intrude upon another's privacy. For strict practitioners of this ethic it would be dreadfully bad form, it would be a fairly substantial violation of *enryo*, to introduce yourself by name on first meeting another person. And so it was with this gentleman; he addressed us politely and clearly surmised that we were moving in next door to his house, but he was not quite ready to go so far as to tell us his name.

What he did do, though, was answer our questions about ice cream. Yes, there was in fact a place within walking distance where we could get ice cream. And it was American ice cream, at that; we would feel right at home. If we would wind down the hill and around the corner, past the pachinko parlor and the Mitsubishi Bank, we'd see a big billboard with English written on it. Beneath that sign would be the ice-cream shop—a place called Satay-Wan.

Satay-Wan? It sounded more like a Malaysian beef house or a Chinese noodle stand than an American ice cream shop. But we set out on our trek, curving through the narrow, seemingly random streets of our new neighborhood, past Shinto temples and futon shops, past a vending machine that offered five-kilogram bags of rice, past a guy selling tacos from a wagon on the street. (Actually, they weren't really tacos, although the vendor kept shouting "Taco! Taco!" In fact, he was shouting not "taco" but "*tako*," the Japanese word for "octopus." It turns out he was selling *tako-yaki*, or fried octopus balls.) Eventually, we found the Mitsubishi Bank, and just up the street from there we saw a big billboard written in English. Well, sort of English. Something vaguely related to English.

That big sign, which stands over the same corner to this day, said:

FINE BOYS
SINCE 1987 SAYS
LETS SEX!

We concluded that this must be the "billboard with English written on it" that the white-haired gentleman had told us about. Because right under it there stood a Baskin-Robbins ice-cream store. It looked like any Baskin-Robbins in any little shopping center in any American town, with the big red "Baskin-Robbins" sign on top and a huge red "31"—that means thirty-one flavors—in a white circle on the shop window.

The minute we saw it, of course, we understood that mysterious "Satay-Wan."

One of the problems facing American businesses that come to Asia is how to preserve the corporate name after it is rewritten in Chinese characters or another local alphabet. The matter is further complicated because a lot of Asian languages have fewer distinct sounds than English uses. Japanese, for example, has exactly forty-seven different sounds, and Japan's home-grown alphabet has one symbol for each of the forty-seven. But English mixes and blends its twenty-six letters to produce more than one hundred different sounds. As a result, strange things happen when English names or words are rendered into Japanese.

The Japanese are famous for their problems with *R* and *L*, because their language doesn't have either letter. Japanese doesn't have an *F* sound, either, and as a result Japanese people find this sound extremely hard to master. They can say "moo," "shoe," "sue," and "goo," but not "foo." When a language teacher first pointed this out to me years ago, I was astounded; indeed, I refused to believe it. After all, the most famous geographical entity in all Japan, the tallest and most beautiful mountain in the whole archipelago, is Mount Fuji. One of the most important postwar Japanese prime ministers was a man named Fukuda Zenko. How can you call your greatest mountain Fuji or your prime minister Fukuda if you can't pronounce the first letter?

The answer is that the "fu" in "Fuji" is actually not a "fu" at all. The Japanese pronounce that name "Hoo-ji." But when the first Westerners came to Japan about 150 years ago, they heard a heavily aspirated "hoo" sound and thought they were hearing "foo." (If you exhale fairly forcefully while saying "hooji" out loud, you can hear this, too.) And that's why the "hoo" sound is transliterated into English letters as "fu."

The inability to make an *F* sound produces some interesting problems when the Japanese try to speak English. I was talking to a man in a sushi bar once about American movies, and he told me, gushing over with enthusiasm, that his favorite Hollywood star was "Hen Lee Honda." Oh, sure, I said, trying to be agreeable, uh, Hen Lee Honda. Hen Lee Honda? Was this some Asian-American character actor whose career I'd managed to miss? "I like him best in *Twelve Angry*

Men," the guy went on, and that was the tip-off. His favorite actor was Henry Fonda. My Japanese friend Togo had a similar pronunciation problem. He had lived in America and studied English for years. His grammar was nearly perfect, and he had a strong grasp of American slang. He had a temper, too. And when he got really mad at me, he would turn on me the full force of his Americanized vocabulary, filtered through Japanese pronunciation. "Huck you!" he would shout at me. "Huck you!"

These pronunciation difficulties posed serious problems for some, but not all, Western food chains. A place called, say, Burger King is fairly lucky, because the Japanese can pronounce something fairly close to the real name: "Bah-gah Kingu." The situation was tougher for another burger chain, Wendy's, when they came to Japan, because neither of the syllables in "Wendy's" exists in Japanese. There's no way to write those sounds using the Japanese alphabet. And so the simple, friendly name Wendy's was turned into a four-syllable mouthful: "Oo-EN-day-zu." (Say it fast and you'll hear it.) "McDonald's," rendered into Japanese, became a seven-syllable word: "Ma-ku-do-na-ru-do-zu." Somebody in the hierarchy of Japanese McDonald's decided that seven syllables was one too many, so they chopped off the final *s* in the name. This was evidently a sound idea, because McDonald—Ma-ku-do-na-ru-do—is today the biggest restaurant chain in Japan, and in the rest of Asia as well.

The problem was even tougher for the hyphenated, multisyllabic business called Baskin-Robbins. In Japanese pronunciation, this name becomes "Basu-keen Low-Beans." Since "Low-Beans" did not sound very ice-cream-like, even in Japanese, the chain rather cleverly advertised itself in Japan not by its corporate name but rather by its most salient feature, the famous thirty-one flavors. All over Japan, Baskin-Robbins ice-cream stores are known not as "Basu-keen Low-Beans" but rather, more simply, as "Thirty-one."

There's a perfectly good way to say the number thirty-one in Japanese. But saying the word in the native language—*san-ju ichi*—doesn't have the spark, the cachet, the worldly flavor that comes from saying the same thing in English. So Baskin-Robbins has never been known as San-ju Ichi. From the very first, the corporate image-makers decided to call their store Thirty-one. Baskin-Robbins is the

biggest ice-cream-store chain in Japan, and everybody refers to the
place as Thirty-one. But there's no *th* sound in Japanese, and of
course that *ir* sound is a tough one as well. So "Thirty-one," in standard Japanese-style English pronunciation, comes out "Satay-Wan."
Which is exactly what that nicely dressed white-haired gentleman
had told us.

(Although it has nothing to do with my story, I can't resist pointing
out here that the same twist of the tongue that turns thirty-one into
"satay-wan" also explains why March 9 has become an important day
on the Japanese calendar. Everybody in Japan–probably almost
everybody in the world, for that matter–knows that the way to express
gratitude in English is to say "Thank you." But in a nation that can't
make the *th* sound, "thank you" turns into "san-kyu." Now, that word
san means "three" in Japanese. And *kyu* means "nine." So when the
Japanese say "Thank you," and it comes out "San-kyu," what they
hear is "three-nine"–that is, March 9. That gives rise to one of the
great old chestnuts of Japanese humor, Japan's equivalent of "Why
did the chicken cross the road?" To wit: "What's the most thankful
day of the year?" Answer: March 9, the *san-kyu* day.)

Having found the mysterious Satay-Wan, and having discovered
that it really was an American ice-cream place, we began to worry a
little about what this ice cream might taste like. In fact, the satay-wan
flavors available included some perfectly normal choices–vanilla, ba-
nana, lime daiquiri, and so forth–that tasted exactly like the real thing
back home. More interesting, though, were the Asian flavors. There
was an offering called Ogura Cream, which turned out to be a sweet-
ened bean-paste-flavored ice cream, and not something you'd want to
try twice. There was Green Tea ice cream, which was as awful as it
sounds. But then there was the sublime Acerola Sherbet, a tart
cherry-fruit flavor that would sweep to the top of the charts in a
minute if it ever got to America. The pumpkin ice cream was surprisingly good, and the honeydew was heavenly.

We had the same mixed reaction–partly charmed, partly revolted–
time and again all over Asia as we built up the courage to try the
Eastern variations on other familiar Western foods. We found pizza
everywhere, for example. Almost all Asian pizza, whether it's from a
Domino's outlet in downtown Tokyo or a guy we met selling pizza

from the back of a bicycle on the southern outskirts of Kuala Lumpur, comes with kernels of corn sprinkled on top. It seemed strange to us at first, but eventually we all had to admit that it was a tasty addition. In fact, the best vegetarian pizza we've had in any country is the famous Combination Number 3 at Shakey's in Japan: eggplant, corn, and shimeji mushroom. We had more trouble adapting to the shaved seaweed they sprinkle over pizza in Japan and Korea—but at least pizza there is generally served with chopsticks, which you can use to pick off the seaweed.

We grew to like the the shrimp curry crepes we found at International House of Pancakes in Mitaka, Japan, and the apricot-custard cream puff that sells under the mysterious name of My Father's Fist at the Mr. Donut in Seoul. After some hesitation, we finally tried something called *yaki musubi*, which is served in place of french fries at the Kentucky Fried Chicken stands in Japan. *Yaki musubi* turned out to be a fried rice ball. Not bad, either.

Kentucky Fried Chicken was probably the most successful of the major fast-food chains in terms of sheer marketing to Asians. Somehow, the KFC folks successfully sold Japan, Korea, and parts of China on the notion that fried chicken is the classic American fare for Christmas dinner. (One of my own daughters, American born and bred, saw the commercials so often that she came to believe this.) The idea has gone over so well in Japan that you actually have to make a reservation, a week or two in advance, just to get a carry-out box of chicken at any time on December 24 or 25. Beginning in early December, KFC puts up giant signs outside each store telling how many reservations are still available.

Over time, we grew so accustomed to these Orientalized delights that we were actually disappointed on our trips home to the United States when we discovered that we couldn't get, say, Domino's to deliver that spectacular teriyaki-chicken-with-corn pizza that we had grown to like in Tokyo.

One summer, when we were headed home to make the annual rounds of relatives and home offices, the five of us all piled out of the plane in New York after one of those endless flights from Tokyo. Since our kids wouldn't touch airline food, we decided our first stop would be McDonald's—the closest McDonald's to Kennedy Airport, wherever it might be. We stepped out the doors of the international terminal and hailed a cab. A guy pulled up and stopped for us. Then we stood there waiting. And waiting. And waiting. Finally, the driver screamed something extremely rude in an arcane foreign tongue and squealed furiously off.

Only then did we realize what we'd done wrong.

In high-tech Japan, when the taxi driver pulls over, the rear door of the cab pops open automatically. You get in, and the door automatically swings shut. After a couple of years of this, it never dawns on you to reach out and open the taxi door for yourself. So when this guy in New York pulled over, we naturally waited for the door to open. The driver, meanwhile, was naturally waiting for us to open the door and get in. We turned out to be considerably more patient than he was. He's probably still ranting about it in some taxi garage somewhere.

Eventually, we got to a McDonald's, only to walk right into one more round of international culinary confusion: Willa Reid stepped up to the counter and ordered a "Mac-chao." This was one one of the all-time classics of Japanese McDonald's, a spicy fried rice served in a straw basket. I can still remember the look–half astonishment, half irritation–on the face of that woman behind the counter at McDonald's in Queens when a customer came in and ordered fried rice. I can also remember the look on my daughter's face when they told her, in blunt New York fashion, that you can't get fried rice at McDonald's. "But I *always* get Mac-chao at McDonald's," Willa said, with perfect logic, if you think about it.

This incident prompted me, after we got back to Japan, to do some serious reporting on the Asianization of American fast food. I enlisted the whole family to work on this story with me, and we set out across Tokyo on an eating binge. With five hungry Americans on the prowl, this kind of thing can be pricey. Depending on the value of the dollar at any given time, a Big Mac can easily run to $6.00 or so in Japan. A Domino's medium (with corn) costs $27.50. Even plain old Denny's charges $4.00 for one cup of coffee. Refill? You want a refill? That'll be another $4.00. I solved the money problem–brilliantly, I thought–by billing the whole excursion to my newspaper.

As we started in on our "reporting," something we all noticed was that not just the flavor of the food but also the style of the stores has been adapted to Asian tastes. That's why McDonald's in Japan always has a uniformed staffer employed full-time to bow a greeting to cars entering the Drive-Thru lane. That's why every take-out box of chicken at KFC in South Korea was personally signed by the cook–to convey that Japanese notion of a personal commitment to quality. That's why a lot of burger joints in Japan have karaoke rooms; at McDonald, they're called (what else?) MacSong. That's why, the one time we ran into Ronald McDonald prancing around outside one of his restaurants in Nagoya, he gave us his business card.

The Asian outlets of American fast food also introduced us to another central aspect of the Asianization of Western ways (or perhaps it was the Westernization of Asian ways; it's not always easy to say which is which). All over East Asia, we found our native language, English–but a whole new form of English, an English heavily spiced with Eastern flavors.

The basic dynamic at work here is that native speakers of Chinese, Japanese, Korean, Bahasa Malaysia, Thai, think of English as seriously cool. It is the global language of big business, after all, but also the language of the global American culture: of *Baywatch* and Big Bird, of Michael Jackson, Michael Jordan, and Mickey Mouse. Just like those Americans who wouldn't dream of carrying a handbag without the Louis Vuitton symbol stamped all over it, Asians these days like to throw around English words and phrases to prove how cosmopolitan they are.

This is evident, as we quickly learned, when you place an order at one of the fast-food chains. Since fast food itself is considered a Western phenomenon, transactions in the fast-food trade must be carried out in English, or at least quasi-English. The first time I tried to order a small Coke at McDonald, I had no doubt about how to do it; of course I knew how to say "small" in Japanese. "Coke," I said. "*Chiisai* Coke." The friendly young woman behind the counter gave me one of those vacant looks that means communication is not taking place. "Coke!" I repeated, somewhat louder. *"Chiisai!"* A few more repetitions ensued, and finally this Japanese person figured out what I wanted to say. "Ahhhhh," she said, with a bright smile of recognition. "Coke, *essu.*" Essu! I should have known! "Essu" is the Japanese pronunciation of the English letter *S*. And as everybody in Japan knows, *S* stands for "small" on American fast-food menus. So you jettison the perfectly good Japanese word for "small" and use "essu" instead. If you're too thirsty for a small Coke, you can order an "emmu"—or even an "erru," which is the closest Japanese can come to saying *L*.

Most of the Asianized English we were to encounter over the next few years was considerably less utilitarian than "essu" and "emmu." For the most part, English is used more for decoration than for communication. Its role is not to convey specific meanings but rather to set forth a vague feeling of internationalism. Consequently, it doesn't matter a whit whether the English on somebody's T-shirt or key-holder or corporate logo is grammatical English, or even logical English. If it's written in Roman letters and uses English words—or words that bear some vague relationship to English—that fills the bill.

Of course, we didn't understand this at first, and so we spent a good deal of time staring in confusion at labels and phrases that appeared, on first glance, to be written in a language we could understand. At one of those superluxe department stores on the Ginza, Tokyo's Fifth Avenue, I bought a sleek, expensive suitcase of dark blue leather. Inscribed on the side, in orange letters, was this message: "The Moment Grace varies to sublime Hazard Leads the way. Blooming ahead, Intensive Gelande Gaily." I still have this piece of luggage, and I still wonder now and then whether that message is supposed to mean anything. I suppose it has as much meaning as the label inscribed on the briefcase I bought in China, which says "Elce Bird—Always and everyway, I want to be quick response."

The real mother lode of Asianized English, however, is found on sweatshirts, T-shirts, jackets, baseball caps, and any other piece of clothing with space for a message. One of our chief frustrations in traveling around Asia was that it was just about impossible to find a shirt or hat inscribed in Japanese, or Korean, or Malaysian—something that would look exotic when we got back home. The clothes simply have to be inscribed in English. It would be much too boring for a young Malaysian woman to wear a T-shirt that said something in Bahasa Malaysia, the national language. Rather, she'd want to wear something like the shirt I saw crossing a busy street one day in the heart of Kuala Lumpur, a yellow T-shirt with blue letters that said "I love you guitar to dying."

I once attended a gathering in Tokyo where the minister of education gave out awards to the nation's top high school students in several academic disciplines. The boy who won the math award attended one of the new, avant-garde private schools in Tokyo that have dropped the requirement for school uniforms. And so it was that this budding genius came up to the stage to receive his high honor wearing a sweatshirt that said "Snot House."

Some other messages we spotted on shirts were equally simple: "Let's Get Vacation!" "Hope Today is Happy Day!" "Since Baby" "High Touch Town" "We are Fashion Boy." But some were quite prolix, like the following, spotted on a ski parka: "Slowing dance on snow stage. We love enjoying, to plays in active sportive Land with Fashion Girls! High Sense since 1994!"

Over time, as we saw more and more of this fractured English prose, certain patterns began to emerge, and we realized that some of these slogans actually had meaning, in a manner of speaking. For example, that sign we spotted the first night we were in Tokyo—"Fine Boys Since 1987 says Lets Sex!"—seemed like total nonsense at the time. Gradually, though, we realized that this slogan was full of meaning for the Japanese.

In Japanese English, the words "boys" and "girls" are used to describe trendy, popular young people of dating age, roughly from eighteen to thirty-five. The words "fine" and "fashion" are adjectives that suggest "up-to-date," or "cool." (The terms "high-sense" and "high-touch" also convey a sense of living on the leading edge of the latest fashions.) The expression "since 19xx" is used for precisely the opposite purpose of its use in English-speaking countries. In England, snooty shops and manufacturers of luxury goods like to use "Since..." on their labels to suggest they have been around forever: "Purveyors to the Royal House Since 1734." In Japan, "since..." is used to suggest that a store or product is brand-new, like "since 1996." In fact, the "since 1987" on that billboard was the oldest "since..." I ever saw in Japan.

As for the concluding phrase, "Let's Sex," this is simply a translation of a common pattern in the Japanese language. The Japanese verb *shimahshō,* meaning "let's do it," can be used with any noun: *benkyo shimahshō,* "let's study;" *ryoko shimahshō,* "let's travel." And so it seems perfectly normal for the Japanese to take the English translation of their verb "let's" and combine it with any English noun. You see patterns like this all the time: "Let's Skiing." "Let's Business Meeting." "Let's Recreation." "Let's Sex."

So if you want to get across to youthful Japanese consumers the message that your company is a fashionable new endeavor targeting a market of upscale young men with romance on their minds, there's a perfectly clear way to convey this information: "Fine Boys Since 1987 says Let's Sex." What could be more obvious?

It always mystified me how the Japanese determine what to call some new phenomenon that enters their world. Will it be a Japanese word, a real English word, or some rough mix of the two? As a rule of thumb, a new idea or gadget that comes to Japan from the West is known simply by its English name (or the Japanese pronunciation of the English name). Radio is known in Japan as "rah-jee-oh." Television is shortened slightly to "te-re-bi." But for some reason the telephone, which arrived in Japan about the same time as the radio, is known by the thoroughly Japanese word *den-wa*, a word formed by combining two characters that mean "electric talk." When the cellular phone came to Japan in the early 1990s, I thought for sure it would be known as a "se-ru hone," which is what a Japanese speaker would say if he was trying to pronounce "cell phone." In fact, a cell phone is called a *keitai-denwa*, a term that is written with four characters meaning "the electric talker you hook on the belt of your kimono."

A fighter jet is known as a "jetto fy-tah," which is simple enough; but then another piece of modern weaponry, the nuclear submarine, gets a completely Japanese name: *genshiryoku sensuikan*, a mouthful written with six characters that mean "primary-nucleus-powered-under-water-warship." An automobile is known by the Japanese word *kuruma*, an ancient Japanese word that used to mean "oxcart." But a truck is called a "to-rah-ku."

The feeling of familiar-yet-strange we used to get seeing these bizarre English slogans all over the place was heightened by the widespread use of all sorts of English words and phrases that do not exist in the English language. With the same ingenuity that created the Walkman and the fax machine, the Japanese have created new forms of English that we English speakers never thought of. Frankly, some of these words ought to exist in English. A lot of Japanese people who use these new Anglicisms every day are amazed to learn that native speakers don't even know the words.

I remember a fairly spirited argument with a distinguished college professor named Fukuda—a man who had studied at Harvard and translated Spenser's *The Faerie Queen* into Japanese—over his refusal to believe that I didn't know the common English verb "to cost-up." "Cost-up." This is a Japanese verb, pronounced "coasto-ahppu." It is one of countless variations on the English words "up" and "down" that are constantly used in Japanese speech. (One reason for the popularity of these "-up" and "-down" words is that both are fairly easy to pronounce in Japanese. "Down" comes out as "down." "Up" becomes "ahppu," which is reasonably close to the real thing.)

So if a Sony, for example, announces a 5 percent price increase for CDs, the newspapers will report that there was a major "coasto-ahppu." When a retailer cuts prices, that's a cost-down; sometimes the newspapers have big advertisements telling about some store's "coasto-down fay-ah," or cost-down fair. If the taxi driver is playing the radio too loud, you tap him politely on the shoulder and ask, would he please "boh-rume-down?" and he will turn down the volume. When a Japanese politician gets snared in one of the country's recurrent payoff scandals, the newspapers invariably report that he has suffered a significant "ee-may-ji-down," which means his image has declined. Politicians can "ee-may-ji-ahppu" as well, although this seems less common. Nowadays, many Japanese women try to achieve an image-up of their own by seeking out a plastic surgeon who can provide them with a more Westernized bustline; this operation is known, inevitably, as a "bahsto-ahppu."

Among those most likely to have a "bahsto-ahppu" are the legions of young women who work as general helpers around a Japanese office. These women, generally dressed for work in dark blue corporate uniforms, flight-attendant style, are there to make copies, serve tea, run down the street to buy office supplies, deliver important packages to clients, and so forth. They aren't secretaries—that's a separate line of work—but rather just ladies around the office who help out. Their job title is one of those made-in-Japan English terms: "office lady," or O.L. (pronounced "oh erru"). The classic office romance in a Japanese company occurs when a cute young O.L. starts dating a junior executive, or "salaryman." At first the pair go out in a group with everybody else in their section. But eventually the time comes for them to head off together, as a couple; that's called a "two-shot."

At first, these encounters with English that didn't sound like English, with hot dogs that didn't taste like hot dogs (they were made of fish sausage), seemed little more than amusing aspects of daily life in a distant culture. The Inscrutable East, and all that. Given the economic, political, and cultural clout of the United States all over the world, it was to be expected that Asian countries, too, would mimic Western ways. And given societies that remembered and celebrated thousands of years of Asian culture, it was no big surprise that Westernization would come with a decidedly Eastern flavor. But gradually we came to see that our initial taste of cultural coupling had been nothing more than an appetizer, a preview of something considerably bigger than mysterious T-shirts and seaweed-speckled pizza. We came to see that there was another and more fundamental sense in which the countries of East Asia were emulating and adapting Western ways.

I wish I could say it was due to brilliant planning on my part, but in fact it was largely by coincidence that we happened to move to Asia just in time to witness the beginning of the historic transformation of Asia's role in world affairs—the emergence from centuries of colonial rule, and the insistence on a significant role in shaping and governing global affairs. That is, we were watching the phenomenon described in the previous chapter: the Asian renaissance, or the East Asian miracle, or whatever you want to call it.

This Asian renaissance began in Japan. Japan's almost unbelievable turnabout from total rubble to vast riches—achieved in about half a lifetime—became the great dream and the model for all the rest of the Orient. In Japan, they called it the *sengo kiseki*—the postwar miracle. Personally, I like that term, because it seems to me indeed a miracle that the Japanese were able to claw their way back from the self-inflicted disaster of World War II that destroyed their country.

Perhaps you've seen the photographs of those shocked, weeping masses of Japanese people listening to their emperor's radio broadcast of August 15, 1945. War-weary, starving, sick, and sad, people dressed in makeshift smocks made from old newspapers sank to their knees and bowed their heads when they heard–virtually all of them for the first time–the imperial voice croaking through the static. Hirohito didn't tell his subjects all that had happened: that the Japanese empire had been completely lost, that the Imperial Army and Navy were totally destroyed, that five million Japanese had died, that thirty million had no homes, that every Japanese city was a wreck, that there was virtually nothing left to eat and no intact roads or railroads to deliver food even if there had been some, that once-proud Japan was the most despised nation on earth, that millions around the world had cheered when atomic bombs were dropped on Japanese cities, and that an occupation force of enemy soldiers would soon arrive to run the country. Rather, the emperor set forth the state of things in a classic piece of Japanese understatement: "The situation has developed not necessarily to Japan's advantage."

No, not necessarily. By August of 1945, Japan had nothing. Its formidable prewar industrial base was gone; even in remote areas, nearly every factory was destroyed. Railroads had been shattered so badly–partly by U.S. bombs, and partly by the Japanese military, which ripped up the rails to make artillery shells–that there were few stretches in the whole country where a train could transit more than ten miles. And to make matters worse, the island nation had no natural resources to fall back on. A series of volcanic islands with few natural resources, Japan has never had any measurable amounts of petroleum, iron ore, aluminum, copper, or other minerals. The war years had used just about all coal and timber reserves. There was no food–people were so hungry they ate the bark off all the ginkgo trees–and there wasn't enough land in the entire country to grow enough food to feed everybody. Japan was a ruined nation, with no resources at home and no friends anywhere.

That was 1945. Ten years later, Japan was still one of the poorest third-world countries. Hats in hand, a delegation from Tokyo approached the World Bank in 1955, seeking a loan of a few million dollars to build a new transit project, the "bullet train," which would race at high speeds between Tokyo and Osaka. The bankers thought about it and gave their answer: No. The country known in the West as little Japan was too poor, they concluded, and too backward to carry off such a high-technology endeavor.

Thirty years later, in the mid-1970s, when my wife and I first lived there, Japan was no longer desperately poor, but it was hardly rich. In the southern city where we lived, Kumamoto, there were still war ruins lying around, because nobody could afford to clean them up. We signed up for telephone service the day we moved into our little house and were asked to wait a few days until the local utility could get a shipment of phones. We were still waiting more than a year later. The stores and businesses in downtown Kumamoto turned their neon signs off about nine o'clock because the country didn't have enough fuel to provide electricity through the night. In 1975, Japan's per capita income–roughly speaking, the amount of money a single worker makes in a year–was about one-third the figure for the United States.

But by 1975 the foundation for growth was firmly in place. Since then, Japan has lived the miracle. Today, this crowded, isolated island country with no natural resources is a global economic superpower. It is the home of eight of the world's fourteen biggest banks and two of the four biggest securities firms. It is the world's biggest maker of steel, ships, home electronics, and countless other high-tech products. Even now, after a long recession, the Japanese are rich; the country's per capita income is the same as America's. Tokyo in the 1980s became the world's number one market for firms like Gucchi, Chanel, Rossignol, and other makers of luxury goods. Today the neon signs–huge, absurdly bright and colorful neon signs–flash and gleam all night long in every city. Today sleek bullet trains race the length and breadth of the Japanese archipelago. One day in 1993, aboard the fastest train from Tokyo to Osaka, I met a European gentleman who told me he worked for the World Bank. Hat in hand, he had come to Japan to ask for a few billion dollars to beef up the bank's assets.

He had gone to the right place, because Japan is the world's biggest donor of foreign aid to poor nations, and the world's leading lender to rich ones. The United States is also a country of vast wealth, but it happens to be deeply in hock to Japanese lenders. Japanese banks, insurance companies, and government agencies have loaned so much money to Washington–about $500 billion–that when Japan's prime minister vaguely suggested one day in 1997 that his countrymen might want to sell their U.S. Treasury bonds, the Dow-Jones average fell 200 points, which was then Wall Street's biggest drop in a decade. (The prime minister quickly announced that he didn't mean it, and the market went back up 150 points the next day.)

It was a miracle, all right. Japan's economy has performed in considerably less than miraculous fashion for most of the past decade–and even so, the country has easily maintained its position as the world's second-richest nation. Judged by the economic data, no country in history has come so far so fast. The real story, though, lies not so much in the data as in the lives of ordinary people, the millions of Japanese who lived through the transformation. Of all these people, the one who personifies Japan's miracle for me is Nosaka Akiyuki, a witty, talkative man who also happens to be the country's greatest living novelist.

Nosaka Akiyuki, whom I came to know in the 1990s, was born in 1930, when Japan controlled a vast Asian empire. He lived through the war and its painful aftermath, and wrote a series of books chronicling the unbelievable changes his country experienced. They are marvelously readable tales, gritty, funny, honest, and occasionally filthy–which perhaps explains why Nosaka got the shaft from the Nobel committee.

It was an open secret that the Nobel Prize committee wanted to give the Nobel Prize in Literature, in the fiftieth year after Hiroshima, to a Japanese author, preferably one who had lived through, and written about, the war and the Bomb. In the summer of 1994, as the judges were considering the choice, there were several potential candidates. The Japanese press was full of speculation. One favorite among the prognosticators was Endo Shusako, author of passionate, moving tales (*Silence* would be my recommendation, if you can read only one) dealing with the complexities of religious faith. The problem for Endo was that he's one of the minute percentage of Japanese who are Roman Catholic. The oddsmakers back in Tokyo figured that the Swedes would not want to seem so narrow-minded as to pick out a Catholic in a non-Christian Asian country. Another strong contender was Oe Kenzaburo, whose sparse, rather foggy novels and stories are suffused with the pain and anger of World War II. Oe's problem was that his books are so convoluted that almost no reader can finish them. (If you want to try, *A Personal Matter* is perhaps the best choice.) Of course, this was not a disqualifier for Nobel Prize candidates.

And then there was Nosaka, an acerbic type who dabbled in politics, television, and humor magazines when he wasn't writing more serious stuff. The serious Nosaka produces prose seared in the heat of the atomic bomb; for him, as for many Japanese people his age, the nuclear blast remains the dominant fact of his time on earth. To make a buck on the side, Nosaka also wrote lighter stuff—comic novels, laced with violence and sex. Not many of Nosaka's novels have been translated into English. One that was translated (and thus was available for perusal by the Nobel judges) was a funny and outrageous story called *Erogotoshitachi*, a title that was rendered into English, with perfect accuracy, as *The Pornographers*. Those of us who are Nosaka fans feel to this day that the existence of this translation probably cost our man the Nobel Prize; the judges, according to our theory, couldn't bring themselves to bestow their great honor on the author of a book that was primarily about ejaculation.

In the end, it was the foggy Oe Kenzaburo who won the Nobel Prize as the world recalled the fiftieth anniversary of the end of World War II. For some reason, the Nobel committee didn't ask me for advice, but if they had, I would have told them that before they reached a decision they should read Nosaka's *America Hijiki*, the finest story yet published about what the war and its aftermath did to the people of Japan.

America Hijiki, set mainly in the fall of 1945, is based on Nosaka's memories of his wretched village near Kobe in the first years after Japan's surrender. Everybody is starving. Quite often, the only meal people get in a whole day is one stick of chewing gum, tossed from a passing jeep by American GIs from the occupation force. The pain of hunger is matched, perhaps exceeded, by the pain of begging for food from the erstwhile enemy. One day, a U.S. B-29 flies over the village; people cower in fear beneath the canvas roofs of their makeshift shacks, but then realize that the bomber has dropped a long line of parachutes, with wooden crates dangling from the chutes. Inside the crates are large cans, which contain "some wrinkled black stuff like little pieces of thread."

Nobody in the village has ever seen this stuff before, but curiosity and sheer hunger drive a few brave souls to scoop up some and eat it.

The stuff is parceled out to every household, and for the next few weeks each meal consists of this grainy black food that is hard to chew. The villagers don't know what it is, but they put more salt on it and keep eating. One of the wise village elders decides that this food must be the American version of *hijiki,* a shredded brown seaweed served with tofu in fancy Japanese restaurants. Everyone is so full of questions—since when did Americans eat *hijiki?*—that the mayor eventually asks an American soldier. And thus the village learns the English name for this strange black food: coffee. The proud people of Japan have been eating ground coffee for dinner, because there was nothing else to eat.

Just about fifty years after the events of that novel, I had a very late supper in Tokyo with Nosaka-san. A tuxedoed waiter brought us coffee in delicate china cups no bigger than a thimble. As we sipped, Nosaka told me that much of *America Hijiki* was true. People had been eating ground coffee—not enjoying it, but eating it, because they were so poor they had to eat whatever handout they received. It wasn't just handouts, either, Nosaka said, deftly wielding his teak chopsticks over a silver tray covered artistically with small slices of tuna that cost $20 per ounce. Some people were so hungry back then, he told me, that they would pluck a silkworm off the mulberry tree and swallow it whole, just to have something in the stomach.

How was it that this man and his fellow Japanese, trapped in a shattered island country with no resources, had pulled themselves up from abject poverty to enormous wealth? There are two basic answers.

Japan had no natural resources, but it did have some assets to draw on. Japan's postwar miracle sprang mainly from its most important resource: Japanese people. With their well-known penchant for hard work, respect for education, and habits of thrift and saving, the Japanese threw themselves with total commitment into rebuilding their nation and its economy. With a cultural propensity to put the group first and individual needs second, the population willingly accepted governmental schedules that gave factories, shipyards, and warehouses priority over housing, shops, and stores. (These priorities were still in effect in the 1970s, which is why we couldn't get a home telephone.) Long-term growth was the watchword, and everybody deferred gratification to build for the future.

Japan's other great resource was its only friend in the world: the

United States. For a variety of reasons—a sense of responsibility, basic human decency, a need to maintain Japan as a non-Communist outpost just offshore from Russia and China—victorious America took on the role of big brother and adopted Japan for a makeover. Americans wrote the Japanese constitution and gave the country a democratic government that guaranteed fundamental freedoms. American experts, dispatched to Japan for months or years at a time, taught willing pupils how to build banks and highways and state-of-the-art factories. America fed the Japanese—not just gum and coffee, but huge quantities of wheat, vegetables, and meat from the midwestern grain belt, which literally kept the nation alive until the first decent rice crop came in 1946. The United States, having learned a lesson at Pearl Harbor about Japanese military prowess, forced Japan to hold its military budget to minute levels and provided American forces to defend the islands. Japan poured the money saved into its industrial build-up. And when finished goods started pouring off those Japanese assembly lines, America became the biggest and richest market for Honda, Panasonic, Sony, Toyota, Nikon, and thousands of other Japanese firms.

It was probably the most generous response that any conqueror has ever shown to a once-hated enemy. I sometimes wonder whether the United States could do the same thing today. It's hard to imagine an American president today providing similar aid and comfort for an enemy like Iran or Iraq, and neither of those countries ever attacked American soil, as Japan did in 1941. Even in those optimistic years after World War II, it was hard for the rest of the world to believe what the Americans were doing for Japan. In Britain, the whole unlikely scenario prompted a small gem of the silver screen, *The Mouse That Roared,* starring Peter Sellers as the prime minister of a tiny, impoverished country that declares war on the United States so it, too, can cash in big after the inevitable defeat and surrender. (Naturally, things go awry; Sellers and the Army of Grand Fenwick accidentally capture New York.) The film was a hit in America in 1959 but never caught on in Japan; people evidently didn't get the joke.

The Japanese, knowing a good thing when they saw it, took advantage of their big brother's help and went to work. Their love for constant tinkering, their endless zeal for improving whatever they worked on, gradually overcame the world's contempt for the phrase "Made in Japan." By the 1980s, consumers in every country were clamoring for Japanese cars, cameras, computers, cassette players, chemicals, camping gear, karaoke machines, and so on. And global dominance came extremely fast. In 1960, Japanese automobile firms had about 2 percent of the world market—essentially, all the cars they could sell in Japan. Just twenty years later, the Japanese had a 30 percent share of the global market, and American buyers willingly signed their names to three-month waiting lists to get the latest-model Honda. Japan's share of global semiconductor sales went from about 10 percent in 1980 to 50 percent ten years later.

So much money poured back to the isolated island nation that it became a force in the world almost in spite of itself. When the six richest nations of North America and Europe decided to form an organization to protect the interests of the world's well-to-do, they had almost no choice but to invite Japan to join. The group of developed nations became the G-7, and the Japanese prime minister had a seat at the table. For the first time in history, an Asian nation was being treated as an equal by the Western powers that ran the world.

THE REST OF ASIA reacted to this stunning development with ambivalence. "I don't think anybody will forget the moment when we knew that Asia would be represented in the bloc of the most-developed countries," a South Korean diplomat told me once. "But we might have picked a different representative." Looking at that photo of Prime Minister Sato lined up on the steps of some grand European palace with the leaders of the great Western nations brought out intense feelings of Asian pride—coupled with intense feelings of Asian hatred. Most of the East Asian nations feared and loathed Japan, and with reason. For the first half of this century, the Japanese had made no secret of the fact that they considered themselves superior to their fellow Orientals on the continent. It was the Japanese emperor, they said, who had a divine right to rule all of Asia. In his august name the Imperial Army conquered, colonized, and enslaved Manchuria, Korea, Malaysia, Singapore, Burma, the Philippines, Vietnam, Laos, Cambodia, Taiwan, and as much of mainland China as they could

reach. On the mainland, the Japanese called themselves the liberators of Asia–the Asians who had finally driven the Western colonial-
ists out of the Orient. Back in Tokyo, the "liberators" had their own
term for the Japanese role on the continent: *toyo meishu*, or lord of
the East.

In many cases, the new colonial "lords" were crueler than the
British, Dutch, Portuguese, and French rulers they defeated. Japan
outlawed the local languages, forced schoolchildren to take Japanese
names, and made everybody bow humbly twice each day toward the
emperor back in Tokyo. They built up infrastructure and strength-
ened their defenses using slave labor from the conquered cities, and
forced perhaps 200,000 Chinese, Korean, and Filipino women to work
as "comfort women"–prostitutes for Japanese soldiers. The resulting
ill-feeling (to put it mildly) toward Japan has been mitigated somewhat in recent years, partly by time and partly by the massive quantities of financial aide that Tokyo distributes all over East Asia. But a
good deal of rage still smolders.

How long can an entire country stay angry? You might want to direct that question to the former president of South Korea, Kim Young
Sam. On August 15, 1995, fifty years to the day after Japan surrendered, President Kim celebrated Korea's Liberation Day in the following manner: He set up bleachers on a major thoroughfare of
downtown Seoul. With 100,000 Koreans cheering, a gleaming gold
wrecking ball flew through the summer air and smashed the graceful
fluted dome of the neoclassical building that had long ago been the
headquarters of Japan's imperial governor in Korea. This elegant
structure was the most attractive building in downtown Seoul. It had
served for years as Korea's National Art Museum, and since there was
no other suitable building available, the museum's collection had to
be removed from public display and stacked in a warehouse. But
none of this mattered to President Kim; half a century after the
Japanese left the country in abject defeat, South Korea was still nurturing, indeed celebrating, its hatred of the former conquerors by
smashing buildings to smithereens.

But for all the rancor, there was no denying Japan's success. And
gradually, other Asian countries decided that they, too, could succeed
the way the Japanese had. "In the 1970s, 1980s, a new generation of

leaders came along in East Asia," said John Malott, a veteran Asia hand in the U.S. foreign service who is currently American ambassador to Malaysia. "These people didn't remember much about the years when Japan had occupied their countries. They used the memories of the war quite skillfully to get aid money from Japan. But the fact is, the younger leaders were less interested in waving the bloody shirt of World War II and more concerned about learning what they could from Japan's model."

And so a second wave of Asian enrichment began, built on the principle that "anything Japan can do, we can do too." In the 1980s, four more Asian states–Taiwan, Singapore, South Korea, and Hong Kong–adopted the Japanese model and worked their way to prosperity. These four stars of East Asia's second act were known as the Four Little Dragons (with Japan evidently considered a Big Dragon on the global economic scene). In the early nineties, similar patterns of rapid growth and modernization were seen in Malaysia, Indonesia, and Thailand. As the 1990s come to an end, the current Asian champion is China, which has leaped from abject poverty into the ranks of the world's richest nations–and is quite likely to become the Biggest Dragon of all. The path to prosperity was not always straight or smooth, and some of the countries–Indonesia, Malaysia, South Korea, Thailand, and Japan–are currently in dire straits. But these setbacks are probably temporary. The overall trend is clearly toward more growth and more prosperity. Asia is growing rich.

OUR FAMILY SAW this transformation almost everywhere. When my wife and I traveled through East Asia in the early 1970s, we used to come upon huge snarls of two-wheeled traffic as people in simple cotton smocks and loose shirts made their way through the impossibly crowded streets on bicycles or motorcycles. When we traveled to those same teeming cities a quarter century later, in the 1990s, they looked a lot more like home. Of course we still soaked in the exotic sights, sounds, and smells of the Asian bazaar on many big streets: people selling fried rice balls and garlic-grilled ginkgo nuts from wooden pushcarts, Buddhist monks with round straw hats holding out earthen vases for alms. But now, on those city streets, we saw more people in pin-striped business suits, in attractive dresses with patent-leather pumps, traveling to work in their cars (which made the impossible crowding that much worse), or riding the subways with the newest-model Walkman hooked to their pockets and leather handbags over their shoulders (in East Asia, both men and women wear handbags). We were looking at a phenomenon that was familiar to the Western democracies but fairly new in Asia: a middle class. In fact, with a billion members already and several hundred million more people about to join, Asia's is the biggest middle class the world has ever known.

To some Western visitors seeing Asia for the first time in the 1990s, this change is a source of disappointment—a letdown like that our family felt when we first arrived at Narita Airport. You fly sixteen grueling hours from the United States to a glamorous Asian capital like Kuala Lumpur, and what do you see? A bunch of people in business suits walking busily into a glass-and-steel office tower that has "Citibank" over the door and a Starbucks Coffee in the lobby. "For this," a friend of mine from Nebraska told me once, as we strolled past the Mr. Donut stand—it's right next door to Dairy Queen—on Tokyo's famous Ginza, "I could have stayed in Omaha." In some ways, in fact, Tokyo feels more American than America. In all of the United States, there's only one retail outlet for that quintessential yuppie merchant L. L. Bean. Tokyo has four of them. Of course, when you get there, there's a big sign in the tent department that says "Let's Camping!"—but it is still L. L. Bean.

We, too, felt we had come to a Disneyland model of contemporary America when we first got to Japan. But fairly soon we began to realize that a great deal of what makes Asia so Asian has survived and thrived, in small ways and large.

Books, magazines, and newspapers are all backwards (by our standards); what would be the back cover of a magazine in the West is the front page in Asia, and you read through it turning the pages from left to right. Names are confusing. Most Asian people write their family name first; that is, there's Tanaka Taro and his sister Tanaka Hanako. But in Malaysia and Indonesia, which are primarily Muslim countries, Islamic citizens don't use last names at all. The name is Mohamad. If some Westerner insists on a "last name," then you take on the first name of your father: Mohamad bin Ali.

We came to admire and adapt some of these Asian ways. The plastic models of food in the restaurants, with lifelike spaghetti sauce and nicely browned fried rice, provided a much better introduction to unknown new dishes than a menu could. We loved the vending machines everywhere–roughly one machine for every twenty people; in the United States, the figure is one machine for every two hundred people.

The idea of taking off your shoes at the front step whenever you enter a home–your own or someone else's–just seems so sensible now that we feel incredibly gross, back in the United States, tracking the dirt and mud from outside over people's floors. Taking off your shoes at the door, still standard operating procedure in most Eastern countries, stems from a time when Asians sat and slept on straw mat floors. Today, most people have Western-style beds and carpeting, but the shoes still come off when you go inside a house. No matter what. One day in Tokyo two guys came to our house to deliver a piano; it weighed, probably, twice as much as the two of them combined. With enormous effort, they huffed and puffed that big instrument out of their truck, up the front steps, and across our front porch, where I was holding the door open for them. They stopped at the door, still hefting the piano, slipped off their shoes, stepped into a pair of indoor slippers we had ready for this purpose, and proceeded into the house with their cargo.

IN SHORT, it wasn't just in the fast-food stores that we encountered Western staples flavored with a decidedly Eastern spice. And that's not surprising, because East Asia itself was for centuries an involuntary blend of East and West. Western nations began imposing their ways by force on East Asia some six hundred years ago–and it was only yesterday, in historical terms, when they finally stopped.

Actually, Western Europe's first response to the world of Asia was respectful, even deferential. Marco Polo, who walked from Jerusalem to Beijing at the end of the thirteenth century–and became an official of Kublai Khan's diplomatic corps, if *The Travels of Marco Polo* is to be believed–reported back about a land full of marvels, well ahead of the West in fields ranging from manufacturing to cosmology. Silk and spice traders who traveled East in Polo's wake naturally treated the khans and their successors with the deference a businessman tends to show a client. They even assented to the most elaborate form of kowtow—falling to the knees and knocking the forehead to the floor nine times—when introduced to the Chinese emperor.

When St. Francis Xavier, Matteo Ricci, and other Jesuit missionaries went East—initially to Goa, the first European settlement in India, then on to Malacca, in what is now Malaysia, and eventually to China and Japan—they expressed genuine admiration for Asian scholarship, philosophy, and literature. The Jesuits devoted years, indeed lifetimes, to the chore of learning Chinese and Japanese for the purpose of translating the Bible into those languages. But these sacred projects were delayed for decades because once the fathers started reading the great books of the Orient, they decided it was equally important to transmit the teachings of Asia back to Europe. The Catholic fathers chose Latin as their vehicle. Gradually, the libraries of great European cathedrals and universities came to include titles such as *Antiquissimus Sinarum Liber* ("The Most Ancient Text of China"), which was a translation of the *I Ching*. Naturally, they also translated the most important of the Chinese classics, the *Lun Yü*, or collected discourses, of the sage Kung Fu-tzu—a volume which was given the Latin title *Confucius Sinarum Philosophus sive Scientia Sinensis* ("Confucius, the Philosopher of China, or, The Wisdom of the East.")

Not all the Europeans who had the strength and courage to take the long, treacherous voyage east were so deferential. Conquest and plunder started early. On the Magellan voyage of 1519–21, the first circumnavigation of the globe, the crews stopped for water at a small chain of islands south of the Philippines. There they found two lovely spices unknown to the Western world. They filled the hull of their last remaining ship with these two plants, clove and nutmeg. That sweet, fragrant cargo drew such high prices that every crew member became wealthy. Several of them quickly chartered ships to head back and extract more spice from these "Spice Islands." (They are now known as the Molluca Islands, and make up a segment of the long arc of islands composing Indonesia.)

It wasn't long before a thousand ships per year were leaving Europe for the Orient. The Europeans set out not just to take from the East but to tame it and to teach it Western (i.e., Christian) ways.

Western technological superiority in navigation, business organization, and firepower made the colonial endeavor not only easy for the Europeans but attractive to some Asians. Some embraced their foreign masters, grateful for schools, hospitals, railroads, police, courts, and other trappings of Western civilization. Others resisted–not by force, for no Asian country could stand up to the twelve-inch guns of a man-o'-war, but rather through diplomatic ploys. The king of Siam balanced adeptly between the jealousies of the British (to his south, in Malaya) and the French (to his north, in Indo-China) to remain free of both. The Japanese shogun allowed Dutch traders, and no one else, to call at the port of Nagasaki, and thus neatly manipulated one European power into keeping the others away. After the American navy all but blasted its way into Tokyo Bay in 1853, Japan maintained its sovereignty by playing one Western power against the other, while quickly becoming a "Western power" in its own right. By 1890, the Japanese had a modern army, locally owned banks and railroads, and an emperor who sipped French wine and danced the minuet in white tie and tails at lavish balls in the palace in Tokyo.

In Beijing, the Son of Heaven and his imperial court continued to denounce the colonial powers as barbarians. Since China was clearly the biggest and richest prize in the Asian game–and since the Manchus of the Ching Dynasty were recognized by Europe's various courts as a genuine imperial family–it simply would not do for the Middle Kingdom itself to be colonized by one Western nation. Rather, the Europeans divided this sovereign empire into smaller pieces for their own benefit: a dozen military bases, thirty-eight treaty ports, and hundreds of "concessions," each governed by the rule of "extraterritoriality." For instance, in the British "concession" of Shanghai, roughly a square mile in the heart of the city, British law applied (for Chinese as well as foreigners); disputes were settled and criminals tried in British courts, under British law. Where this piecemeal system failed to serve the colonial powers, they assumed broader responsibility. From 1861 to 1942, China's minister of foreign trade was an Englishman. No doubt this gentleman was referred to in the Forbidden City as a barbarian. But he had power, and the imperial courtiers had almost none.

Looking back on this now, when colonialism is seen as a historical evil, when terms like the "Age of Empire" evoke sailing ships, snuff-boxes, and powdered wigs, it is remarkable to realize how long the colonial regime lasted in East Asia. When the American foreign correspondent John Gunther published his marvelous survey *Inside Asia* in 1939, he noted that across the whole vast expanse from the Red Sea to Tokyo Bay, only two countries—Siam and Japan—were free. "As everybody knows," Gunther wrote, without a trace of irony, "the greatest Asiatic power is Great Britain." And in 1939, it was true.

But not for long. By the time Gunther got the second edition of *Inside Asia* into print in 1942, the "greatest Asiatic power" had lost all its East Asian colonies to the onslaught of the Japanese army—that is, the Imperial Japanese Army, for the Japanese had learned the lessons of colonialism quite clearly from their teachers in the United States and Europe. For the people of East Asia, "liberation" by the brutal Japanese proved no better—in most cases, even worse—than colonial rule by the West. Almost immediately, Britain, France, Holland, and the United States began recruiting partisans and resistance fighters in their former colonies to help drive out the Japanese invaders. On August 15, 1945, when Japan surrendered, East Asia was free of colonial rule for the first time in four centuries.

And then, amazingly, the old Western imperialists came back. Within months of Japan's surrender, Holland reclaimed the "Dutch East Indies." The French went right back to "Indochina." In Malaysia, Singapore, Burma, North Borneo, those bright young lads from Britain's Foreign Office moved back into their old colonial offices, swagger sticks in hand. The portraits of Emperor Hirohito were removed from the schoolroom walls, to be replaced with pictures of George VI. Having won the heroic battle against Japan, Europe was determined to return forthwith to the status quo ante. "I did not become the king's First Minister," Winston Churchill famously declared (or infamously, depending on your vantage point), "to preside over the demise of the British Empire."

For the Asians, who had fought and died side by side with the Western Allies against Japan, it was an unbelievable betrayal. Dr. Mahathir, the Malaysian president, was a twenty-year-old student when the war ended. The saddest day of his life, he says, was the dark day in the fall of 1945 when he realized that the British were coming back to rule again—and that the people of Malaya were powerless to stop them.

It took anywhere from four to forty years for the various East Asian colonies to gain their independence—some through decades of warfare, as in Vietnam, and some through diplomacy and the sheer force of public opinion in a world that had decided imperialism was no longer admirable. About a third of the population of these newly independent East Asian countries today is old enough to remember the various Independence Days—the parades, the fireworks, the speeches and music, the Union Jack or the Tricolore coming down and the new national flag proudly hoisted for the first time. On Malaya's Independence Day, on August 31, 1957, the new government celebrated this long-awaited moment by erecting the world's tallest flagpole—a 311-foot monster that just happens to stand in the middle of the cricket field at the old British colonial club in Kuala Lumpur.

To understand what is happening in East Asia these days, it's crucial to realize that the colonial era is not ancient history for contemporary Asians. Americans threw off colonial rule almost ten generations ago, and it would be hard to find anyone in the United States who still nurtures resentment toward England because of the excesses of King George III. But East Asia is not even one generation removed from colonialism. The current generation of business and governmental leaders grew up in a world where Westerners were the colonial masters, the major employers, the teachers, the preachers, the founders of the great colleges and the major business enterprises. Little wonder that, to this day, many East Asian leaders carry a chip on their shoulders roughly the size of the Great Wall. They grew up in a world where Asians were, in the words of a great imperialist, "lesser breeds without the Law."

Most educated adults in Europe's former Asian colonies know that line of Kipling's. They know about the "White Man's burden" and all the other rationales that the West used to justify domination of the East. Asian history books are full of antique slights and atrocities that most Westerners have never heard of. The Chinese, in particular, love to wallow in the old stories of how badly they were treated. When Hong Kong reverted to Chinese control in 1997, one of the chief ele-

ments of the celebration was the premiere of a new action movie
about the Opium War, that rather inglorious episode when the queen
of England called out the gunships to force the Manchu emperor to
permit British drug dealers to sell narcotics in China. The film hewed
fairly closely to historical facts, evidently because the Chinese considered the truth so appalling that they didn't need to make anything up
to show how evil the West had been.

Today, Asian leaders want their former colonial masters to realize
that they are nobody's subjects anymore. They have not been subtle
about making the point. Among much else, they are building towering monuments to mark their new wealth and independent stature.

We Americans used to do the same thing, of course. At the dawn of
the twentieth century, when we had something to prove to our former
colonial masters in Europe, Americans made sure that the world's
tallest building stood in some great U.S. city. First there was the
Woolworth Building (lower Manhattan, 1911), which was topped by
the Chrysler Building (midtown Manhattan, 1930), which was surpassed by the Empire State Building (midtown Manhattan, 1931),
which gave way to the World Trade Center (downtown Manhattan,
1970), which gave way in turn to the Sears Tower (Chicago, 1974). But
in the twenty-first century, the world's tallest buildings will be in Asia.

Since 1997, the tallest buildings on Earth have been the two
Petronas Towers, rising above the lush green parks of Kuala Lumpur,
Malaysia. The world's tallest buildings are a matched pair of glass-
and-chrome cylinders with a stark and menacing look, like twin mis-
siles ready for firing on the launch pad. When our family stood on the
sidewalk below and gazed up, up, up at these shining behemoths, we
all agreed on one salient fact about them: They're ugly. (Actually, you
can't blame the Malaysians for that; the design came from a Yale architect named Cesar Pelli.) But that's not the point; the buildings
serve the exact purpose they were meant for, which is to shout out to
the world that Malaysia has made it.

The Petronas Towers (Petronas is Malaysia's national petroleum
company) are eighty-eight stories tall, but that wasn't enough to win
the record. So the builders hoisted a long, long needle of stainless
steel–241 feet long, to be precise–atop each building. And with that,
the twin towers reached a height of 1,483 feet (451.9 meters). This

passed the Sears Tower by only ten yards, but that was enough to get an Asian building in the record book (which is maintained by an outfit called the Council on Tall Buildings and Urban Habitat at Lehigh University). Of course, one of the two towers has been just about completely vacant since it opened, and the whole complex has been a bath of red ink as a real estate project. But profit was never the point; those tall buildings were all about national pride, about asserting a place in the world. In any case, those Malaysian towers won't be at the top for long. In Sichuan, the Chinese have a skyscraper in the works that will reach 1,508 feet (457 meters); that one will subsequently be topped by Shanghai's World Financial Center, currently under construction and scheduled to top off at 1,518 feet (460 meters). Hong Kong, Jakarta, and Seoul all have blueprints for towers even higher.

The severe economic setbacks that struck some East Asian countries in the late 1990s meant that some of the ambitious plans for growth had to be cast aside. But there is still a lot of ambition on Asian drawing boards. By the twenty-first century, Asia will be able to claim not only the tallest but also the world's *longest* building–the so-called Linear City, planned to extend 1.2 miles under one roof along the Kelang River in central Kuala Lumpur. It will have the world's biggest airports, at Shanghai and Hong Kong. It will boast the world's biggest dam as well, the world's longest undersea power cable, not to mention bridges, power plants, nuclear accelerators, and countless other massive projects that will qualify as "bigger than anything in the Western world." When you travel around Asia these days, the travel guides invariably point out these wonders; they spin out the heights and lengths and tonnage of concrete with particular gusto, it always seem to me, when there are Americans in the tour group. It brings to mind Annie Oakley singing "Anything you can do, I can do better." When it comes to long, tall, heavy, glitzy, or expensive, the Asians can do–and they want us to know it.

IT'S FAIRLY EASY for Westerners to snipe at those ugly buildings in Kuala Lumpur, just as Europeans no doubt sneered at the Empire State Building when it first went up. If Asians want to spend their money on massive dams and mile-long office buildings, we can smile indulgently and let them do it. But we should not be so indifferent to the intellectual side of East Asia's lunge for recognition and respect on the world stage.

For a decade or so, a group of scholars, statesmen, and business leaders in East Asia have been promoting the notion that Asian cultural traditions are just as worthy of attention around the world as the Judaeo-Christian ideals the Western missionaries and conquerors carried with them during the age of imperialism. As we've seen already, they call this body of Asian knowledge the Asian spirit or the Asian way. When East Asia's financial boom first came to the attention of Western economists and financiers, there was a brief flurry of interest in an Asian way in the Western media. As long as we could make money with it, the theory seemed to be, we'll think about it some. But as soon as the Asian crisis of 1997 began reversing the economic charts, the Asian way became as outmoded in the West as last week's newspapers. But it shouldn't be. Whether or not we still believe in Asia's economic miracle, the social miracle is alive and well. And the Asians tell us that the social miracle, too, is a reflection of this Asian spirit. So when East Asians try to talk to us about their philosophical and cultural traditions, we ought to pay attention.

For example, people in the West should be paying attention to Kishore Mahbubani, the Singaporean diplomat I quoted in the first chapter of this book. This Mahbubani is an important figure in the emerging Asian consciousness. As a serious thinker and an outspoken advocate of his nation's ideological foundations, he fills a role, in these opening days of the Asian century, somewhat like the role played by Henry Kissinger in the waning days of the Cold War. He is a small but imposing figure—smart as all get-out, articulate, engaging, and friendly. He studied at (where else?) Harvard and lived in New York City for most of the 1980s, when he was Singapore's ambassador to the United Nations. That experience gave him a deep, if biased, view of American life.

Mahbubani has developed a strong following among East Asian bureaucrats, business leaders, and scholars with his argument that the Asian way is different from Western cultural patterns. But Mahbubani and his many disciples take the argument a step further than that: the Asian way is not just different from Western culture, it's better.

In a series of articles and lectures bearing titles like "The Dangers of Decadence" and "Go East, Young Man," Mahbubani tells his fellow Asians that "the American boat is sinking" and that the West needs a strong dose of Confucian values to set things right: "If Americans were to try to begin learning from Asians, their nation would be a better place."

The world is at a point of fundamental change, he says. "In a major reversal of a pattern lasting centuries, many Western societies– including the United States–are doing some major things fundamentally wrong, while a growing number of East Asian societies are doing the same things right. . . . East Asia's gross domestic product is already larger than that of either the United States or the European Community, and it will exceed both combined in the year 2005. Such economic prosperity, contrary to American belief, results not just from free market arrangements but also from the right social and political choices."

Mahbubani is one of many East Asians whose idea of a fun evening is to sit around trashing the Western world in general and the United States in particular. He knows by heart the FBI crime statistics for the number of rapes, robberies, and murders in the United States over the past thirty years; he can cite chapter and verse on Americans' penchant for drugs, alcohol, and extramarital sex. He knows all about O. J. Simpson, Monica Lewinsky, and the woman who won a million-dollar settlement when she spilled McDonald's coffee on her legs. He likes to contrast the "deep value placed on family in Asian societies" with "the disintegration of the American family," as shown in high rates of divorce and out-of-wedlock births.

For all that, Kishore Mahbubani is a genial, charming fellow–easy to like, even for an American. Maybe that's why I (stupidly) let myself get dragged into a sort of debate with him once at a symposium on "The New Asia." I was listening to Kishore talking about "American decline," and suddenly I snapped. I had heard just about enough of these hyperconfident Asians expostulating on what was wrong with my country. So I fired back.

"Ambassador Mahbubani is a thoughtful observer of our country,"

I started in, "but he is missing perhaps the most important fact about American society: our resiliency. Sure, we have social problems. But we face up to them. We report them in our media and debate them in Congress and try everything we can think of until we find solutions." I went on to say that "other countries" lack this resiliency, because they don't tolerate criticism. Of course the "other country" I had in mind was Kishore's own Singapore, where people who point out social problems tend to end up in exile or jail.

I should have quit while I was ahead. But I thought I was on a roll, so I kept going. "Anyway, if Asia is so wonderful and America is so rotten," I said, "how come hundreds of thousands of Asians every year get on the boat to America? How come every time you turn the corner in New York you find a Korean family running a deli or a Cambodian selling newspapers? They're coming to America because they know if they work hard in our country, they'll have the greatest standard of living in the world."

With that, Mahbubani stood up like a tiger ready to pounce. "Yes, I'm glad you mentioned the American standard of living," he replied, soft-spoken and amiable even as he plunged the rhetorical dagger.

"Yes, it's true, if standard of living means the number of square feet in your home, or the number of channels on your television set, or the number of horsepower in the driveway—then, yes, America leads the world. But if standard of living means not being afraid to go outside that home after dark, or not worrying about what filth your children see on all those channels, or not wondering when you get up in the morning if all that horsepower will still be in the driveway—if the standard includes safety and decency and security, then our East Asian societies have the higher standard."

Many Asian leaders share this conviction that Western countries have stumbled into a quagmire, while Asia's value structure has saved it from a similar fate. To some, the Confucian ethic is the only thing standing between Asian societies and Western-style social decay. "By following the insights of Confucianism," says the Japanese scholar Katsuta Kichitaro, "we can avoid the social catastrophe befalling the West, the result of centuries of individualism and egotism."

They feel it so strongly, in fact, that there is a growing movement to export Asian values to the United States and Europe. In effect, the

Asians want to do for us—or, perhaps, to us—what, as Christian missionaries, we did to the nations of Asia through four centuries of evangelization. In Malaysia there have been proposals for a "reverse Peace Corps" which would send young Malaysian volunteers across the Pacific to show Americans how to get along without murdering each other.

One of Japan's ranking diplomats, Ogura Kazuo—a man of considerable importance in East Asia, because he helped supervise the distribution of Japanese foreign aid—has called for the nations of the region to set up a formal process for the export of Asian values. "Now that this part of the world is emerging as a real economic and political presence," Ogura wrote in an open letter to his fellow Asians, "we should reexamine its traditional spirit and transmit our worthy Asian values to the rest of the world. This is what the 'Asian renaissance' should be about."

Ogura's Asian spirit manifesto notes with evident pride that Western business interests have been studying Japanese manufacturing and management methods for many years. Now the time has come, he says, for the West to learn Asian social and ethical values as well—"especially including the maintenance of family relationships and the relationship between the group and the individual." What that means, he goes on, is "exporting the social systems of East Asia to the rest of the world." Americans may not be receptive, Ogura adds, but it is now "necessary for America to Asianize itself in the same way Asia has Americanized itself."

To some extent, this is nothing more than good old Americabashing, a familiar pasttime for politicians around the world. With the exception of Japan, where much of the population still feel a sense of gratitude toward their country's chief ally and largest market, politicians all over Asia understand the value of a good verbal swipe at the United States. Great Britain, France, and Holland, the former colonial masters, are also useful foils now and then. But America is clearly the target of choice. For people who have spent their lives looking somewhat fearfully toward the leviathan across the Pacific, it feels good to hear somebody saying "Asia good, America bad."

Further, a little burst of anti-Americanism can be a useful way to change the subject. I was in Malaysia one April when the U.S. State

Department released its annual "Human Rights Report," a thick document outlining the state of legal and civil rights around the world, country by country. Malaysia got high marks overall for its free elections, minimal corruption, police respect for the law, and generally unbiased courts. But the State Department also noted, quite accurately, that freedom of the press is restricted because publications had to be licensed by the government, and that basic legal protections tend to get thrown out the window when the accused is one of the regime's political adversaries.

President Mahathir–a former physician who is known to Malaysian headline writers as Dr. M.–responded with a tirade. "*They* are lecturing *us* about human rights?" he roared. "The United States? Here's a country that tolerates the murder of twenty thousand of its citizens every year, where one million citizens are held in jails, where a man can kill his wife and go free if he gets the right lawyer–and they have the gall to lecture us about human rights?" Dr. M. never dealt with the State Department's criticisms of his government. He didn't have to. In domestic political terms, he had already run up the score.

When the Asian countries have economic reverses, they blame the West for that as well. In the fall of 1997, when a chain of currency crises spread from Thailand to Malaysia to Indonesia to South Korea, many political and financial leaders complained that the problems had been engineered by Western speculators flexing their economic muscle. Even as the troubled countries were turning to a Western institution, the International Monetary Fund, for bailouts, they were denouncing stock and currency trades in the United States and Europe for causing the problem in the first place. (Most economists, in contrast, said the crises were the natural result of bad loans and sloppy fiscal regulation on the part of the Asians.)

With all this tiresome anti-Americanism floating around, I sometimes got fed up with the Asian-way advocates and their insistence that they had found the right path. But still, there has to be something in what they said. Those admirable social statistics I cited in the previous chapter have to come from somewhere. And so I set out to learn something for myself about Asian values, about the cultural and philosophical underpinnings of contemporary East Asia. I put a lot of time and miles into the quest. I talked to politicians, professors, police chiefs, preachers all over East Asia. I spent hours, weeks, months, in libraries trying to get a feel for the Asian cultural classics.

In a sense, though, there was no need to go that far. The most valuable lessons I received about Asia's social miracle came from the man next door.

Pine Tree by
the Rice Paddy

CLOSETED UPSTAIRS IN A BEDROOM about the size of a tea towel, the
fifteen-year-old Bon Jovi wanna-be in our family was twanging hor-
rendously on an electric bass. Magnified to the megadecibel level by
an industrial-strength amplifier, the noise—a fifteen-year-old might
call it music—exploded down the stairwell and reverberated painfully
off the walls. You could almost see the paint peeling. But we were
used to this; in fact, the noise level here in our house in Japan was a
lot more tolerable than it had been back in the United States, where
our son had a whole rock band rehearsing in his room most of the
time. Compared with that, these solo twangs seemed mild. In any
case, we were loath to stop a child who was voluntarily practicing his
music, so we fastened our seat belts and did our best to ignore the
raging thunder rolling down the stairs.

Somehow, amid the din, we were just able to hear the sound
of a gentle tapping, tapping, tapping. It was the door—somebody was
knocking at our front door. I went to open it and found a distinguished
figure: a short, kindly-faced, white-haired gentleman in a handsome

blue suit, with a dark tie knotted perfectly against the starched collar of his white shirt and a crisp white handkerchief folded into three perfect peaks in his breast pocket. Almost wordlessly, he stepped inside onto our *genkan,* the little porchlet at the entrance to every Japanese residence where visitors remove their shoes. Our genteel guest removed his black wing-tipped shoes, stepped up into our living room, and accepted the inevitable cup of tea we offered him. He started chatting. He was terribly sorry to intrude on our honorable family when we must be extremely busy, and by the way, the summer was hot and muggy, autumn might be cooler, although you never really know, he was sure the weather must be better in our honorable home country, he hoped to get in a game of golf next Sunday, his wife was not feeling well, hadn't really been herself for months now. Eventually, he took a sip of tea and mouthed the magic words "*tokoro ga.*" This phrase—it means "as for the matter at hand . . ."—marks the pivotal moment in a Japanese conversation. Once somebody says "*tokoro ga,*" all the ritual preliminaries, all the casual and irrelevant talk required to avoid the unspeakable rudeness of getting to the point, have come to an end, and it is time at last to get to the point.

"*Tokoro ga,*" this gentleman of immense politeness began, "I am terribly sorry, Reido-san, to intrude on your honorable family at a time when people as important as you must be extremely busy. It is an unconscionable impertinence on my part, but I felt it was perhaps best to tell you, honorable Reido-san, that the noise coming from upstairs in your house—well, of course, I know that my humble family, too, must be unspeakably noisy and must be an extreme disturbance to your honorable family. But, Reido-san, that noise coming from upstairs in your house—that noise is a *meiwaku.*"

It was the first time I had ever heard the term *meiwaku,* but it wouldn't be the last. The term, and the sensibility inherent in it, was to become a close acquaintance, something we ran into almost every day on the western side of the Pacific. Over time, I came to think of *meiwaku* almost as a person—a young woman with a Chinese name, Ms. May Wah Koo. As we were to discover, developing an understanding of *meiwaku* would be a crucial step in understanding the basic social dynamic of Japan and most other East Asian societies. In short, our visitor had delivered a message of considerable importance.

•••

BUT BEFORE WE DELVE into the message, a few words about the messenger. Our polite and perfectly dressed visitor was the same white-haired gent we had met on our first night in Tokyo–the one who steered us to the ice-cream store known as Satay-Wan. He was our next-door neighbor on that steep, narrow street. His name was Matsuda, a common Japanese family name that means "the pine tree by the rice paddy." It was Matsuda Tadao, in full, but the given name, Tadao, was basically irrelevent. Although I was to become quite friendly with this gentleman over the next seven or eight years, I would never, never dream of calling him Tadao. In Japan, you might use the given name for somebody who is about your age and whom you have known from preschool days. But generally, in that decorous society, it is much too intimate, too "wet," as the Japanese put it, to re- fer to somebody you've known for only a decade or so by his first name. It is better to keep things "dry," to maintain a discreet distance, to show respect for the other person, by using family names. To me, then, this gentleman was, is, and always will be Matsuda-san, or Mr. Matsuda.

One result of our warm but dry relationship is that to this day I don't know much about Matsuda-san's life. And it would be hope- lessly impertinent to ask. What we did learn was that Matsuda Tadao was born in Tokyo–was born, in fact, on the street where we lived–in the year the Japanese call Taisho 6, which is to say the sixth year of the reign of the Emperor Taisho, the father of Hirohito. That was the year 1917 by Western reckoning, so Matsuda-san was seventy-three when we met him. In his twenties, he had apparently served in Asia in the Imperial Japanese Army, but this was a period of his life we were never to learn much about. In the bitter years after Japan's defeat, he, too, endured abject starvation. The Matsuda family had planted yams and daikon (long white radishes) in the stony rubble of the postwar remnants of our neighborhood; on many days, Matsuda- san had lived on a single radish, parceling it out to make the sem- blance of three meals. Eventually, he got a college degree and went to work for an oil company; his role in the postwar miracle was to work virtually around the clock, searching for petroleum anywhere in the world to fuel the factories that would produce manufactured products, which could be sold around the world to get the money to buy more oil and thus produce more goods for export and thus bring in more money, and on and on, working day in and day out, like everyone else, until the nation grew rich.

Matsuda-san carefully saved a portion of his regular salary and every yen of his twice-a-year bonus, and eventually made a brilliant financial move. He tore down his old wooden house on our narrow street and erected a new structure of white stucco. The new place had three apartments—one for Matsuda and his wife, one for his married son, one for his married daughter. With the savings he accumulated during the miracle years, plus the rent he was getting from his two tenants, Matsuda-san was comfortably set for life when we met him. He was seventy-three and still put on that perfect blue suit every morning, sometimes to head to his old company, where he had some kind of post-retirement emeritus position, and sometimes to spend a few pleasant hours at a nearby golf-driving range, a fenced-in enclosure on the roof of a hospital down the street.

Although you can never really tell, I think Matsuda-san was pleased when a family of Americans moved in next door. He had traveled a good deal overseas in his work, and was comfortable with foreigners. We added a sort of cachet to the block, which was an otherwise unremarkable block on Tokyo's central west side.

Unremarkable to the Japanese, at least. To us, our street was striking in several respects—not least the street itself, a steep and skinny strip of bumpy concrete. It was a two-way thoroughfare for Tokyo drivers but was in fact so narrow that it wouldn't pass for a one-car driveway in the United States. In all the crowded cities of East Asia, residential streets are like that—tiny little alleys about the width of a pencil, as if nobody wanted to waste any precious land on something as unimportant as a public thoroughfare. There were no sidewalks, of course. Cars, pickup trucks, motorcycles, bicycles, and pedestrians all shared that thin strip of street, and it wasn't easy. The street was so narrow that at some points, where the electric poles took up part of the precious pavement, there wasn't enough space left for a single car and a single pedestrian to pass side by side.

If you were walking or riding a bike up the street at one of those points when a car came along, you had to squeeze flat against the wall. The driver, meanwhile, would flick a switch on the dashboard that made the car's outside mirrors fold in flat against the door of the car. These motorized folding mirrors are standard equipment on almost all cars made in East Asia. (One of the many reasons the Detroit automakers have flopped in Asia's markets is that they don't offer this simple feature. Of course, an automotive engineer whose drive to work follows the broad curving boulevards of Grosse Pointe and the eight lanes of the Edsel Ford Freeway through Detroit would never consider an outside mirror that folds in toward the car to be an essential design feature. But in a crowded metropolis of East Asia, the two inches of free space you gain on both sides by folding in the mirrors can often mean the difference between navigating the street and getting stuck there against the front wall of somebody's house.) Our street was so narrow that on Monday, Wednesday, and Thursday, when the Tokyo trash collectors came around, the garbage truck couldn't drive down our block. So the driver would stop his truck on the (slightly) wider street above our house, and the garbage men, in their perfect gray uniforms with black helmets and white gloves, would come bounding down the hill to gather our block's refuse and run it back up to the waiting truck.

I refer to this skinny concrete passage simply as our street because there was no other name for it. In fact, there was no name for any street in our neighborhood. In all of Tokyo, with its tens of thousands of winding streets, there are only a few dozen that have names. And this turned out to be true in almost all the major cities of Asia. At the very center of some cities, there were street names—often Princess Beatrice Road or Wellington Avenue or some other legacy of Western colonization. And the new towns and suburbs, built in the past ten years or so, tend to have street names, along with other housing innovations like front yards and central heating. But in the traditional Asian cities, it evidently never occurred to anybody to name the streets. To find a particular home or shop or temple that you haven't visited before, you get yourself to the general area (e.g., "near Kokubunji Temple") and ask some local fruit vendor or the neighborhood policeman for directions. Since this method can often lead to frustration, it is commonplace in Japan and most other Asian countries to include a detailed map on an invitation, solicitation, advertisement, business card, matchbook, etc. My American friend Elisabeth Bumiller told me once that she could understand perfectly why it was Japanese and Korean electronic firms that developed–and made a global fortune on–home fax machines, even though the basic technology was invented in the United States. "Everybody had to have a fax machine in Japan," she said, "because nobody would come to your cocktail party if you didn't fax every guest a map of how to get there."

But the most remarkable thing about our street, about our whole neighborhood–and, indeed, about nearly every other residential neighborhood in Tokyo–was the plain ugliness of the place. Over time, we would find that our neighborhood was overflowing with quirkiness, kindness, civility, and a not inconsiderable charm. But those were human qualities. Physically, the place was ugly. It was a ragtag collection of squat, drab concrete buildings in a fairly uniform shade of dirty gray; many homes and businesses had a low concrete wall–usually an even dirtier gray–a few feet in front of the main structure. There was a park down the street, a little postage stamp of asphalt; its one plaything, a pink fiberglass octopus that turned out to be a sliding board, was generally teeming with kids, who seemed to think that all parks consisted of asphalt and fiberglass. Above our street was an almost impenetrable spaghetti of electric wires, telephone wires, and electrical transformers, with a jungle of radio and TV antennae jutting out above them. And the whole unchanging vista was made even grayer, most of the year, by a pall of urban haze that hung low over the rooftops.

This concrete shabbiness seems to be almost a design requirement for major cities throughout East Asia.

Vast sections of many major Asian cities were destroyed in World War II, either by the Japanese conquerors or by the American/ British/Dutch/Australian forces that came along to batter Japan into submission. After the war, the priority was to get roofs over people's heads as quickly and cheaply as possible. In the postwar era, most of the construction money that was available was poured into developing the industrial base–factories, railroads, ports–with little left over for housing. And so the grimy, nondescript housing stock from right after the war still stands, one gray concrete cube flush with the next, so that a yard or garden of any kind is a luxury. There are, increasingly, suburbs and "new towns" scattered outside Asian cities, but suburban living is still an unusual and somewhat suspect concept for most Asians.

We used to watch a Japanese quiz show on TV that featured strange or wonderful sights from around the world. There would be a video of something fascinating, and then the panelists were supposed to guess where on earth this could be. One week, the program's host, a clever, engaging comedian who calls himself Tokoro George (that is, "George Location"), was shown camping out in a bright orange tent on a broad green meadow. "Ah, this is the life," Tokoro George declared from the tent door. "Out here in the wide open spaces of . . ." And that was the gimmick: the panel had to guess where Tokoro-san was. Nobody could get the answer, though, and eventually the camera began to pan back, away from the tent. Now we saw more green grass, trees, shrubs, and eventually, perhaps fifty feet from the tent, a medium-sized brick house. It was residential house on a fairly normal residential street on the west side of Seattle. The strange and wonderful thing was that this ordinary residence in America had a yard—both a front yard and a back yard, in fact. "And you know what?" Tokoro George said from his tent. "This is completely normal in America!" (With that, the camera spun around and spotted something else on the lawn that was normal in America: a small metal sign reading "Warning! This home protected by Acme Security Services." This, too, was amazing to the Japanese, and Tokoro George had to explain that Americans routinely install burglar alarms because they are afraid of thieves.)

But most Asians live in drab and lawless city neighborhoods, often surrounded by elevated rail lines or highways, with the rumble of passing trucks and a fragrance that mingles soy sauce, garlic, and exhaust fumes to remind all that they live amid a vast sea of humanity and commerce. I never quite figured out what preserves this state of affairs in a time of rapidly increasing wealth. When I think of Japan today, I think of those businesswomen downtown in their sleek designer suits, their Ferragamo shoes and Chanel handbags, chatting with someone on a cell phone outside one of the world's most lavish department stores. But I also think of the places those young women go home to at night–some small concrete structure with a red hose leading out the front window to a washing machine set up on the front step of the house, because there's no room for it inside.

While the streets didn't have names, the neighborhood as a whole did. We lived in Tokyo-to Shibuya-ku Hiro-o san-chome, which is to say, Subsection 3 of the Hiro-o Precinct of the Shibuya Ward of the Tokyo Administrative District. It seemed a perfectly fitting name for our neighborhood, as spartan and functional as the surroundings.

It was our neighbor Matsuda-san who taught us to stop looking at the physical setting of Subsection 3 and focus on the more important aspects of the neighborhood. We looked around and saw a drab collection of small cement houses lining narrow, busy streets. When Matsuda-san described the neighborhood to us, however, it was clear he saw something different. He saw a community. He saw a few thousand people–the residents, the merchants, the students and teachers at our local schools, the mailman, the two cops who watched over our neighborhood and the adjacent Subsection 2 from their little booth a few blocks down the street–who worked together to make a community. To him, Subsection 3 was a group of people.

This was a thoroughly Asian way of looking at things.

For Matsuda-san and all the others who lived and worked in Subsection 3, the neighborhood was just one of the many groups that crisscrossed and overlapped in their lives. The hierarchy of groups in each person's life begins with the basic unit, the family. It extends outward to include neighborhood, school, job, union, Sumo wrestler's fan club, karaoke singing circle, ikebana society, and so on. Each group is entitled to loyalty from its members, and these various loyalties essentially define a Japanese life. The groups you belong to make up who you are. Your group is your identity. That's why the Japanese always introduce themselves with some group affiliation. It's never just "Hello, I'm Matsuda." That sentence would be considered wholly inadequate–and rude, to boot–because it doesn't convey the essential information. It's always "I'm Matsuda, of Tanigawa Sekiyu, Inc.," or "I'm Matsuda, of the Construction Supplies Section," or "I'm Matusda, of the class of 1923," or "I'm Matsuda, of the Elementary School No. 6 Parents' Club," or simply "I'm Matsuda, of Subsection 3."

Generally, but not always, during my years in Asia, I resisted this pattern. I wore my American individualism on my sleeve. I wanted to let people know—or maybe I wanted to convince myself—that I was strong enough to stand on my own, with no need for my company or my university or my subsection of Shibuya Ward to prop me up. My Japanese friends, or at least those who understood something about Americans, seemed to realize that it was a need to preserve my individual identity that prompted me to introduce myself with the starkly simple "I'm Reid." One day, though, Matsuda-san told me, in his oblique way, that this was too stark for Japanese sensitivities. My refusal to identify with a group didn't strike the Japanese as an indication of strength. To them, it was selfishness. Everyone belonged to groups; to deny that truth was both unrealistic and self-centered. Loyalty to these groups was a fundamental human obligation.

To me, it was simply a twist of fate and timing and the complexities of the Tokyo rental-property market that had brought us to Subsection 3. To Matsuda-san, this was irrelevant. "Whatever brought you here, you are part of the neighborhood now," he told me in his quietly insistent way. We had become new members of the neighborhood group, with all the privileges and responsibilities appurtenant thereto.

You could spend a lifetime—in fact, people in East Asia do spend a lifetime—figuring out what those rights and responsibilities are. But at least two aspects of membership became clear to us. We had two basic responsibilities toward our fellow members of Subsection 3, or of any other group.

We learned the first basic responsibility that day when our son's electric bass was shaking the neighborhood, and Mr. Matsuda came calling. By inflicting this noise on the neighbors, we had committed a *meiwaku*—and it was clear that avoiding *meiwaku* was a duty incumbent on all human beings.

The Japanese dictionaries spend a lot of space explaining this concept, but the basic definition is simple: a *meiwaku* is something that causes trouble or shame for other members of a group you belong to. The various types of *meiwaku* range from something as innocent as walking in late to a meeting or a luncheon engagement—an occurrence that requires the latecomer to erupt in a series of melodramatic apologies, along the lines of "I am terribly, terribly sorry that a person of my wretched status should keep someone as important as you waiting in the midst of your honorable day"–to considerably more serious offenses. One of the staples of Japanese TV news is the video of a tearful politician or corporate executive who has just been caught embezzling from the treasury, pocketing a bribe, or causing an accident while driving the company car. Invariably, these wrongdoers apologize to the other members of the company, the agency, or the party: "I deeply, deeply, regret that a person of my wretched status inflicted a *meiwaku* on my esteemed fellow members." Quite often, the guilty one gets down all fours, in his pin-striped suit, and presses his forehead to the floor.

If you are jolted out of a pleasant afternoon nap by the stinging twang of some teenager's electric bass, or if the money needed to pay your salary has been spirited out of the company's bank account by a crooked corporate treasurer, it is obvious that you've been wronged. But the concept of *meiwaku* goes much further than these direct injuries. Let's say, for example, that you are employed at Tanaka Enterprises, and you and your family live in Apartment 102 of Building 3 of the firm's employee housing complex. And let's say that some mechanic in the truck garage at Tanaka, a fellow who lives in Apartment 756 of Building 9 of the same housing complex, gets caught shoplifting at the local 7-Eleven. You may not know this mechanic. You may have never met the guy. But he has seriously wronged you. He has brought shame on your company and on your housing complex. He has besmirched the reputation of the entire group. This is major-league *meiwaku.*

Sometimes, a *meiwaku* occurs on a national or even global scale. When it does, what is required is one of those heartfelt apologies, on a global or national scale.

One day in early December of 1994, my job took me over to the grungy concrete building that houses Japan's Foreign Ministry. More or less by accident, I happened upon a statement, in Japanese, that had been issued that morning by the foreign minister, Japan's equivalent of our secretary of state. It appeared to be an apology for Japan's sneak attack on Pearl Harbor, which had occurred precisely fifty-three years ago that morning.

This was mystifying. Although some diehards insist to this day that the raid, which left 2,400 Americans dead, was a legitimate act of war, most Japanese decided long ago that their country was wrong to attack the United States at a time when the two countries were at peace and engaged in negotiations. For years now, usually on the anniversary of the raid, Japanese prime ministers and diplomats have been apologizing to the United States, with varying degrees of sincerity, for that infamous surprise. Naturally, these apologies have been issued in English, and the Japanese deliver them to all the foreign media outlets to show the world that Japan feels remorse for what it did.

But the statement that came out for the Pearl Harbor anniversary in 1994 was in Japanese, with no accompanying English text. And nobody had bothered to tell the American media about it; it was strictly by accident that I saw it at all. Perplexed, I went to see a senior Japanese diplomat, a friendly fellow named Terada Terusuke, to ask what was up. "There's no reason to issue that apology in English," Terada-san told me. "That statement was directed to the people of Japan." This explanation left me more perplexed. Why did the government feel a need to apologize to its own people for deceiving another nation a half century ago?

"It's obvious, isn't it?" Terada-san said. To him, at least, the answer was so obvious he had to stop and think for a minute before he could explain things to me. "You see, the Foreign Ministry created a *mei-waku*," he said slowly, watching me carefully to make sure I grasped this essential point.

In the fall of 1941, Terada-san continued, the United States and Japan were engaged in extended negotiations to resolve their angry dispute over Japanese aggression against China. While these talks continued in Washington, a Japanese naval attack force secretly sailed toward Pearl Harbor. Near the end of November, the Japanese made their fateful decision to bomb the U.S. fleet. But just to be quasi-fair about it, they also decided they would formally end the Washington negotiations before going to war.

Early in the morning of December 7–or December 8, on Japan's side of the international date line–the Foreign Ministry in Tokyo sent a final message to the Japanese embassy in Washington. This was supposed to be delivered to the secretary of state at 1:00 P.M. Washington time, just twenty-five minutes before the raid was to begin. With characteristic vagueness, the cable did not clearly declare war or threaten attack. It said Japan "cannot but consider that it is impossible to reach an agreement through further negotiations." In Japan, where indirection is an art form, that's a pretty clear statement that talking was over and war was imminent.

Historians to this day are debating whether the American government would have taken this roundabout message to be a clear warning of attack. We'll never know, because the message didn't get delivered on time. It was a Sunday morning, after all, and the typing pool at the Japanese embassy had the day off. The diplomats who were at work that morning took so long typing the English version that the message didn't reach the State Department until an hour after Pearl Harbor had been bombed.

Although the tale of this delayed message is a staple of Pearl Harbor movies, it is not widely known among Americans. In Japan, though, it is conventional wisdom that the failure to deliver this vague message as planned, twenty-five minutes before the attack, is the reason that Americans to this day do not trust the Japanese in negotiations. "The delay in delivering that announcement," the Japanese newspaper *Asahi Shimbun* explained once, "sparked a widespread belief among the American people that the Japanese are sneaky. Long after the attack, that feeling lingers. Even in economic disputes it has a profound impact on Americans' deep distrust of Japan."

In short, those rusty typists at the Japanese embassy on a Sunday morning in 1941 had besmirched the reputation of the entire Japanese nation. To do something that brings shame to your group is a *meiwaku*. A *meiwaku* requires an apology, even if it happens to be fifty-three years after the fact. "It's obvious, isn't it?" Terada-san said to me.

Avoiding the dreaded *meiwaku*, then, is one responsibility that every individual holds toward every group of which she is a member. But there's another duty that is perhaps even more basic: preserving the *wa*.

Wa is harmony—not musical, but social, harmony. It is the mellow feeling that comes when people are getting along. It is working together in a state of mutual understanding. It is the absence of confrontation. For the Japanese in particular, and for the people of Asia in general, it is the preeminent social value, the summum bonum. The basic word *wa* is written with the Chinese character meaning "peace." In Japan, the idea is more commonly conveyed with the compound word *chowa*, made from two characters that mean "a neat arrangement" and "peace." When the affairs of a family, or a neighborhood tea-ceremony society, or a classroom, company, or croquet club are neatly arranged so that all the members are getting along smoothly, that is a state of *chowa*.

When my neighbor Matsuda-san used to give me lectures on *wa*, I was resentful. Of course I recognized the virtues of group harmony. You didn't have to be Japanese to know that it is more pleasant, and more effective, to work on a unified team than in the midst of warring camps. There's nothing un-American or un-Western about this idea. In fact, one of the best definitions of *chowa* I ever saw was uttered by the quintessential American individualist Huckleberry Finn, as he and Jim were floating down the Mississippi, sharing their raft with a pair of grifters: "For what you want, above all things, on a raf' is for everybody to be satisfied, and feel right and kind towards the others."

But there was, perhaps, a difference of degree. In America, this sense of "feeling right and kind towards the others" in the group is a virtue to be balanced against each member's right and stature as an individual. In Japan, much of the time, there's no balancing of these interests. The *wa* tends to win out over other interests. It's not that *chowa* is valued simply because it makes a raft trip easier, or because working together is the best means to achieve the ends of the club or corporation; rather, that state of easy, harmonious personal interaction is an end in itself in Japanese society. Social harmony is the highest goal of human endeavor. With local variants here and there, this, too, tends to be a pan-Asian phenomenon. The early British colonist who first stamped Asia with that infamous label "the inscrutable East" would have found the East a lot more scrutable if he had realized that many seemingly unfathomable aspects of the Orient were established to preserve the *wa*.

Since the end of World War II, for example, Japan has established a solid democracy, with a free-swinging press, competing political parties, and wide-open, hard-fought elections. But one democratic ideal that has still not taken strong root in Japan is majority rule. The

Japanese just don't feel comfortable if a club or committee or board of directors decides on some action by a vote of, say, 20 to 4. The presence of those four dissenters is a continuing disturbance in the *wa*. In a Japanese organization, the only acceptable basis for action would be a "vote" of 24 to 0.

A TV sitcom we used to watch centered on a young third-grade teacher named Ueno. Ueno-sensei (that is, Teacher Ueno) was immensely popular with his students and their parents. He had a calm, reasoned approach to every classroom crisis. In one episode, a boy in the class started causing trouble–throwing other kids' papers on the floor, deliberately spilling the milk at snack time, and so forth. The whole hour was spent with Ueno-sensei reminding young Hiroshi of the requirements of class membership. By the end of the episode, Hiroshi was back in his seat and studying; his mother dropped by to bow her appreciation to the teacher.

A few weeks later, though, this sunny weekly drama took a dark turn. The teacher, Ueno-sensei, contracted a mysterious brain disease. He began having hallucinations in the middle of class, interrupting the lessons and terrifying the kids. Ueno insisted that nothing was wrong, but it became increasingly clear that he was a menace in that classroom. Finally, the principal called all the teachers and the parents' association to a general meeting to discuss the crisis. Everyone who spoke up agreed that the teacher, unfortunately, had to go. When the principal asked for a pro forma show of hands, the vote for terminating Ueno was 37 to 1. And who was the one holdout? It turned out that young Hiroshi's mother, out of sympathy for the man who had set her own boy right a few weeks earlier, simply could not agree to fire him. The result was considered inconclusive; this being Japan, it was better to take no action than to act on a 37 to 1 vote. The teacher went back to his classroom. This being television, though, he was gradually cured of the ailment and became a wonderful teacher again. *Chowa* had been preserved, and a happy ending was enjoyed by all.

This need to act on consensus explains why a business meeting in Japan is a sharply different experience from an American-style meeting. In appearance, the sessions are about the same: Everybody sits around a table sipping coffee (or green tea, as the case may be), the person in charge brings up the issue at hand, and a few people make presentations. But the basic purpose of the meeting is fundamentally different in the two cultures. In the United States, the big meeting is a time for people to hash out problems, debate alternatives, and finally decide on a course of action. In an American meeting, people are supposed to ask tough questions and raise objections; the young upstart in the corner of the room who comes up with a brilliant ploy midway through the meeting is a standard cliché in novels, plays, and movies about the business world.

In Japan, no upstarts, young or old, are welcome. At the Japanese company, it is a given that alternatives will have been considered, objections raised, and the final decision made long before the decisive meeting can be called. These things are done quietly, through the exchange of written memos or discussions in the hallway. At the meeting, everybody pipes up and expresses agreement with the decision they've already agreed to; the person in charge then declares a consensus to move ahead. The point is not to make a decision; only a fool would hold a meeting before the decision had been made. The point of the exercise is to get the entire group publicly committed to a course of action. Sometimes, the document setting forth the predetermined decision is passed around the table so that each participant can stamp it with a personal seal and thus enhance the public commitment to the general goal. That way, the entire group is marching in the same direction, and everybody has an interest in seeing the project succeed.

One of the key instruments for preservation of the *wa* in Asian societies—particularly Japan and China—is language.

You can be rude to people in Japanese, but it's not natural; politeness is built into the language. From morn to midnight, just about every conversation in Japan is draped in a heavy blanket of obeisance and courtesy. This, in turn, maintains a basic level of decency in human contact. I used to get up early enough some mornings to see the young woman on the bicycle bringing our morning paper; she would say to me, in a perfectly easy and natural tone, "Good morning, honorable customer! Thank you, thank you for reading our humble paper in the midst of your busy schedule. Now please excuse my terrible rudeness, but I'm afraid I must move on to the next house." I would put the newspaper under my arm and stroll down the narrow streets of Subsection 3 to the subway station. While waiting on the platform for the train, I'd hear the greeting from the stationmaster over the PA system. I liked it so much, I wrote it down verbatim in my diary: "Thank you, honorable passengers, for taking time from your busy day to ride our humble train. The next train will be here shortly; we're terribly sorry to keep you waiting."

It mystified me, but pleased me at the same time, that the operators of trains, buses, boats, and planes in Japan were constantly apologizing for keeping me waiting, even though virtually every public conveyance in Japan runs right on schedule. But then, there's a lot of apologizing going on in Japan all the time. When somebody walks into your home or office, he has to apologize–even if you've been pleading for weeks to get him to visit. "Please excuse me, but I'm about to commit an intrusion," your visitor will say before passing through your door. If you call Ms. Tanaka at her office, her secretary will immediately say, "Please excuse my terrible rudeness, but..." That's all she says. You're supposed to know, however, that she's actually asking your name. It would be much too direct, too crude, to come right out and say "Who's calling, please?" So you get an apology instead: "Please excuse my terrible rudeness, but..."

In the ruined city of Kobe after the earthquake there in 1995, government officials and businesses were apologizing like crazy, as if the earthquake had been somebody's fault. At a branch of the Seiden appliance chain, where the front windows were smashed and crumpled refrigerators had toppled out onto the sidewalk, I saw a printed sign attached to the front door: "It is a terrible inconvenience and handicap to our respected customers, but because of the earthquake we have been forced to close this humble store." At several points in the city where the steel rails of the railroad had been twisted and snapped like toothpicks, uniformed employees of the West Japan Railroad Company stood around with bullhorns, saying "We're terribly sorry, but we humbly ask our honorable customers to tolerate the enormous inconvenience of switching to a bus at this point."

Apologies are couched, of course, in honorific language. A few readers of this book may be old enough to remember Charlie Chan movies, a popular Hollywood product of the 1930s and 1940s. Chan was a detective in San Francisco who used the wisdom of the Orient to solve crimes; he was always saying things like "Ancient sage say, wrongdoer always return to scene of evil deed." The venerable Mr. Chan was assisted by a fast-talking youngster whom he inevitably introduced as "Honorable number one son." This is a standard language pattern in Chinese and Japanese; people constantly attach honorific syllables to ordinary words.

In direct translation, this can sound ridiculous. The instructions on a package of instant soup we used to buy in Japan began as follows: "Please fill your respected pot with honorable water before putting in our humble noodles." But that kind of translation misses the point. It's not that Charlie Chan considers his son honorable, or the soup company thinks my cooking pot is worthy of respect. They are using that language to show regard for the person being addressed. The real meaning is "You are a respected person, I feel honored to speak to you, and by the way, this is my oldest son."

As an American, and thus a small-*d* democrat, I felt a little edgy being addressed this way all the time. I certainly did not feel any more honorable or respected than my thoughtful, decent neighbor Matsuda-san, but he always laid on the honorifics with a trowel. "Honorable Reido-san, you are such an important person that I feel guilty intruding on your busy schedule by knocking on your door this way, but I have an honorable letter here that was unfortunately delivered by mistake to my wretched home next door." It didn't feel right to have this kind, older man kowtow like that to me. But to Matsuda-san, it did feel right. That's the way you talk to other people.

Japan is the native home of the euphemism. Softening the blow of bad news is an essential function of the Japanese language. Many times, I would have preferred the frank, direct answer, but this was simply not forthcoming in an Asian society.

When Mariah Carey came to Japan—like most American pop idols, she is explosively popular there—we raced over to the ticket booth to buy seats for her show. "I'll take five tickets for Tuesday night," I said. The ticket seller responded as follows: "*Okyaku-samu, sore wa chotto . . .*" In English, that would be "Honorable customer, that's a little . . ." That was all she said. "Honorable customer, that's a little . . ." To any Japanese, this conveyed a crystal-clear message. But I was too

thick to catch on. "Five for Tuesday," I repeated. "Honorable customer," the ticket-seller replied, speaking slowly this time so this
dull-witted foreigner could comprehend, "please excuse me, but that
may be a little difficult." We went on along this line for some time before I figured out that the reason it would be a little difficult to sell me
tickets for Tuesday was that all the tickets for Tuesday, and for every
other performance, had been sold days before I got to the window. It
would have been unspeakably rude for the ticket lady to come right
out and tell me that, however, so she launched into her polite eva-
sions until I finally caught on.

As that experience suggests, it is considered impolite in Japan to
come right out and say the word "no," even if "no" happens to be the
correct answer. At a summit meeting once, Bill Clinton leaned over to
Boris Yeltsin and warned him to be on guard when negotiating with
the Japanese prime minister. "He says 'yes' when he means 'no,'"
Clinton noted. The remark was picked up by an open microphone
and prompted a temporary trans-Pacific diplomatic crisis. The Japanese took serious offense at this suggestion that their prime minister
was a liar—but in fact, Clinton was right. All Japanese people avoid
saying "no," not because they are dishonest, but because saying a flat
"no" might cause disappointment and ill-feeling. It might disturb the
wa. So the Japanese fall back on their arsenal of euphemisms: "That
may be difficult." "We'll give your request careful thought." "Excuse
me, but . . ."

As long as both sides of the conversation understand what's going
on, there's no problem. But when a politely evasive Japanese and a
frankly direct American get talking, this can be the stuff of international incidents. U.S.-Japan relations were sour for years during the
Nixon administration after Richard Nixon asked Prime Minister Sato
Eisaku to open Japan's rice market to American imports. The prime
minister hemmed and hawed for a moment, and then said, *"Zensho
itashimasu."* A translator told Nixon exactly what the words meant: "I
will respectfully give your proposal positive consideration in the future." The elated Nixon went back to Washington and declared victory
on the rice issue. Sato, meanwhile, assured everybody in Japan that he
had said "no." And indeed, any Japanese would know that "I will give
your proposal positive consideration in the future" is the same thing as

"no." Anyway, as a Japanese diplomat pointed out to me much later, Japan did eventually give Nixon's proposal positive consideration. The rice market was opened to imports a mere twenty-eight years after that conversation–a few months before Nixon's death.

Not many people get fired from their jobs in Japan, but it happens on occasion. The Japanese have a particularly vivid expression for losing a job: *kubi da*, which means "to get it in the neck." This is obviously too brutally direct for any Japanese boss to say to any employee. I once asked a group of Japanese middle managers what language they would use if they had to fire somebody. Everybody stuttered around for a while, but eventually I got some answers. Here's the proper way to tell some poor underling that he has just gotten it in the neck: "Tanaka-san, I hope your trip to work was pleasant this morning, and I hope you didn't have the inconvenience of a long walk into the office from our humble company's totally inadequate parking lot. Now, to get to the matter at hand: It has become a matter of somebody here being fired, Tanaka-san, and this relates to you."

Another essential role that language plays, particularly in Japan and China, is the maintenance of the hierarchical structure of the society. To people whose identity stems from membership in groups, it seems only natural that there should be rankings within each group, that one person will be a leader, another a deputy leader, and so forth down the line. Hierarchy begins in the family, where it is generally determined by age. That's why the Oriental languages have two different words for "brother," and two for "sister." There's a major difference between an "older brother" and a "younger brother," and this has to be recognized. A two-year-old in Japan will always refer to his three-year-old sister as "older sister," a term of respect–and he'll still be doing it when he is ninety-one and older sister is ninety-two.

It's not just that the nouns differ, either. There's a whole different language for greeting somebody who stands above you in the hierarchy, and a whole different language for ordinary conversation. That's why the Japanese are always exchanging business cards, even with people in their own company. There's a kind of ritual ballet that takes place when two Japanese businesspeople meet. At first, almost nothing is said. Business cards are exchanged, and read. By looking at the position and title on the other guy's card, each person can determine where he ranks relative to the other. Only then can they bow a greeting (for the lower-ranking person must bow deeper) and start conversing with each other. Without knowing where the other person ranks, you don't know how to talk to him.

THERE'S SOMETHING MECHANICAL—in fact, there's something arguably phoney—about all the flowery verbiage that marks normal discourse in Japan. When the PA system in the subway apologizes every thirty seconds for keeping me waiting, I know that it's just a tape recording apologizing to me. When a ticket seller says, "Honorable customer, that would be a little difficult," I know she's just repeating a phrase her boss told her to use. After a few decades of the same boilerplate niceties, people may not even hear them anymore. Even so, the language makes a difference.

Hardly anybody on an airplane is really listening when the flight attendant's prepare-for-landing announcement, "Please return your tray tables and seat backs to their full upright position," floats out over the PA system. But suppose the same announcement came out in words like "Get those damn seats up where they belong, and I mean NOW!" It would make a difference, not in meaning, but in feeling. It would destroy the *wa* within that airplane. If the woman behind the ticket window finally got tired of the polite formula "Honorable customer, that's a little . . ." and said instead, "Fahgeddaboutit, you idiot, we sold out weeks ago," the meaning would be essentially the same, but the feeling wouldn't.

This is the purpose of all the linguistic rigmarole in East Asian societies: to maintain good feeling, to make everybody feel copacetic, so the overall group can continue to function in a state of harmony. And it works. Good manners and polite language are contagious—as are rudeness and cruelty. Listening to the convoluted language of polite discourse all around me in Japan, I used to feel that I was living in the middle of one of those colloquies on the floor of the U.S. Senate: "It is with the greatest respect to my distinguished friend the senior senator from California that I rise to say she is unfortunately dead wrong." There's a certain deliberate excess of courtesy, and it sounds about the same whether you hear it on the Senate floor in Washington or the subway platform in Tokyo. In both places, this ornate language is used for the same purpose. It soothes feelings. It heads off anger. It preserves the *wa*.

To violate the harmony of the group, to undermine the *wa*, is shameful, and shame must be avoided at all costs.

In Asian cultures, where the well-being of the community as a whole outweighs the interest of any single individual, it seems logical that notions of right and wrong will also be determined by the overall group rather than by the individual. That, at least, is the thesis of a distinguished group of sociologists and psychologists, both Asian and Western, who argue that the—or, at least, a—fundamental difference between East and West is the difference between shame and guilt. This view was set forth famously in one of the most daring anthropological tracts of the twentieth century, Ruth Benedict's *The Chrysanthemum and the Sword*.

Benedict, a cultural anthropologist at Columbia, was assigned by the U.S. government in 1944 to produce a sociological profile of Japan. This was supposed to aid military planners as America geared up for the final push against the Imperial Army and Navy, and to assist those thinkers who were already making plans for a military occupation of Japan after the home islands were captured. Benedict knew no Japanese; she had never been to Asia. But she accepted the mission. She read Japanese novels, watched Japanese movies, and talked for days at a time to Japanese-Americans. The result was a 300-page study that is still readable, and still being read, today. It's an intriguing work, particularly for a reader like me, with years of experience living in Japan. On some pages, Benedict strikes me as brilliant; on others, totally wacky.

Benedict argued that Asian societies, such as Japan, rely on shame as the chief guardian against improper conduct, while Western society relies on guilt. She saw a big difference. "Shame cultures rely on external sanctions for good behavior," but "guilt cultures [rely] on an internalized conviction of sin." In a shame culture, that is, something is wrong only if others see it and consider it wrong. In a guilt culture, like the one the Puritans brought to the United States, an evil deed is wrong whether or not anybody else knows about it. If a tree falls in a forest, it's a fallen tree, whether anybody heard it fall or not. Benedict drew from this distinction the conclusion that the Japanese have a flexible, relative concept of morality, whereas Western societies have fixed ideas of what is right and wrong.

Was this distinction ever accurate? And is it a fair comparison to make today?

It's certainly true that the notion of shame is alive and thriving in Asian cultures; you see it writ large every time one of those corrupt politicians or business executives gets down on his knees before the TV cameras and bangs his forehead on the floor to express mortification about taking a bribe. You see it writ slightly smaller when the ashen-faced mother comes to the elementary school to tell the principal how ashamed she is that little Yong-sam failed to turn in his homework on time. Back in the United States, in contrast, it does sometimes seem that people have no shame; they kill their parents or cut off their husband's penis and then set off on a coast-to-coast promotional tour autographing the book in which the whole sordid affair is set forth for all to admire.

But people in the United States also apologize and express their shame for doing wrong. And a lot of people in Asia confess to crimes that nobody saw them commit, suggesting that they may have been driven by some "internalized conviction" that they did something wrong. The distinctions seem fuzzy, and many people at least as knowledgeable as Ruth Benedict don't see the sharp difference she did. One of the wisest American observers of Asia, Edwin O. Reischauer, the Harvard scholar who basically invented Asian studies as an academic discipline in the United States, disagreed with Benedict, but in a diplomatic way. The shame-guilt distinction "should not be pushed too far. Shame and guilt easily blend in the feelings of the average person," Reischauer wrote, in one of his last pronouncements on this perennial question. "The end effects of shame and guilt may not be very different."

Somewhere in the middle on this crucial point was our neighborhood sage, Matsuda-san. I asked him about it all the time. He was, shall we say, equivocal.

One day, for example, I happened to mention to Matsuda-san that those bicycles we left unlocked at our house every night in Subsection 3 never got stolen. "Well, Reido-san, that's not surprising, is it?"

Matsuda-san said to me. "If somebody did steal one of your bikes, what would he do with it? If he tried to use it, his family and neighbors would ask where he got it. And he'd be ashamed to tell. And if they figured out that he had stolen it, it would be shameful for the whole family." Clearly, this answer put Matsuda-san on the "shame" side of the equation. People refrained from doing wrong, such as stealing my mountain bike, because it would cause shame for themselves and other members of their group. But I pursued the point. "What if the thief lived alone, or what if he lied about where he got the bike?" My neighbor gave me one of those these-foreigners-never-catch-on looks. "Even if he lied, it wouldn't do much good to a thief. He would probably feel too guilty about stealing the bike to get any pleasure out of it."

I SPENT THE better part of six years in these calm and pleasant discussions with Matsuda Tadao, pondering *chowa*, membership, *mei-waku*, and the like. Then our family left Japan to move home to America. A few months later, I was back in Tokyo for a visit. The morning after I arrived, I found myself winding through the steep, narrow streets of Subsection 3, past the grimy concrete houses and the vending machines selling bags of rice, to pay a call on my old neighbor.

There was a reason. Shortly after we left Japan, I received a card from Matsuda-san apologizing for the fact that he would not be able to send me his annual New Year's card. In Asian cultures, where New Year's Day is the biggest holiday of them all, there's only one reason why that would happen. There must have been a death in the family.

So I was not surprised, when I arrived at Matsuda-san's house, took off my shoes on the *genkan*, and stepped up, to find that his tiny living room had been turned into a shrine. The room was dominated by a Buddhist altar adorned with candles, pine boughs, and fragrant fresh oranges. In the middle was a photograph, framed in black and draped in a thick black ribbon. It was a picture of Matsuda-san's wife, Chioko. She had died, at the age of seventy-eight, a few weeks earlier. Having had some experience with Japanese funerals, I knew basically what I should do. I laid the flowers I had brought along on the front edge of the altar. I knelt silently to say a prayer. Matsuda-san whispered to his wife's picture, "Cho-cho, it's Reido-san," just in case she had forgotten me.

Then the widower and I sat down in a pair of matching oversized easy chairs and took up our old conversations about groups and societies and communities, and the responsibilities of their members. It felt like old times, back when there wasn't a Pacific Ocean between the two of us. I was glad to be there, and I could see that Matsuda-san, too, was enjoying himself. After a pause, he looked at me with a wry smile, a sort of testing smile. He said, "Isn't it a pleasure when you can make practical use of the things you have studied? Isn't it a pleasure to have an old friend visit from afar?"

I looked back at him with a wry smile of my own—actually, more like a smile of triumph. I knew that line. It was not for nothing that I had spent twenty-five years of my life studying Asia. What Matsuda-san had just recited to me is one of the most famous literary passages in all Eastern culture. It is the Asian equivalent of "In the beginning, God created the heaven and the earth" or "Arms and the man I sing" or "Call me Ishmael." He had recited the opening lines of the basic text of what it means to be an Asian. It was Chapter 1 of Book 1 of the Analects of Confucius:

> Confucius said: Isn't it a pleasure when you can make prac-
> tical use of the things you have studied? Isn't it a pleasure to
> have an old friend visit from afar? Isn't it the sure sign of a
> gentleman, that he does not take offense when others fail to
> recognize his ability?

"Why, that's Koshi-sama," I said. (The ancient Chinese scholar Kung Fu-tzu, the man we call Confucius, is known in Japan as the Honorable Koshi.) I tried to be calm about it, but in fact I was thrilled to have spotted this literary allusion.

"Well, of course," Matsuda-san replied, clearly less impressed than I was with the depth of my knowledge. "Didn't you know? What do you think we've been talking about all these years? Everything I've tried to teach you, Reido-san, everything anybody knows about building a successful society—it all comes from Confucius."

FOUR

The Master Kung

IN THE DISTRICT OF TSAU, in the province of Lu, on the twenty-eighth day of the harvest month in the twenty-first year of the Duke Hsiang's reign—or so we are told by ancient chronicles of fair-to-middling reliability—a child was born to a seventy-year-old retired soldier and his youthful bride. The boy was given the formal name Kung Chiu and the nickname Chung-ni, but he would eventually come to be known throughout Lu, and later throughout the whole of China, as Kung Fu-tzu: the Master Kung. After the Jesuits translated his works (and his name) for Western readers, this "Confucius" would come to share global stature with the likes of Socrates, Jesus, Muhammad, Jefferson, Gandhi, and other great teachers. He was one of the most influential human beings ever to walk the earth.

The Chinese have always been fantastic record keepers, and as a result we know a good deal about the births, careers, and deaths of people who lived long before there was written language in other parts of the world. Confucius's traditional birthday—still celebrated on September 28—is perhaps just a guess, but his family background and the year of his birth can be determined through official records, memoirs, and other documents. It was 551 B.C. (give or take a year or so), a time of turbulence and squalor in the Middle Kingdom.

This was a century before the golden age of Greece, five centuries before the Roman Empire, a period when Europe, Africa, and the Americas were inhabited mostly by unlettered nomadic tribes. But China was already an ancient civilization. It was the oldest and biggest "nation" on earth, ruled (at least in theory) by a single emperor and unified by a common language, a writing system that had been in use for nearly a thousand years, and a fairly extensive literature of music, poetry, and history.

Although Confucianism has sometimes been called a religion—and the town in Shandong province that purports to be Confucius's birthplace is now dotted with imposing shrines to his memory—the Master Kung was not a spiritual leader. He was simply too down-to-earth to start a religion. He focused on the here and now. When a student asked what happened to humans after death, Confucius brushed the query aside: "We have a hard enough time trying to understand human life," he said. "How can we possibly understand death?" But when it came to the art of life, he took on the core questions: ethical behavior, good government, loyalty, friendship, truth, and the meaning of human existence. His answers are so full of wisdom and decency that he is still being read, for pleasure and for personal improvement, twenty-five hundred years after his death.

He became a timeless prophet, but Confucius was very much a product of his time—a time when the central government had lost control and the proud empire of China had been reduced to a collection of warring states. It wasn't the first era of civil war in the Middle Kingdom, and it wouldn't be the last. In fact, the whole of China's long, long history is a back-and-forth pattern of order and disorder, of powerful central dynasties giving way to decades or centuries of war and unrest. The last great dynasty, the Ching, ended in 1911 and was followed by decades of civil war, which killed millions of innocent people. The current regime, begun by Mao Zedong, has ruled for fifty years—the merest blink of an eye in Chinese history, but the longest consolidation of power in the past century. Does today's government in Beijing represent a successful new era of central control, or just another blip in a period of internecine struggle? That question is beyond the scope of this book—which is just as well, because I don't know the answer.

Confucius knew China's ancient history. The contrast between those long periods of peace and prosperity he read about in the annals and the dangerous chaos he saw in his own day caused him endless anguish. His goal was to teach the people of China how to find the way—the ethical way that would take his country back to the good old days. He leaves no doubt about which good old days he had in mind. He reminds his students about the benevolence of the rulers Yao and Shun, the heroics of the Great Yu, and the wisdom of the ancient kings Wen and Wu.

The history texts that Confucius had before him in 500 B.C. reached way, way back in time, so far back that history merged into myth. The rulers Yao and Shun may have been real people, just as King Arthur may have been a real person, but they had been draped with a veil of legend as rich as the tales of Camelot. They were men of virtue, and ruled by example. Knowing that the king himself would do the right thing, ordinary people went out of their way to be honest in their business dealings and helpful to neighbors. A strong moral standard at the top, Confucius concluded, made for far more effective government than strict laws and harsh punishment: "Guide them with edicts, keep them in line with punishment, and people may stay out of trouble but will have no sense of shame," he taught. "But if you guide them by your own virtue, and keep them in line with acts of decency, they will develop a sense of shame and control themselves." The Great Yu, another ancient role model, is roughly equivalent in Chinese legend to the Old Testament's Noah. He saved mankind at a time of a great deluge, not by building an ark but by directing construction of levees and canals that spared the paddy fields, an act that would make anybody a hero in a land periodically swept by killing floods. Yu was said to be the founder, in about 2200 B.C., of China's first great dynasty. But the key point for Confucius was that this king did not just sit around accepting tributes. He earned the loyalty of his subjects by showing loyalty to them; he got up from his throne and worked on the levees, to enhance the common good.

The Confucian role models King Wen and his son King Wu can be placed more solidly in the realm of actual history. Around 1100 B.C., when the ruling family was seriously corrupt and China was struggling through one of its periodic stretches of anarchy, Kings Wen and Wu launched a civil war and began a new dynasty, the Chou. The Chou dynasty brought order and prosperity and still held the imperial throne when Confucius was born in the province of Lu. But Chou, too, was well past its golden age by then. The emperor was a figurehead, and his provincial rulers cringed before the power of great feudal lords. In the province of Lu, Duke Hsiang was nominally in charge, but he was essentially just a spectator as three rich and ruthless clans battled for control.

Turbulent times often produce lasting treasures, and sixth-century China produced two schools of thought that have endured and flourished. Lao-tzu, the founder of Daoism, was roughly a contemporary of Confucius; there is a tradition, probably mythical, that the two sages knew each other personally. They certainly were not in agreement, though, as to the best way for a man to respond to the upheaval and corruption of their time. To simplify tremendously, Lao-tzu's Dao (it means "the Path") was a mystical retreat from the real world. He preferred meditation over action: "Do nothing, and everything is done." Confucius was a man of action. We know that he was an accomplished archer, charioteer, debater, hunter, and musician. Well into his sixties he kept setting out on dangerous and exhausting trips to distant provinces. He longed for a chance to take an active role in running the state, to set an example of virtuous deeds and thus restore respect for government.

Perhaps this was in the blood, because the records say that the Kung clan had been aristocratic at one time, with close ties to those at the top of the Chou hierarchy. By the sixth century, the family was considerably less exalted. The master's father was a midlevel soldier. He died when Kung Chiu was a small boy. In the Analects, the master tells us that he grew up in fairly spartan circumstances. He realized as a teenager that he had the makings of a scholar, for he loved learning and had a passion for passing along the wisdom of the ancients. But the Kung family fortunes were such that he needed a job. When he was about twenty he secured a post as a petty bureaucrat in the provincial granary, and a few years later he was promoted to overseer of public grazing lands. He resigned this job in 527 B.C. because his mother had died and the appropriate filial response was to leave work and go into mourning. He began teaching history, the classics, and what we might call political science to a group of young men. In a society that revered a sage, he gradually became a famous and sought-after figure, throughout Lu and its neighboring province, Chi.

A new ruler in Lu, Duke Ding, now gave Confucius his first chance at serious government work. His initial post was as a local mayor, and he proved so successful that he was made police commissioner of Lu. The evidence suggests that he practiced what he had preached. He ruled with a dignified and gentle touch, urging people to goodness and eschewing the death penalty. Whatever he did, it must have worked, for we are told: "The men and women of Lu walked at a distance from each other. Things left behind by their owners were never taken, and at night, doors were left unlocked without fear of robbery" (a description that sounds like many East Asian cities today). But Duke Ding did not live up to Confucius's notions of a moral ruler, and so in 497 B.C. the Master Kung quit his provincial position.

The remaining eighteen years of life must have been frustrating for Confucius. He traveled from one state to another, seeking a feudal lord who might need a commissioner or an adviser on governmental affairs. Although he was honored everywhere as a great scholar and teacher, he never again got a chance to put his beliefs into action. Everywhere he saw China sinking into decay and despair, but he was not given the authority to do anything about it. He finally came back to Lu when he was about seventy. He continued the dialogues with his growing band of students, but it is reported that he suffered deep sorrow over the deaths of a son and an esteemed disciple. He died in 479 B.C.

This is not to suggest that the Master Kung was a grim or bitter man. At one point in the Analects, a rather dim-witted student, Tzu-lu, says that the governor of a nearby province had asked him what sort of man this Confucius might be, but he was too tongue-tied to answer. What should he have said? Confucius replies that the best word to describe him would be "enthusiasm." "Why didn't you just tell the governor," he says to Tzu-lu, "that Master Kung is a man driven by so much passion [for learning] that in his enthusiasm he often forgets to eat, and seems completely unaware that he is growing old?" This enthusiast for learning was also a fervent fan of music. Once he was so struck by the beauty of a musical performance that "for three months, he forgot the taste of meat." He was the embodiment of the "philosopher" in the original sense of the word: *philosophos,* a "lover of knowledge." But he was interested in knowledge people could use— for, say, governing a state. He relished relationships and spent most of his life surrounded by loving friends. He failed to win the trust of the various rulers he approached, but at least each rebuff served as a test of his character; he would not let these setbacks wear him down. All of these traits are summed up in those famous opening lines of the Analects, the passage Matsuda-san recited to me:

> Confucius said: Isn't it a pleasure when you can make practical use of the things you have studied? Isn't it a pleasure to have an old friend visit from afar? Isn't it the sure sign of a gentleman, that he does not take offense when others fail to recognize his ability?

For the past twenty centuries or so, in the nations of the Chinese cultural sphere, almost every schoolchild has memorized these words. They learn the opening lines of the Analects to this day, in the same way that American students learn "When, in the course of human events . . ." and English students learn "My kingdom for a horse!" What's really striking is that in China, students still write and recite Confucius using the same words and the same characters that he used. This is one of the reasons for the sage's continued power: the continuity of Chinese culture and of its chief vehicle, the Chinese language. It is hard to think of any other nation where schoolkids can still read and understand something written 2,500 years ago. In Japan, the wonderful *Tale of Genji,* written about A.D. 1000, is discernible only to experts; students today use a modern Japanese translation to access its marvels. In English-speaking countries students generally use a similar translation to read Chaucer, who composed his poems in English a mere six centuries back. But the Analects are read in the original. The language sounds weird to a modern-day Chinese person, just as the works of Shakespeare and Jefferson sound a little archaic to modern English ears. But the very words of Confucius are still alive.

Confucian learning goes far beyond this one book, however. There are nine works that the Chinese have traditionally honored as the Confucian classics. All nine of these books, plus centuries of analysis and commentary by scholars of various stripes, constitute the corpus of Confucianism today. Confucius laid the foundation for the ideas that are known as Confucian, but the total package is larger and more complicated than the sayings of the master himself. It has also acquired a large number of internal contradictions along the way. In short, the corpus of Confucian writings is as rich and complex as the Bible.

The nine basic works are divided, with that characteristic Chinese zeal for categorization, into the Five Classics and the Four Books. The distinction seems to be that the Classics were texts that Confucius himself knew and used in his teachings, while the Books are compilations of the sayings of Confucius, his students, and his great disciple Meng-tzu (whom the Jesuits named Mencius).

Of the *Wu Ching*, or Five Classics, the earliest is probably the best-known: the *I Ching*, or "The Classic of Changes," a book of divination and fortune-telling. For some reason, this obscure treatise discussing the counterbalanced forces (the famous yin and yang) to be found in 64 six-line shapes (the hexagrams) enjoyed a boomlet in the West during the hippie era. The mystical, majestic English translation by Cary Baynes has remained a strong seller ever since then. The book seems to date back to the dawn of the Chou dynasty, in 1100 B.C. or so—and indeed, there was an old Chinese tradition that the *I Ching* was written by King Wen and King Wu themselves.

There followed the *Shu Ching* ("The Classic of History"), the *Shih Ching* ("The Classic of Poetry," or "The Book of Odes"), the *Li Chi* ("The Classic of Ritual"), and the *Chun Chiu* ("The Spring and Autumn Annals"). This last classic is a year-by-year history of the breakdown of the Chou dynasty from about 770 B.C. to Confucius's time; the "Spring and Autumn" classic was traditionally said to be the work of Confucius himself, and it took its name because he supposedly finished the text in a single summer by working full time from spring to fall.

The most important of the *Shi Shu*, or Four Books, is the *Lun Yü*,

whose title means "dialogues" or "conversations," but has traditionally been translated into English as "Analects" (from a Greek word
meaning "gleanings" or "selections"). Since Confucius himself apparently did not write down his teachings, the *Lun Yü* is probably the
purest record there is of the Master Kung's actual words. It was compiled by his students, or by students of his students, in the century after his death. And it reads that way. It feels exactly as if a group of
eager students sat down over rice wine one evening, taxed their
memories, and started exchanging stories of the great things their
teacher had said. Sometimes, the *Lun Yü* moves logically from one
topic to the next; sometimes, completely new subjects suddenly pop
up in the middle of a chapter. Some anecdotes start and never end.
There's a lot of repetition, and some key transitional sections seem to
have been lost somehow over the centuries.

And yet there is a fundamental unity to the Analects. There's a con-
sistency of style and method that makes it clear we are listening to a
single powerful voice, no matter how muddled the message has
grown over time. Anyone who has read and appreciated the Christian
Gospels or the dialogues of Socrates–both records written down by
disciples after their master's death–will be perfectly at home with the
conversations of Confucius.

It's a shame–it's almost a tragedy–that the Analects are not required reading in the West as well as the East. I say that partly because of the book's universal appeal: It is one of the greatest
collections of ethical wisdom in the history of mankind. Its truths fit
the contemporary West as well as they fit the ancient East. But it is
also essential as a key to the thinking of East Asia–a key that has become even more important for those of us in the West with the coming of the Asian century. "No book in the entire history of the world
has exerted, over a longer period of time, a greater influence on a
larger number of people," wrote Pierre Ryckmans, one of the greatest
contemporary scholars on China and the author of a terrific new
(1997) translation of the *Lun Yü*. "With its affirmation of humanist
ethics and the universal brotherhood of man, it inspired all the nations of Eastern Asia and became the spiritual cornerstone of the
most populous and oldest living civilization on earth."

The remaining volumes of the Four Books are further compilations of Confucian teachings, although they don't have the immediacy of the *Lun Yü*.

The *Ta Hsüeh* ("The Great Learning") is a brief restatement of one of the master's key ideas–that a state can only be healthy to the extent that the ruler maintains a high personal standard of virtue.

The *Chung Yung* ("The Doctrine of the Mean") is a broader philosophical tract that takes its name from a Confucian idea not very different from what Western philosophy calls the Aristotelian mean. Aristotle summarized the concept as "Moderation in all things"; Confucius said, "To overshoot is as bad as to fall short." In the Confucian formulation, this idea is connected to the virtue of group harmony: avoidance of confrontation, resolving disputes by negotiation, searching for solutions that serve all interested parties rather than total victory for one side and total defeat for the other.

The *Meng-tzu* ("Mencius") is the basic Confucian text on political science, written in the fourth century B.C. by the Confucian scholar known in China as *ya sheng*, "the second sage." If we can compare Confucius with Socrates, then in the same sense Mencius is Plato. Each of these famous pupils recorded and organized the master's ideas, and then expanded them into a politics of his own. The *Meng-tzu* is something like Plato's *Republic*, in that the author sets forth the basic principles of governance, drawing from the central teachings of the earlier master. The key point about Mencius for modern readers, as we shall see shortly, is that he recognized and expanded the democratic ideals set forth by Confucius.

From these four books–and particularly from the Analects–we can draw a fairly clear picture of the Confucian ethic as set forth by its founder twenty-five centuries ago. I say "fairly clear" because it's a simple truth that the path through ancient Chinese texts is never as direct or as logical as a Western reader might hope.

This is partly because of the rather haphazard way the Analects were composed, a century or so after the conversations recorded therein took place. It's partly because of the ancients' habit of sprinkling their conversations with fleeting references to the Five Classics (and particularly "The Book of Odes"), on the assumption that any learned person would understand these poetic or historical allusions. It's partly because puns and wordplay have always been a key part of

Chinese (and Japanese) literature, and any speaker or writer is expected to throw them around fairly liberally.

At one point, for example, Confucius seems to put himself on a par with the mighty King Wen: "King Wen is dead," he says. "Does that not mean the future of our culture rests on me?" The language here seems fairly easy to understand—but there's a problem with it. The statement is totally out of character for the humble Confucius, who would never suggest that he ranks with the ancient heroes. In fact, just one paragraph before he says this, it is noted that "the Master absolutely eschewed four things: capriciousness, dogmatism, willfulness, and self-importance." So why is he now making this dogmatic, self-important claim about being the successor to King Wen? The answer is that the line is a pun. The Chinese word for "culture" is *wen*, which is pronounced the same as King Wen's name (but has a different written form). So that line is not so much a boast as a joke—the kind of thing lecturers in China are supposed to use now and then just to keep everybody awake. A translator who hoped to preserve the spirit of wordplay in this Confucian joke would have to produce an English sentence along these lines: "When Wen is gone, where and when will we find *wen*?"

There's another factor that can make Confucius's words either easy or impossible to understand. This is the extreme simplicity of written Chinese, a language without case, gender, plurals, tenses, moods, or grammatical devices used elsewhere to convey degrees of nuance. Confucius is full of nuance, or course, but it is not always conveyed in the bare characters on the page. "The general meaning of a Chinese sentence is often plain," noted Confucius's first great English translator, James Legge, "and yet we are puzzled to supply exactly the subjects, auxiliaries, etc., which other languages require." That famous opening line of the Analects ("Confucius said: Isn't it a pleasure when you can make practical use of the things you have studied?") is written with seventy-nine letters in English, but only eleven in the original. That's one reason for the enormous accretion of interpretative notes on the Analects over the centuries. A contemporary Chinese or Japanese text of the *Lun Yü* will have two or perhaps three lines of Confucius on each page, followed by thirty lines of exegesis and debate over what the master must have meant.

The situation reaches new dimensions of ambiguity for those of us reading translations of Confucius in foreign languages. Things get so confusing that some potential scholars have closed the ancient books for good out of frustration and moved on to other, less mysterious, pursuits. This is not always a net loss to mankind. Thanks to an early experience with the complexities of Confucian translation, the world lost a scholar but gained an outstanding novelist, Jorge Luis Borges. Before he embarked on his career in fiction, Borges was a student of ancient China—but not, as he tells us, for long:

> Around 1916, I decided to apply myself to the study of Oriental literature. As I was reading with credulous enthusiasm the English translation of the great Chinese philosopher, I came upon this memorable passage: *"It matters little to a convict under a death sentence if he has to walk on the edge of a precipice; he has already given up living."* To that phrase, the translator had appended a footnote, and indicated that his interpretation was to be preferred to that of a rival sinologist who had translated the same line this way: *"The servants destroy the works of art so as not to have to adjudicate on their merits and defects."*
>
> At that point . . . I did not read any further. A mysterious skepticism had crept into my soul.

Still, we don't all have to be skeptics when it comes to Confucius. Since he makes the same points over and over in different ways, it's possible to skirt around the many ambiguities in the Confucian classics. There are a few basic points that the Master Kung sought to convey, and they are easy to find.

Living in a world that seemed to be going to hell in a handbasket, Confucius was searching for ways to stop the decline. He wanted to take his world back to the days when China was a stable, civil, unified, and virtuous community, where men and states did the right thing because they realized that proper conduct would produce the best results for the society as a whole, and thus, for the individual members of society as well.

Confucius said that one of the key requirements for turning a decadent society into a virtuous one is respect for the truth. Any group, company, school, or state that refuses to face the truth about it-self, or refuses to permit its members to speak the truth, is doomed to suffer, because without a knowledge of true conditions it's impossible to correct problems. There's nothing uniquely Confucian about this observation. "You shall know the truth, and the truth shall set you free." "Congress shall make no law... abridging the freedom of speech, or of the press." But Confucius had a unique way of stating it.

In Chapter 3 of Book 13 of the Analects, Tzu-lu, the dim-witted disciple we met earlier, comes up to Confucius and asks—for the umpteenth time—for a simple explanation of all the master's teachings. Suppose, Tzu-lu says, the Duke of Wei were to call on you to take over the government of his country. What's the first thing you would do? In response, we are told, "the Master said, 'It would certainly be to rectify the names.' "

"To rectify the names." The phrase has an exotic, antique ring to it; it's the kind of mystical pronouncement you'd expect some Oriental sage to be uttering around 500 B.C. "To rectify the names" is a straightforward rendition of what the Chinese text says, and it has been the standard way to translate the passage since the first English translation in 1860. (The British scholar Arthur Waley took a more modern approach: "It would certainly be to correct language.") But in fact this exotic declaration can be stated in the plainest English. "To rectify the names" means to tell the truth; to call a spade a spade; to resist the temptation to paper over unpleasant truths with politically correct euphemisms; to avoid the tendency, which exists in any organization, to silence critics who tell uncomfortable truths. Because, as Confucius goes on to say, nobody can do a job correctly if he's lying about it: "If language be not in accordance with the truth," he tells Tzu-lu, "affairs cannot be carried on to success."

Facing the truth, whether or not you like it, is a recurring theme in the Analects, but the specific conversation where Confucius says "to rectify the names" has a particularly topical sting on this point. This exchange evidently took place when the sixty-nine-year-old Confucius had returned to Lu after his years of wandering. Tzu-lu, mean-while, had been retained as an adviser by the Duke of Wei. Confucius could hardly approve of one of his students taking such a position—even a dullard like Tzu-lu—because this Duke of Wei had seized the throne by force, overthrowing his own father to gain power. In other words, the man who called himself the Duke of Wei was living a lie. He had seized power but had not earned it. Everyone in Wei knew this, of course, which made it impossible for them to feel any respect for their ruler—and made it impossible for the duke to maintain order in his province. If the names were rectified, the title would be restored to his father and the son would be branded an impostor. That would confound the power structure in Wei, of course, but it would put the state in harmony with the truth. So when Confucius says that Wei needs a "rectification of the names," he is proposing the one thing that the Duke of Wei dare not do.

Facing the truth is a sine qua non of good government, Confucius adds. Thus the state must protect those who point out unpleasant truths. It's not that people enjoy being corrected. "Well, I guess you could call me a lucky man," Confucius says wryly to his students. "Whenever I make a mistake, there's always somebody to point it out to me." The higher-ranking a person is, the more important it is that people challenge him. "If the ruler is right, and nobody challenges him, that's fine," Confucius says. "But if the ruler is wrong, and nobody dares say so—that's the one thing the could ruin a country." It goes without saying that "rectification of the names"—calling things what they really are—is as necessary today as it was when Confucius had this back-and-forth with Tzu-lu in 475 B.C. One day when I was a political reporter covering the U.S. Congress, I sat in the gallery watching the House of Representatives debate and vote on a bill titled "The Tax Reform and Relief Act of 1980." Like much "tax reform" legislation that reaches the floor of Congress, this proposal was in fact a collection of special-interest provisions designed to dole out tax breaks to assorted lobby groups. A bipartisan group of do-gooders stood up to oppose each amendment, but the power of the interest groups was too strong, and one by one the new tax breaks breezed through to easy passage.

Finally, one of the embattled minority, a congressman from the suburbs of Pennsylvania, stood up and offered an amendment of his own: He proposed that the words "Tax Reform" be stricken from the title of the bill, since the legislation was not "reforming" the tax code but was making it more complicated and unfair. This quixotic proposal prompted fairly vigorous debate on the floor. The members pushing the tax bill were outraged. What a frivolous amendment! How could the gentleman from Pennsylvania waste the valuable time of this House worrying about the title of the legislation? What difference could it make what the bill was called? And I can still remember, nearly two decades later, how that U.S. congressman from Pennsylvania stood up and said, in essence, "A great man named Confucius taught that government cannot operate honestly if the names are dishonest. This amendment to the title of the bill is an attempt at a fundamental goal of good government: the rectification of the names." Naturally, this effort at truth-in-legislation went down to overwhelming defeat. And Congress is still regularly passing bills called "The Tax Reform Act."

For Confucius, as for many other great teachers who would come later, a key aspect of facing the truth was recognizing the limits of one's own knowledge. In Book II of the Analects, Confucius turns to Tzu-lu and says, "Shall I teach you what knowledge is? When you know a thing, to recognize that you know it, and when you do not know a thing, to recognize that you do not know it. That is knowledge." Just one hundred years after Confucius, Socrates would make the same point in his *Apology:* "I decided that I was wiser than the man who . . . thinks he knows something when he knows nothing. Because while I may not know anything, at least I never pretend that I do." About twenty-five hundred years later Chief Petty Officer Prendergast told me the same thing when I was learning to become a naval navigator: "The best thing is to know where you are. It's a little worse not to know where you are. But the worst thing is to think you know you are someplace when you really ain't there."

Confucius himself was successful in rectifying one crucial name– a word that shows up constantly in the Analects, beginning with the opening lines that Matsuda-san recited to me. The Chinese word is *chun-tzu.* It is written with two characters that mean "royal" and "person." This tells us that traditionally *chun-tzu* referred to a prince, an aristocrat, someone who obtained a position of stature and power through birth. Confucius accepted the basic principle that certain people have the right to hold elite positions, but then he completely changed the rules for joining the ranks of the elite. To Confucius, the *chun-tzu*–the term has been variously translated as "the noble man," "the superior man," "the gentleman"–was a person who had *earned* elite status. To be a gentleman, a person had to spend a lifetime studying and following the rules of virtuous conduct. Just being born right was not enough. A gentleman should be judged–just as Martin Luther King, Jr., would put it twenty-five centuries later–on the content of his character.

In essence, Confucius stole the status of "nobleman" away from the few elite families and gave it to everybody–at least everybody who earned it. There's no original sin in the Confucian cosmology. All humans are good, and thus any person has the potential to become a member of the ruling elite. But nobody–not even the son of a king– could automatically claim the title of gentleman. A true gentleman is made, not born, the master said. A true gentleman is a person who works hard at education. He makes the effort to study history, and the ancient rites, and the art of government, and then makes practical use of the things he has learned. And only these gentlemen, people with a finely honed sense of ethical conduct, are entitled to govern.

Because the Confucian gentleman is to be entrusted with so much authority in running the state, the master spent a great deal of his time teaching what a real gentleman should be. As we have already seen, he has to be a big enough person to brush off the slings and arrows of lesser men: "Isn't it the sure sign of a gentleman, that he does not take offense when others fail to recognize his ability?" Beyond that, the Analects are chock full of prescriptions and guidance for the would-be gentleman. Confucius offers fashion advice for the *chun-tzu:* "A gentleman does not wear purple or mauve lapels; red or violet should be used for daily wear at home. In the heat of summer, he wears white linen, fine or coarse, but never goes without putting on a gown." He offers tips on table etiquette: "Even if his rice is of the finest quality, he does not gorge himself. . . . Even if there is plenty of meat, he does not eat more meat than rice."

But most of the guidance for those who would be leaders falls squarely in the realm of ethical conduct:

> The gentleman by his culture collects friends about him, and through these friends he promotes goodness.

A gentleman is dignified, but never haughty. The lesser man is haughty, but never dignified.

It is easy to work for a gentleman, but not easy to please him. Try to please him by immoral means, and he will not be pleased. But he never demands anything that is beyond your capacity.

He who behaves with honor, and, being sent on a mission to the four corners of the world, does not bring disgrace to his lord, deserves to be called a gentleman. . . . His word can be trusted; whatever he undertakes, he brings to completion.

There are nine points on which a gentleman must take care: when observing, to see clearly; when listening, to hear distinctly; in his expression, to be amiable; in his attitude, to be deferential; in his speech, to be loyal; when on duty, to be respectful; when in doubt, to ask questions; when angry, to ponder the consequences; when gaining an advantage, to consider whether it is fair.

The key breakthrough here was the thoroughly democratic insistence that anybody could become a *chun-tzu*–a principled man of virtue. The opportunity and the duty to serve as a leader were open to all. To make sure that everyone had a fair chance to develop the virtuous character required of a gentleman, Confucius put enormous emphasis on the role of education. Any man could be virtuous, but the elements of virtuous conduct had to be taught. In modern Western societies, with our emphasis on the individual, we might argue that universal education is an obligation owed to each person as a basic human right. Whether or not Confucius might have agreed with this viewpoint is hard to say. But his rationale for educating people was a different one. He advocated education for the good of the collective society. Only by making training available to all could the state be sure that its best people were trained in the arts of virtue and government. The ruling elite had to be drawn from the best–not the richest or the highest born, but the best. Thus the state had a responsibility to provide education to everyone; parents, in turn, had a responsibility to see to it that their children pursued an education; the children, in turn, had a responsibility to take schooling seriously. Whatever the rationale, Confucius's insistence on education for all still resonates powerfully in East Asian societies. Thus Chapter 39 of Book 15 of the Analects, although it is one of the shortest chapters, ranks as one of the most influential lines in all the Chinese classics: "Confucius said, 'In teaching, there should be no distinction by classes.'"

Since Confucius and his followers over the centuries felt that government was the highest calling, it became necessary to devise a mechanism for placing the most talented and hardest-working people in the society in government jobs. To choose these people, the Chinese invented the civil service exam, a long written test in which applicants were expected to demonstrate comprehensive knowledge of the Confucian Classics.

Examinations for picking members of the governing bureaucracy were in use well before the birth of Christ. A single national test was standardized in China in A.D. 1321; it remained in use, more or less unchanged, until 1905. It was given every three years, and was open to all (male) applicants, regardless of background. Naturally, the sons of current officials or wealthy families tended to dominate, since it was they who would have the time for the necessary years of study. But at every examination sitting, a few bright young men from poor, rural backgrounds would also pass the tests and gain admission, by merit, to the elite governing cadres. The young hopefuls were required to write out large chunks of the Four Books from memory, and answer analytical questions on the Five Classics as well. The ordeal was brutal, as a nineteenth-century account makes clear:

> Throughout the Canton examinations, the candidates were confined, without a break, for days on end, in cells only four feet square. In these they had to endure the trials of the examination as well as the extreme discomfort of the humid August heat. Such was the cumulative effect of both the physical and mental strain to which the candidates were subjected, that, when the cells were opened at the end of the examinations, it was not unusual for the examiners to find that many of the candidates had not survived the grueling test.

This system of appointment by merit moved to Korea, Japan, and other nations with the spread of Confucian doctrine. To this day, in most East Asian societies, nearly all schools, government agencies, corporations, newspapers, etc., choose their new entrants each year through competitive examinations. Nowadays, the tests tend to cover science, geography, and current events rather than quotations from the Analects. But the Confucian principle remains the same. By using a test of merit rather than birth or wealth as the gateway to a privileged position, societies can make sure that their leaders constitute an elite of the brightest (or at least hardest-working) members of society.

The whole framework of the Confucian state, with a coterie of decent, virtuous people earning the right to rule, is itself a form of national education. For Confucius was a strong believer in the notion of teaching by example. The twentieth-century U.S. Supreme Court justice Louis D. Brandeis was precisely in accord with the ancient Chinese sage: "Our government is the great, the omnipresent teacher. For good or ill, it teaches the whole people by its example.... If the government becomes a lawbreaker, it breeds contempt for the law." In the same way, Confucius always said that a leader teaches his subjects through his own conduct. If the people see that their ruler is a gentleman, then they will follow his example. The state will flourish. "Raise the straight and put them above the crooked, so that they may straighten the crooked," the master tells his student Fan Chi.

At one point in the Analects, Confucius is asked for advice by the Lord Chi Kang, leader of one of the three powerful clans then battling for control of Lu. Confucius clearly did not approve of this upstart and his challenge to the authority of the established government. And so, with no apparent concern for Chi Kang's strength, the humble teacher responds curtly to the powerful warlord.

"Lord Chi Kang was troubled by burglars," relates Book 12 of the Analects. "He asked Confucius about the problem. Confucius said, 'If you yourself, Chi Kang, were not on the take, nobody would be trying to steal from you.'"

Later, Chi Kang asks Confucius to authorize capital punishment: "Suppose I were to kill the bad to help the good; how about that?" Confucius responds with a famous metaphor: "You are supposed to govern, not to kill. If you yourself desire what is good, the people will be good. The moral power of the gentleman is the wind; the moral power of the common people is the grass. The grass will always bend in the direction of the wind."

Confucius constantly emphasizes that the relationship between ruler and subject is actually just one of many relationships that affect every choice a person makes. Every human being lives within a web of overlapping relationships—family, friends, village, country—and has specific responsibilities as a member of each group. The wise human being is the one who recognizes his position (that is, who rectifies his own title) within each group and meets the responsibilities that come with it. If each person does what is expected, then all of his various groups will thrive.

Confucius—or, more likely, the disciples who came after him—organized the rules of social behavior around the Five Basic Relationships, or the Five Basic Loyalties: (1) the relationship between ruler and people; (2) the relationship between parent and child; (3) the marital relationship; (4) the relationship between older and younger siblings; (5) the relationship between older members of any group and their juniors. Within each of these pairings, the younger or lower-ranking member was expected to offer respect, obedience, and an attitude of deference toward the elder. But that's only half the story. The crucial point—one that has been conveniently ignored by Asians who seek to justify authoritarian regimes—is that the Confucian loyalties run both up and down.

The subject has an obligation to the ruler, but the ruler has equally strong obligations to the subject. The underling must be respectful and obedient, but the superior has a duty of benevolence. He is required to protect and educate his subjects, to provide the conditions they need for a safe and prosperous life. In the same way, parents have obligations to the children, and a husband to his wife; an older sister has to look out for her kid brother, and senior members of a club or company are expected to train and protect the younger members. Naturally, one of the basic tests of a good person, a gentleman, is fealty to these basic loyalties. The disciple Tzu-kung asks Confucius, "How does one come to deserve the title 'gentleman'?" The answer is no surprise: "His relatives praise his filial piety and the people of his village praise the way he respects the elders."

The emphasis on loyalty—in Chinese, *chung*—brings with it the eternal problem of conflicting loyalties. How do you act when, say, your family's best interests are not in accord with the interests of the ruler? The clever dodge for any teacher confronted with this dilemma is to argue that there's no real difference; properly viewed, the interests of both groups are identical. But Confucius is too honest to fall back on this ploy. He has a hierarchy of loyalties, and the top rung clearly belongs to one's family. For Confucius, family is the basic social grouping at the heart of society. All the Confucian texts are filled with the master's emphasis on filial piety and fraternal loyalty. He is constantly praising people for putting family first, and criticizing others who have failed to be good sons, or fathers, or granddaughters, or even distant cousins. The family grouping, and family loyalties, must be preserved. Thus we have this crucial exchange in Book 13 of the Analects:

> The Governor of She declared to Confucius: "Among my people, there is a man of unbending integrity. When his father stole a sheep, this man testified against his father." Confucius said, "Among my people, men of integrity do things differently: a father covers up for his son, a son covers up for his father— and there is integrity in what they do."

In that remark, we see Confucius's basic distrust of law and regulation as a means of assuring goodness. Confucius and his followers were always suspicious of written laws, contracts, courts, and litigation. A dusty book of statutes was simply too inflexible to handle the infinite variety of human experience, the master said. He chose to trust people, not laws—to rely on innate goodness and the benevolent attitudes instilled by education as the best guarantees of a civil society. He saw that litigation, as a means of resolving disputes, only served to make a society more confrontational, more competitive, and less harmonious. "I could adjudicate lawsuits," Confucius says in the Analects, "but I would prefer to make lawsuits unnecessary."

As a result, "the majesty of the law," which plays such a key role in Western society, has never seemed so majestic to East Asians. In Asia, the law is a kind of fallback position, something to be relied on, reluctantly, if people cannot not be taught to act decently of their own will. In Imperial China, Professor Ryckmans notes, "a prefect who had adjudicated a great many lawsuits during the time of his posting could not expect to be commended for his zeal; so much contentiousness among the people under his authority reflected poorly on the quality of his administration." To this day, written laws and contracts play a smaller role in Asian societies than they do in the West. Asian countries—even those ruled for hundreds of years by the British—have about one one-hundredth as many lawyers per capita as the United States has.

Confucius chose to place his trust on the laws of the heart, on the basic moral rules that marked a gentleman. The most important of these, invoked all through the Confucian Classics (hundreds of times in the Analects alone), is the concept of *jen* (the word is pronounced "ren"). This sweeping term is hard to translate, because it combines kindness, charity, civility—every aspect of treating people decently. Over the centuries, translators have used "humanity," "benevolence," "love," and just plain old "goodness" to convey the sense of *jen*. Even Arthur Waley, the most artistic wordsmith of all the translators of ancient oriental texts, was stumped by this term. "*Jen,* in the Analects, means 'good' in an extremely wide and general sense," Waley wrote. ". . . It seems to me that 'good' is the only possible translation."

Many editors avoid the risk of narrowing the meaning by refusing to translate the word at all. It is simply *jen*. With the growing interest in Eastern religions, this ancient Chinese term has become so popular that some unabridged dictionaries now include it as an English word. The unabridged *Random House Dictionary of the English Language* gets it just right, I think: "jen—(in Chinese philosophy) a compassionate love for humanity or for the world as a whole." Confucius would no doubt sympathize with those struggling to translate the term, because he taught that *jen* was too deep a concept to convey in words. It was something a person had to see in others, or feel in the heart. In Book 12 of the Analects, a student named Sou-ma Niu asks the master about *jen*. "A man who has *jen* is wary of talking about it," Confucius replies. (He's using another of his puns here, because the word for "wary" or "reluctant" is also pronounced "jen.") When Sou-ma Niu complains about this evasive answer, Confucius says, "Since doing *jen* is so difficult, how can one be anything but wary of talking about it?"

To anybody who grew up in the Judaeo-Christian culture, of

course, the idea of "a compassionate love for humanity" is thoroughly familiar territory. A Christian would have no trouble inserting this Confucian ideal directly into the New Testament: "And now abideth faith, hope, *jen*, these three; but the greatest of these is *jen*."

But the parallels between the founder of Confucianism and the founder of Christianity go farther than that. In the Analects, a student one day asks the master to reduce all his teachings to one word. With admirable patience, Confucius agrees to do so. "It is perhaps the word *shu*," he says, using a word that means "consideration" or "caring for others." He then goes on to explain *shu*, in terms that will be familiar to any veteran of Sunday school: "Do not impose on others what you do not want for yourself." That is, Confucius taught the Golden Rule, some five hundred years before Rabbi Hillel and Jesus Christ were to teach the same thing, halfway around the world.

Confucius is less Christ-like, though, when it comes to things like loving the enemy and turning the other cheek. The "gentleman" needs to nurture feelings of love, consideration, and charity, of course, but he must also know how to hate those who undermine the social order. "It is only the virtuous man [literally, "the man of *jen*"] who can love people—or hate people." In Book 13 of the Analects, Confucius is asked, "What would you think of a man, if all the people in his village liked him?" The master replies, "It would be better if the good people in the village were to like him, and the bad people to dislike him."

The Master Kung knew both like and dislike in his lifetime. As we have seen, he never managed to find a ruler who would trust him for long with a serious government position. And yet, by the end of his days, he was a famous and respected teacher. Late in his life, when he traveled to the province of Yi, the gatekeeper at the border was thrilled just to have a chance to meet the great sage. "The Empire has long been without the Way," the gatekeeper said. "But heaven is going to use the Master as its bellringer."

On the fourth day of the fourth month in A.D. 479, the annals say, Confucius woke early and recited an ancient poem to his students:

> *The great mountain must crumble;*
> *The strong beam must break,*
> *And the wise man wither away like a plant.*

When the disciple Tzu-kung asked what this was supposed to mean, the master said, "My time has come to die." He then lay down on his couch and stayed there, day after day. And on the seventh day, he was dead.

Duke Ai, who was then the nominal ruler of Lu, pronounced himself disconsolate at the loss of his greatest teacher. "There is none now to assist me on the throne," he wept—an outburst that prompted the bitter Tzu-kung to wonder out loud why it was that the duke had failed to take the great teacher's advice when he was alive. But the duke's lament presaged the ambivalent attitude that the rulers of China would hold for the next twenty-five centuries toward Confucius and his teachings.

Initially, Confucius was hallowed. His students spread through Lu, Wei, Yi, and the other provinces, teaching what they had been taught. The *Lun Yü* was compiled to assist in this task, and the book of Mencius added to the scholarly corpus.

Mencius (roughly 372–289 B.C.) was particularly interested in the political-science implications of the master's teachings. Focusing on Confucius's idea that the ruler owes a debt of benevolence to his subjects, Mencius took the concept to its logical conclusion: If the ruler was not benevolent—that is, if the people decided that their ruler was not protecting them adequately—he could be, and indeed must be, replaced. It was a theory of government that Thomas Jefferson would invoke, almost verbatim, against King George III in 1776: "That whenever any form of government becomes destructive of these ends, it is the right of the people to alter or to abolish it, and to institute new government . . ."

Jefferson and his fellow revolutionaries called this idea "popular sovereignty." Mencius, equally revolutionary, had a slightly different way of putting it. The ruling families of China had always insisted that the emperor was the son of heaven; they invoked the "mandate of heaven" to legitimize their right to power. Mencius, yoking the enormous prestige of Confucius to the democratic cause, declared that "the mandate of heaven is not immutable." If an emperor abused the divine mandate, if a dynasty failed in its obligation to the people, it was the right of the people to alter or to abolish it, and to institute new government.

As Mencius was writing, in the fourth century, the Chou dynasty continued to lose what little power it had. China slipped into one of its Warring States interludes, with various contenders battling for power. The struggle was won–briefly, at least–by the Chin dynasty, formed by a band of warlords from the northwest who conquered all other challengers and seized power under the emperor Chin Shih Huang-ti ("The First Sovereign Emperor of Chin") around 240 B.C. This young emperor was nothing if not energetic; during a reign of less than twenty years he built the Great Wall, standardized the writing system, made all competing warlords his vassals, and dominated the Middle Kingdom so completely that the nation is known around the world to this day as the Chin country, or China. Shih Huang-ti also launched a reign of terror against ideas. Book burnings were held on a massive scale. It was hardly surprising that the two great teachers, Confucius and Mencius, with their dangerous ideas about the duty of benevolence, the primacy of family loyalty, and the rights of ordinary people, should be the chief targets of this purge. The Chin regime did its best to destroy every known copy of the works of Confucius.

But it was one thing to burn the books. It was quite another to immolate the ideas in them. The people would not stand for the harsh Chin version of "benevolence," and sided with a clan of usurpers, the Han. The Chins lost power barely two decades after grabbing the throne. The Hans, who could cite Confucian authority ("the mandate of heaven is not immutable") for their right to take over, established a board of Confucian scholars and scoured the countryside for surviving volumes of the classics. Around 150 B.C. (or so the rather romantic story runs), a complete manuscript of the *Lun Yü*–evidently copied from an earlier text and hidden at the time of the Chin purge–was found wedged between two boards in the wall of the Kung family home in Lu. With this secreted volume and other remnants found here and there around the empire, the Han dynasty was able to save the corpus of the works of Confucius.

For the next two thousand years or so, Confucius, Mencius, and the Confucian worldview went through similar ups and downs as various upheavals, usurpations, and revolutions brought new dynasties in and out of power. There were anti-Confucianists, neo-Confucianists, anti-neo-Confucianists, and neo-neo-Confucianists. And yet, many Confucian elements–the zeal for education, the reverence for history, the preservation of ancient ceremony–remained constant features of Chinese society. The system of merit testing to pick elite bureaucrats was fully established by the first century A.D.—and continues to this day. As Confucianism worked its way deeply into the basic foundation of Chinese culture, it was spread to other Asian countries by traveling Chinese: Buddhist missionaries, the Mongolian (Khan) conquerors, and later the so-called overseas Chinese–the hordes of emigrants who moved to Malaysia, Burma, Singapore, Vietnam, Hawaii, and elsewhere to open new branches of family businesses.

Over the centuries, the Master Kung himself was given a series of increasingly resplendent titles: the All-Complete and Illustrious (about A.D. 100); the Venerable Sage (492); K'ung, the Ancient Teacher, accomplished and illustrious, all-complete, the perfect Sage (1645). Centuries of scholiasts compiled paper mountains of commentary on the *Lun Yü* and other Confucian works, and then later scholars expanded upon their predecessors. Legge, the British translator, compiled a bibliography of Confucian scholarship published in the seventeenth and eighteenth centuries, and the list runs to hundreds of volumes just for those two centuries. Various communities in Lu, vying for the honor of being the hometown of the venerable sage, built imposing shrines where the master and his works were memorialized.

With the fall of the last dynasty, the Ching, in 1911, poor Confucius fell onto hard times. He was branded a reactionary, a counterrevolutionary, a negative force who had repressed innovation. Thus it was Confucius's fault that the Middle Kingdom, facing the greatest external challenge in its history, had been humiliated by the Western barbarians, with their warships and armies and colonial governors. Later, under Chairman Mao's infamous Cultural Revolution, Confucius was relegated to lowly status indeed: he was just one more "capitalist roader." The Red Guards systematically trashed the temples and mansions erected in his memory, and the Confucian Classics became books to be suppressed, not studied.

As has been proven time and again in Chinese history, however, it's hard to keep a good sage down. Today, the Master Kung is once again the Venerable Sage. Mao's successors, moving to erase some of the outrageous excesses of the Communist era, have revived Confucian teaching. President Jiang Zemin quotes liberally from the *Lun Yü*, the Book of Odes, and the other classics in his speeches. Once again, those opening lines of the *Lun Yü* are chanted by memory in classrooms the length and breadth of the land: *Isn't it a pleasure when you can make practical use of the things you have studied?* The current regime has invested millions of dollars to repair the shrines, and quotations from Confucius pop up regularly on banners over the streets in all major Chinese cities.

In Shandong Province (the former Lu), across the Yellow Sea from the Korean Peninsula, Confucius is treated as one of the two most famous local products. Shandong's site (http:\\www.china-sd.com/) on the World Wide Web boasts that it is "hometown of Confucius . . . one of the birthplaces of the Chinese philosophy and oriental culture." (It then moves on to the other local pride, Tsingtao Beer, China's most famous bottled export. In the colonial era, Shandong had come under primarily German control, and the masters taught the colonials how to brew beer.) The center of Shandong's Confucius revival is the city of Qufu (pronounced "Choofoo"), which claims to be the actual site of Tsau, where the Kung family lived. Of Qufu's 600,000 residents, about 130,000 bear the Kung name—and most of them seem to claim to be descendants of the sage.

Surrounded by rice fields and apple orchards, Qufu presents itself as something of a relic, a town dotted with museums and shrines to a favorite son who died nearly twenty-five centuries back. Each year on September 28, birthday celebrations are held for Kung Fu-tzu. At the 2,548th birthday, in 1997, dancers and drummers marched around the lacquer-red Confucian shrine as a speaker in a dark and seemingly ancient robe stood beneath the Gate of Esteeming the Lofty and read selections from the Analects. The birthday crowd then marched solemnly toward the Confucian Forest, where the sage is said to be buried.

"To get rich is glorious" in modern China, and the people of Qufu are doing their best. There's a rich supply of guided tours, museums, and souvenir shops offering memorabilia of the master. Street peddlers offer visitors old coins "that once belonged to Confucius, guaranteed." A man named Kung Quingxi, who says he is in the seventy-third generation of Kungs descended directly from Kung Fu-tzu, is the brewer of San Kung Beer, named for three famous local spots where Confucius is said to have met with students. Mr. Kung says his beer is delicious because of the local water and because of the inspiration the brewery workers derive from studying the master's works during their lunch break. Another local start-up company is making Confucius Family Liquor, a clear grain alcohol somewhat reminiscent of cheap vodka. The label bears the company's slogan: "Isn't it a pleasure to have an old friend visit from afar?"

CONFUCIUS HAS ACTUALLY fared better in other East Asian nations than in his native land for most of the twentieth century. Confucian ideas and the overall Confucian value structure have been incorporated into the social, educational, and governmental fabric of Japan, Korea, Thailand, Indochina, Singapore, Vietnam, Cambodia, and, to a somewhat lesser degree, Malaysia and Indonesia. When the Nationalist Chinese fled to Taiwan in 1949, they took their Confucian texts with them; the more the Master Kung was denounced on the Communist mainland, the more he was sanctified on Taiwan. To this day, September 28 is celebrated on Taiwan as a national holiday (Teacher's Day).

South Korea is dotted with ornate Confucian shrines. There are schools and libraries dedicated to the study of the Four Books. The National Confucian Association is an important institution in the life of the nation—among other things, it constantly monitors the public schools to make sure lessons pay sufficient attention to the Confucian ethical discourses—and the Confucian college, Seongkyunkwan University, is one of the nation's leading private universities. In Japan, the unified national school system, as we shall shortly see, was specifically designed to pass along traditional Confucian values, and has succeeded brilliantly at doing so. "Contemporary Japanese are not Confucianists in the sense that their [feudal] ancestors were, but they are still permeated with Confucian ethical values," noted the great Harvard orientalist Edwin O. Reischauer. "Confucianism probably has more influence on them than does any other of the traditional religions or philosophies." Western civilizations were much slower to recognize the value of Confucius's ethical and political teachings. This was partly a function of language and distance, but it was also the inevitable result of European arrogance. Learn from the Asians? How could these "lesser breeds" have anything to offer Western civilization? Those Europeans who did study the ancient Chinese texts were inclined to find nothing more there than proof of the established Western stereotypes. The Reverend W. E. Soothill, a British missionary, got all worked up about a minor incident in Book 17 of the Analects: A student comes to Confucius's home while the master is playing his lute. Confucius doesn't want to be disturbed, so he tells the student he is sick. For Soothill, this says it all: "That such laxity on the part of China's noblest exemplar has fostered that disregard for truth for which this nation is so notorious, can hardly be denied." It is an enormous credit to the sixteenth- and seventeenth-century Jesuits, who had traveled around the world to convert the heathen of Asia, that they recognized the fundamental humanity of Confucian ethics and undertook the hard work of carrying these Oriental ideas back to the West. The Jesuits' first Latin translation of "Confucius" was published in 1687, and all of the Four Books had been rendered into Latin by the early eighteenth century. French and Italian versions followed fairly shortly thereafter.

Some of the early English missionaries took stabs at translating Confucius, but there was no standard text of the Confucian teachings in English until a force of nature named James Legge arrived in Asia on a sultry December day in 1839.

Legge was born in 1820, the son of a Scottish farmer. A brilliant language student, he won all the prizes in Latin and Greek during his school days. He took a Doctor of Divinity degree and applied for a position as an overseas evangelist. At the London Missionary Society, somebody decided (inaccurately, but fortunately nonetheless) that this young preacher was burning to see the East. And thus it was that young Legge, with no knowledge whatsoever about Asia or its languages, was put on a ship bound for the East Indies.

For the next half century, Legge devoted himself to Asia with that prodigious industry that marked the eminent Victorian. He built and ran the Anglo-Chinese College in Hong Kong, started several private schools, founded, built, and presided over Hong Kong's first Protestant church, made numerous trips to England and back (passing time on the long voyages by reciting the New Testament aloud, from memory), outlived two wives and three of his ten children, and eventually became the first professor of Chinese at Oxford (and the first non–Oxford graduate ever to be made a professor there). He was a central figure in the raging nineteenth-century debate as to whether it was possible to translate the word "God" into Chinese. Legge argued the liberal position, that the Chinese could and did understand the Christian concept of God—and for this he was denounced as a China lover.

Which he was. Legge fell in love with East Asia from the instant of his arrival, and he spent the rest of his life battling to overcome the great enemy: "English ignorance," or the common European perception that the Orient was backward and barbarian. "It is true that their civilization is very different from ours," Legge wrote in 1858, "but they are far removed from barbarism.... For 4,000 years the people have been living and flourishing.... The Assyrian, the Persian, the Grecian, the Roman empires have all risen and decayed, and yet the Chinese empire is still there with its 400 millions of inhabitants. Why, it is clear there must be amongst the people certain moral and social principles of the greatest virtue and power."

Self-taught in Chinese, Legge found those moral and social principles in the Confucian classics, and eventually arrived at a fateful conclusion: "He who would understand the Chinese nation, must know its classical literature." To overcome "English ignorance," he set out to produce English versions of the Four Books and the Five Classics. He began, in 1858, with the *Lun Yü*, which he translated as "The Analects," the disappointingly academic title that has been used by every English translator ever since. By the time of his death, in 1897, he had completed not only those nine books but another ten classics from the Tang dynasty (seventh century A.D.).

Legge's magnum opus, *The Chinese Classics, with a Translation, Critical and Exegetical Notes, Prolegomena, and Copious Indexes, in Five Volumes,* is a stupendous piece of scholarship, an essential tool for Confucian study in both West and East ever since the appearance of its first volume in 1861. Most of its pages carry just a line or two of the Chinese text, followed by a line or two of translation, followed by a thick underlayer of footnotes in English, Chinese, Latin, and French and studded with citations from Chinese commentators, the Bible, and other sources. As befits Legge's disgust with the common European notion of an "inscrutable Orient," his Confucius is clear and straightforward, rendered in a Victorian accent that seems slightly arch to a modern reader but is easy to understand.

Legge always refers to Confucius as the Master. His version of *chun-tzu* varies with context: "the superior man," "the truly superior man," "the man of complete virtue." For *jen*, he uses the English word "virtue." Legge's translation of the opening lines of the Analects reads like this:

> The Master said, "Is it not pleasant to learn with a constant perseverance and application? Is it not delightful to have friends coming from distant quarters? Is he not a man of complete virtue, who feels no discomposure though men may take no note of him?"

Legge's stature and scholarship were so imposing that several decades passed before anyone else set out to translate Confucius into English. In the 1930s, however, an equally formidable literary figure applied himself to the task: Arthur Waley. This British scholar was a master of Chinese and of ancient and modern Japanese; more important, he was a poet with a command of mystery and nuance that fell perfectly on the ear of Europe between the world wars. Waley's translations of Eastern poetry influenced Yeats, Auden, Pound, and other poets. His six-volume rendition of the Japanese epic *The Tale of Genji* was such a fabulous tapestry of romance and intrigue that the nine-hundred-year-old novel about comings and goings at the court of Heian became a best-seller, volume by volume, in the England of the flapper era.

With total confidence in his own interpretive skill, Waley blasted James Legge, the titan of the field, arguing that Legge's rendition of Confucius was too dependent on medieval interpreters. The Waley translation of the Analects, completed in 1938, has the ring of poetry. Where Legge is stilted—"If a man in the morning hear the right way, he may die in the evening without regret"—Waley has perfect pitch—"In the morning, hear the Way; in the evening, die content!" But Waley's rendition seems at some points to be adjusted to Western preconceptions. When Confucius says, "It is only the virtuous man who can love people—or hate people," Waley turns the sense upside down: "He whose heart is in the smallest degree set upon goodness will dislike no one." Waley's translation of the opening lines of the Analects reads as follows:

> The Master said, To learn and at due times to repeat what one has learnt, is that not after all a pleasure? That friends should come from afar, is this not after all delightful? To remain unsoured even though one's merits are unrecognized by others, is that not after all what is expected of a gentleman?

The first important American translation of Confucius was done by a poet who was, if anything, even more self-assured than Arthur Waley. Ezra Pound never formally studied Chinese, but he wasn't the type to be stopped by minor barriers like a language he couldn't understand and an alphabet he couldn't read. He was transfixed by the kanji (characters) used to write Chinese and Japanese. He called the characters ideograms and declared, "In ideogram is the basis of a whole new aesthetic." The key point for Pound was that each Chinese character is—or was, about three thousand years ago—a picture of the thing it represents. The character for "man" looks like a man (sort of). The character for "mouth" looks like a mouth, or at least an opening. The character for "words" is a picture of sounds emanating from a mouth. And when the character for "man" is placed right next to the character for "words," the resulting character means "trust"—that is, a man who stands by his word.

As a poet, Pound felt that he could penetrate this aesthetic—that he could look at Chinese or Japanese with virtually no study, and translate the characters by giving each one the meaning he thought he could perceive in the picture. The notion is absurd on its face. It was hopelessly presumptuous. (It's also rather infuriating to a person like me, who has spent a quarter century studying the language.) Astonishingly, Pound made it work.

Working on an ode by the Chinese poet To Em Mei, Pound was provided with notes from a scholar who had translated a few of the individual characters: "clouds," "rain," "darkness," "eight," "flat," and so forth. There is an English translation of this poem by a serious scholar, Lily Pao-Hu Chung, which begins as follows:

> *How fair, the lingering clouds!*
> *How misty, the seasonal rain!*
> *Darkness fills the universe*
> *Blurring the level pathway.*

Ezra Pound couldn't read Chinese, but he could see something in those characters. And thus he could "translate" that poem into real English poetry:

> *The clouds have gathered and gathered*
> *and the rain falls and falls.*
> *The eight ply of the heavens*
> *are all folded into one darkness*
> *And the wide, flat world stretches out.*

In the 1920s, Pound became obsessed with Confucius. He started dropping references to the Master Kung into his endless series of Cantos, and was determined to produce a new translation of the Analects. By chance, he came upon a copy of James Legge's detailed and annotated version of the Four Books, with the Chinese at the top of each page, English in the middle, and explanations at the bottom. With Legge as his guide, Pound produced his translation, first in Italian and then in English.

This American "Analects" was a popular success but was panned by the scholars; since Pound couldn't read the emendations provided by centuries of commentators, he was frequently befuddled, and it shows. Pound's Confucius, interestingly, is not poetic; it is plain and direct. For "rectification of the names," he translates "call things by their right names." Pound's terse English captures the spare, austere feel of the Chinese text, with a lot of meaning packed into very few written words. Still, the work is thin and lifeless, as if some great Renaissance painting were reproduced in stick figures. Here's how he translates the opening lines:

1. He said: Study with the seasons winging past, is not this pleasant?
2. To have friends coming in from far quarters, not a delight?
3. Unruffled by men's ignoring him, also indicative of high breed.

After World War II, as the number of Americans studying Asia began to increase, more and more American translations of Confucius and other ancient Asian classics began to appear. In some cases, American translators decided to rearrange and "improve" the original. In the wake of the *I Ching* boomlet of the hippie era, the American scholar Thomas Cleary put out a new version of the Analects with all the master's sayings rearranged to follow the order of topics set forth in the *I Ching*. For me, at least, this did not make the *Lun Yü* any more accessible.

Recent years have seen a rush of new Confucius translations, both in Asia and the West. As I write this, there are at least four new translations of the *Lun Yü*, in various stages of completion, floating around on the Internet. Two new English translations were published in 1997, including one of the best I've ever come across: *The Analects of Confucius*–Translation and Notes by Simon Leys. Actually, "Simon Leys" is the pen name of the Australian scholar Pierre Ryckmans. The notes are learned and opinionated, and the text is conveyed in a clear, up-to-date English. Most of the quotations from the Analects appearing in this book come from this new Ryckmans version. He rendered the opening lines this way:

The Master said: "To learn something and then put it into practice at the right time: is this not a joy? To have friends coming from afar: is this not a delight? Not to be upset when one's merits are ignored: is this not the mark of a gentleman?

No matter what the language or who the translator may be, the core of Confucianism–the commitment to truth, the relentless emphasis on ethical conduct, loyalty upwards and downwards, and respect for the family–always comes through clearly. The Master Kung's voice rings clear and true, down through the ages. And yet, the Four Books cover a great deal of territory, not always with total clarity. Latter-day readers have regularly managed to twist and mutate the basic Confucian text for their own purposes. Just like Bible-thumping politicians in the West, who always seem to discover that their own stance is supported by Holy Scripture, people reading Confucius often manage to find there exactly what they had hoped to find.

That first Latin version of the Analects created something of a sensation in priestly circles because the Jesuits thought they had found a prophecy of the birth of Christ in Chapter 27 of the *Chung Yung* ("How great is the path of the Sage! It waits for the Proper Man, and then it is trodden"). In modern America, supporters of supply-side tax cuts have listed Confucius as an ally, thanks to a brief exchange in Book 12 of the Analects. The Duke of Lu tells one of Confucius's students that his government is running a deficit, even with a 20 percent tax rate. The student suggests that Duke Ai should impose a 10 percent tax rate. As anybody can plainly see–or so the supply-siders tell us–this is an unqualified Confucian endorsement of the notion that cutting taxes will increase government revenues.

The most consequential current debate about what Confucius said, or didn't say, is going on right now in East Asia. It is an argument about dictatorship and democracy.

As East Asia has become increasingly democratic, the leaders of the regimes in Singapore, China, and Vietnam need some pillar to support continuation of their autocratic rule. And so they dare to argue that authoritarian control, with rigged elections that always return the same governing clique to power, are in fact models of the Confucian state. Democracy is a Western concept, this theory runs, and it violates something called Asian values. The argument rests on a distorted interpretation of Confucius that magnifies his emphasis on public order and loyalty to the leadership class, while completely ignoring his insistence that government has a duty to satisfy the people.

Invoking the first of the master's Five Basic Loyalties, the loyalty between ruler and subjects, the Asian autocrats insist that they are entitled to unquestioning loyalty from their subjects. "We Asians have always had our own way of organizing a state," says Lee Kuan Yew, the strongman of Singapore. "We feel that what a country needs is discipline more than democracy."

You might think it rather embarrassing for the ruling faction in Peking to lean on Confucius, since their own Communist party spent the past half century savaging the master and denouncing his teachings. Evidently the current Chinese leaders are shameless enough to ignore this inconvenient historical fact, for they, too, invoke "Confucian values"–also referred to as "Socialism with Chinese characteristics"–to demand unquestioning submission to authority.

Singapore has gone much further with the Confucius theme. The island nation's chief neo-neo-Confucianist is Lee Kuan Yew, the first prime minister, who continues as de facto ruler. His official title at the moment is Senior Minister, although the columnist William Safire comes closer to the truth when he calls Lee Kuan Yew the "boss-for-life." Always suspicious of popular will, Lee has mounted numerous campaigns over the years to mold his subjects to be more like him. Thus the government has promoted the National Courtesy Campaign, the Speak Mandarin Campaign, and even, when hippiedom reared its ugly head on the island in the 1970s, the Short Haircut Campaign. In the 1980s, these same campaigners decided to launch a new program to inculcate "Asian values"; this brought more Confucian texts to the schools and quotes from Confucius on the walls of the subway stations. Lee himself was described by his chief deputy as "the modern Confucius."

To the autocrats' distress, however, the campaign backfired. The 25 percent of Singaporeans who are not Chinese decided that "Confucian values" was actually code for "Chinese values," and that the whole program was actually a large campaign of government-sponsored racism. In a small, heterogeneous city-state that prides itself on racial tolerance, this could not stand. Gradually, Lee and his cohorts in the ruling party had to cut back. "Asian values" metamorphosed into "shared values." The government issued a White Paper on Shared Values, insisting that it had no intention of imposing Chinese ways on its citizens. But in the political sphere, Confucius is still invoked by the party as a champion of one-party dictatorship. That White Paper, in fact, said that the government of Singapore was composed of a group of benevolent *chun-tzu*–the precise Confucian term for the "good man," or "gentleman." These Singaporean "gentlemen" claim to be so busy caring for the people that they cannot be bothered to run in free elections.

And yet, elsewhere in Asia, nations that are just as committed to Confucian ideals have embraced popular sovereignty, freedom of the press, and open elections. Japan is a free, democratic country and has been for half a century. In South Korea, which held true to Confucian education all those years when the master had been abandoned in China, the newly empowered middle class rose up en masse in the streets in 1987 to throw out the military dictatorship and demand free elections. The leader of the democratic cause, Kim Dae Jung, had been a university professor of Confucian thought; he always insisted that democratic reforms were required by Confucian teachings. When Kim himself became a candidate, he quoted Confucius in every stump speech. It must have been good politics; in December of 1997, capping a long and often painful career as a campaigner for democracy in his native land, Kim Dae Jung became the democratically elected president of South Korea. In his inaugural address, naturally, he reminded the people of his country that Korea is a Confucian society. In Taiwan, the popularly elected president regularly tells his nation that no Chinese who is true to the Master Kung can tolerate one-party rule. The mandate of heaven, after all, is not immutable.

The basic ethical lessons that Confucius taught–the value of harmony and the importance of treating others decently–are immutable, however. One of the keys to East Asia's recent social miracle has been the region's success at inculcating those ethical values in its citizens. The master insisted that ethical values are the key to a successful society, and that it is government's job to exemplify those values and pass them on to the next generation. And the place to pass along values, as any East Asian can tell you, is the classroom.

FIVE

Yodobashi No. 6

I CAN STILL REMEMBER the look on our daughters' faces, and the you're-just-kidding-aren't-you-Daddy tone in their voices, when we told the girls they'd be going to a Japanese elementary school. The kids raised all the standard objections. But we had done our homework, so we had the answers.

But we'll have to go to school all through summer vacation! Not exactly true. All Asian countries, true to that Confucian tradition, consider schooling a full-time occupation for younger members of the society. Thus the schools are in session pretty much year-round. In Japan, China, and most other East Asian nations, there are about 240 school days per year. That makes the school year one-third longer than in Western countries like the United States, where the average is 180 days per year, with a long break in the summer. (And thus it's not quite so surprising that Asian students score so much higher on standardized tests than their peers in other countries.) Japanese kids go to school all of June and July. But in August, when the weather is hot and muggy over most of the archipelago, there's no school. The break lasts about four weeks, and comes complete with daily homework assignments designed to fill about four hours of each vacation day. A teacher drops by the student's home during vacation to make sure the homework is being done. Still, it is a summer vacation.

But we'll have to go to school on Saturday! Not exactly true. Traditionally, Japanese schools have met five and a half days per week, with Saturday classes from eight in the morning to noon. But in 1994 the National Ministry of Education stunned the nation with the controversial decision to close the schools one Saturday each month. So our girls wouldn't have to go to school *every* Saturday. (As if that weren't shocking enough, incidentally, the ministry later announced a plan to phase out Saturday sessions completely.)

But we'll have to wear a uniform! Not exactly true. Japanese school students–like Japanese adults in many lines of work–are generally required to wear a uniform. This enhances the group feeling, and gives each student the security of knowing that she'll never be in the uncomfortable position of sticking out from the crowd. In public schools, the uniform is usually a dark blue Prussian army outfit for boys, complete with a blue chauffeur's cap, and a blue sailor suit for girls. Private schools, in contrast, have dumped these military-style outfits and hired world-class designers to create new uniforms for the new millennium. The trendy new look in school uniforms is junior executive: blue blazer, blue tie, and gray slacks for the boys; blue blazer, blue bow tie, and pleated tartan skirt for the girls. But uniforms are generally required only for junior high and high school students; most elementary schools don't have uniforms. At least, not in the classroom. On the way to and from school, though, the kids in the primary grades are all required to have the same leather backpack (a handsome, sturdy piece of gear available in any Japanese department store for a mere $160) and a colorful bonnet–sky blue, red, or bright yellow. But that's not exactly wearing a uniform.

Even if we hadn't had such ready answers, though, we probably would have made the girls go to the school anyway. After all, I had made a promise to the Abe-sensei.

Abe Masako, a square-faced, intense, no-nonsense woman of about fifty, was the principal at a public school near our house called Yodobashi Dai-Roku Shogaku, or Yodobashi No. 6 Elementary School.

She was not a person who suffered fools gladly. When I first met her and told her that we lived in Subsection 3 of the Hiro-o neighborhood, she mentioned that we were pretty near Yodobashi No. 6. "Oh, really?" I said, just making conversation. "And where is Yodobashi No. 6?" The principal gave me one of her wilting looks and told me, in a manner that indicated the answer was obvious, that Yodobashi No. 6 is right next to the bus stop called Yodobashi Dai-Roku Sho Mae, which is to say, "In front of Yodobashi No. 6."

In any case, Abe-sensei had the idea that it would be a good experience for her students to have some *gaijin*–foreigners–in the classes to help them adapt to an international age. So she suggested that our girls join the third and fifth grades, respectively, at Yodobashi No. 6. My wife and I were intrigued by the idea. With some misgivings, we decided to give it a try. It would be an interesting cultural experience for the girls, we thought. The school would certainly sharpen their Japanese language skills, we figured, not to mention that famous Japanese educational rigor in math, science, and geography. And so we trundled the girls off to Yodobashi No. 6 when their international school was on summer vacation. In the process, we got both more and less than we had bargained for.

To some extent, Yodobashi No. 6 did provide substantive learning for our daughters; even today, back in an American Catholic school, they draw on concepts from the math or science classes at Yodobashi. But the strongest lesson our kids took away from that Japanese school was something we hadn't counted on. They were taught to be little Confucians. That public school, like all Asian public schools, devoted endless time, energy, and ingenuity to the teaching of moral lessons: community virtues, proper social conduct, appropriate behavior as a member of a group. Confucius and his followers, after all, had insisted that virtue can be taught–indeed, must be taught if the society as a whole is to be a virtuous and civil community. Moral education was much too important to be left to parents, or churches, or Boy Scout troops. It was a job for the whole society to engage in. And this is what the schools do, to this day, in East Asian societies. They teach reading, writing, arithmetic, science, and so forth, but at the same time they are busily turning out Confucian citizens.

Of course, for all the emphasis on citizenship, on civility, on proper group-membership skills, the Japanese schools have a dark side. Two of them, in fact. And both probably stem from that inordinate focus on the group.

One of these problems is called *taibatsu*. My pocket Japanese-English dictionary provides the formal translation "corporal punishment" for this term. To me, *taibatsu* has a more painful connotation than that, perhaps because the word is formed from two characters that mean "beating up the body." In Japanese schools, teachers or principals are known for beating their students—spanking, striking, or slugging children who act up or refuse to fit in with the others. Kids who cause problems, after all, are violating the school's collective *wa*, and that deserves punishment. Corporal punishment has become highly controversial in Japan in modern times, and today the school system prohibits *taibatsu*. Officially, that is.

A far greater concern for anybody thinking about sending children to a school in Japan is the notorious *ijime* (rhymes with "Fiji May"). For this word, that same rather understated dictionary of mine offers the translation "teasing"—you know, boys will be boys and all that. But *ijime* frequently takes on a more malignant flavor; in many cases, the better translation would involve words like "bullying," "harassment," "persecution," or, occasionally, "murder." *Ijime* is what happens when a Japanese group—it's usually, but not always, a group of children—decides that one member doesn't fit in. The outsider becomes an object of torment, emotional or physical. Even if some kids in the main group feel sympathy for the victim, there isn't much they can do. To side with the outsider would put them outside the group, which is bad enough, and might subject them to *ijime* as well, which is worse. In the schools, *ijime* can go on for months. It doesn't end until the wretched victim finds a way to fit in with the group, or a way to get out—switching to a new school, running away, or, sometimes committing suicide.

Suicide by teenagers victimized by this gang-bullying at school is a standard scandal item for the Japanese press, both tabloids and serious newspapers. Over the past five years, there have been about a dozen such suicides annually. Many of the victims leave behind farewell letters or diaries; they are painful, indeed shattering, to read, filled with details about the fear, shame, and despair the child felt after being branded the outsider. To make things worse, every case of *ijime*-induced suicide prompts a great feast of breast-beating in the newspapers and the education establishment. This national sense of trauma may actually make things worse, because a case of teen suicide is frequently followed, a day or two later, by another suicide by another victim of *ijime*, often way off in a far different corner of the country. It's as if these poor children, feeling hopeless because they are outside the group, suddenly find a group they can be admitted to— the group of suicide victims. These bursts of teen suicide in Japan quite frequently prompt tut-tutting articles and editorials in the press around the world, usually pointing out the intense stress that some Japanese schoolkids have to live with. I, too, used to write these stories. American readers seemed to find the horrible tales fascinating, and these reports generally got prominent display in American newspapers.

I was just as happy as the next reporter, of course, to snare a page-one story, and yet it always distressed me to see *The New York Times* and *The Washington Post* giving front-page space to these tales of youthful death in Japan. The entire nation of Japan, with 126 million people, averages less than one murder among school-age children each year, plus a dozen or so of these suicides due to bullying. The United States, with two times as many people, has about five hundred times as many teenage murders (and roughly the same rate of teen suicide). In the United States, these killings are rarely considered newsworthy outside of the school district where they occur. Very few make the front pages of newspapers around the country. Evidently, it is easier to be appalled about violence and death in some other country's schools than to face up to the same problem just down the street.

The fact that *ijime* happens to a relatively small number of students in Japan, however, is totally irrelevant if one of the victims is your own child. And of course, the risk of being tormented as an outsider is greater if you really are an outsider. In a sea of black-eyed, black-haired kids named Hanako and Hiroshi, my two blond, blue-eyed girls named Kate and Erin would be outsiders with a vengeance. We were worried.

And so I told the Abe-sensei we would be happy to have our girls attend Yodobashi No. 6, on two firm conditions: (1) no *taibatsu*; (2)

no *ijime*. Before our conversation on this topic, I had done a lot of work preparing what I wanted to say. This wasn't just some casual social conversation. This was about my daughters' safety. I needed to make my point, without insulting the principal or making her angry at me (and, perhaps, at my girls). When I told Abe-sensei about my concerns, I struggled the entire time to get the correct combination of self-effacing courtesy, Japanese-style, and in-your-face frankness, American-style. I had expected a polite but unsatisfactory answer, with the principal promising evasively to do her best. But the stern Abe-sensei was not the evasive type. She gave me that all-business look of hers and said, "No *taibatsu*. No *ijime*. None at all. I won't allow it."

And so it was that we set out one morning, taking a bus, a train, and finally one more bus that dropped us at the stop called "In Front of Yodobashi No. 6." And there was the school building, a three-story concrete structure of a nondescript architectural style that seemed to blend elements of aging prison and aging factory. The building was gray, of course. The most colorful thing we saw, at first approach, was the playground, a big expanse of red and green asphalt known as the "pu-ray hahbu." Evidently some asphalt contractor had convinced the local school board that a red and green asphalt playground was all the rage in America, where it was known as the "play hub." And so Yodobashi No. 6 acquired its own "pu-ray hahbu." Here the entire student body assembled for mass calisthenics on Monday mornings and singing on Wednesdays. These all-school sings invariably ended with a rousing rendition of the school song, a lively little number that bore the sprightly title "School Song of Yodobashi No. 6 Elementary School of Shinjuku Ward." The lyrics presented an idyllic picture of the school's natural setting:

> A school in this bright village
> Shadowed by lush green trees
> With a vista of Mount Fuji off in the distance—
> Oh, the memories of our alma mater,
> Yodobashi No. 6 Elementary School!

These lyrics suggested that the song must be about as old as the school itself. When our girls arrived there, Yodobashi No. 6 was just gearing up, with maximum esprit de corps, for its seventieth birthday celebration. In the twelfth year of the reign of the Emperor Taisho, or 1923, when it opened its doors for the first time, Elementary School No. 6 was in fact located at the edge of a sunny farming village west of Tokyo. The place was called Yodobashi, or "Bridge over the Stagnant Pond." It's entirely possible that students and teachers back then could have seen, rising far to the west over the rice fields of Japan's central plain, the gracefully curved massif of Mount Fuji, the tallest and most beautiful mountain between Mount Everest and the American continent. But that was a different Japan. In the 1990s, there was no possible vista of Fuji, because Yodobashi has been completely engulfed by urban expansion.

In fact, the school's immediate neighborhood—now known as Nishi-Shinjuku, or the area west of Shinjuku station—is Tokyo's equivalent of Madison Avenue. The little concrete schoolhouse is shadowed today not by lush green trees but by the world's most expensive real estate—soaring towers of glass and steel that house great corporations, banks richer than most countries, and five-star, $400-per-night hotels. The school's dominant vista today is not a distant mountain but rather a next-door neighbor that has become a famous symbol of Japan's leap to global financial power: Tokyo's New City Hall. This stupendous structure, reaching toward the heavens directly in front of Yodobashi's front door, is the magnum opus of Kenzo Tange, the patriarch of postwar Japanese architecture. It was specifically designed, at the height of the so-called bubble economy of the late 1980s, to show the world that Japan no longer took a back seat to the United States or Europe in architecture or anything else. Tange conceived his mission to be the creation of a great urban cathedral. So he built a twenty-first-century copy of the West's most famous cathedral, Notre Dame, complete with twin bell towers 797 feet tall and modern-day flying buttresses connecting the mayor's office to the city council chamber. It is all done in a blue-and-gray grid pattern that suggests the surface of a microchip, and it is one of the most beautiful city halls on earth—to me, at least. Unfortunately for Tange, however, and for the politicians who hired him, the huge new monument has sparked huge controversy among the citizens of Tokyo, who had to pay for the thing. When the New City Hall opened in 1991, it was quickly dubbed "Takusu Towah"—that is, Tax Tower—because the construction bill came in higher than a billion dollars. That billion-dollar city hall became a symbol of bubble-era excess. When Toho Studios, a movie company that keeps a finger on the public pulse, brought out the 1991 version of its annual Godzilla movie, the fire-breathing dinosaur was shown stomping through West Shinjuku and trashing Tange's masterwork. Toho later said that it had spent $700,000 just to build a model of the New City Hall for Godzilla to destroy. This was evidently a wise investment, because Japanese audiences roared their approval, and that one scene made the film *Godzilla vs. King Ghidora* a monster hit at the box office.

The area's transformation from quiet, rural Yodobashi to teeming, urban West Shinjuku is depicted in a series of black-and-white photographs in the small reception room at the school, where visitors can sip green tea and review the history of No. 6 Elementary School—and of twentieth-century Japan, for that matter—through the pictures on the wall. There's a mug shot of every principal the school has had, ranging from one Hasegawa Kakutaro, seen wearing a formal kimono bedecked with his ribbons from the Russo-Japanese War, to my serious friend Abe Masako, who took command in 1989. There's a photo of the school's opening ceremony, on April 1, 1923, with some mothers wearing the latest Western fashions (flapper-style dresses and bent-brim straw hats) and others in kimonos. A snapshot from 1943 shows all the students in military uniforms, and all the windows of the school heavily taped to prevent injuries from broken glass during air raids. Another picture taken just a few years later shows a brand-new school, built by the American occupation force, with a swimming pool and numerous basketball backboards on the playground. The latest photo of the series shows the gray concrete school building as it stands today, dwarfed by Tange's imposing Tax Tower and the area's other skyscrapers.

It wasn't just urban cathedrals that were built with tax money during Japan's rich bubble era, however. True to the Confucian dictate that education is one of the prime duties of the state, Tokyo took advantage of a big increase in tax revenues to pour massive investment into schools. The result was that Yodobashi No. 6, like countless other aging gray concrete schools all over the city, became a gleaming, state-of-the-art educational facility—once you stepped in the door. By the time our kids got to No. 6, the school had hallways of polished white pine, a gleaming new outdoor swimming pool, a bright, comfortable library, and computers all over the place. In a corner of the play hub, the school had its own zoo, with rabbits and roosters; each classroom was required to feed and care for one of these. The school had a fleet of 150 unicycles for gym class. In the music room, every square inch of free space was stacked with shiny new instruments– drum sets and tubas and racks full of recorders, one assigned to each student in the school. One item that confounded me at first was the student desks in the music room. They were bigger than any other desks in the school–bigger than the desktops in the classrooms, bigger even than the desks in the art room. Why such big desks in music? I figured it out when I lifted a desktop and found that inside every student desk there was an 88-key Yamaha keyboard.

A piano for every student! At first, this struck me as another example of the bubble era's wretched excess–until I came to realize that those keyboards were installed out of necessity. They were necessary because of the basic philosophical belief underlying elementary education in Japan, to wit: Every student can master every subject. If the year-end exams at Yodobashi No. 6 ever showed that, say, 298 out of the school's 300 students were reading at grade level, this would be a failure; it would prompt a furious round of meetings and special sessions and worried investigations of the cause. It was just assumed, at Yodobashi and every other Japanese school I ever went to, that each student (other than the small percentage certified to be mentally retarded) had the basic skills needed to learn everything taught there.

When Japanese students get older, there is clear educational tracking. The kids who score best on the entrance exams go to the best high schools with the toughest curricula. But in elementary school, and to a large extent in junior high, everyone is expected to succeed in every class. The secret to success is considered to be hard work. Why does one student get straight A's in math, science, geometry, and language, while her best friend gets all C's? In the United States, almost everybody answers that question by saying that the all-A student is smarter. In Japan, almost nobody would answer that way. The reason some kids do well in school and others don't is almost universally considered to be effort. If you work hard, you'll get

A's; if you didn't get A's, you didn't work hard enough. I've visited hundreds of Japanese classrooms over the years, and virtually every one has the word *doryoku* framed on the wall. The word means "effort."

And that's why the school needed a piano for every student and its own fleet of unicycles. Every kid at Yodobashi learned to read music and play the piano. Every kid was expected to balance on a unicycle. The school would provide the equipment, the teachers would provide the training, and the students were required to provide the effort.

BUT LITTLE THINGS LIKE BALANCING on one wheel or playing a Chopin étude are simple compared with the enormous amount of effort required for the major academic challenge of Japanese elementary school: learning to read and write. Japanese schools are famous around the world for their achievements in math, science, and geography. Japanese students regularly rank in the top two or three countries in the world on standardized tests at every grade level in these subjects, as we saw in Chapter 1. For my money, though, the greatest achievement of Japan's school system is teaching people to read and write Japanese.

Through a series of historical accidents, Japan has been stuck with an absurdly complicated written language. Take a look at a single page of any Japanese newspaper, and you'll see not just one alphabet in use, not just two, not just three, but four different alphabets (actually five, if you count the Arabic numerals as another alphabet). Each of the alphabets is used regularly, and it is common to see letters and characters from four different alphabets used in a single sentence. To read them all, Japanese have to learn, generally by rote memorization, thousands of different letters. It is "possibly the world's most difficult writing system," the Harvard scholar Edwin O. Reischauer noted.

And yet Japan has a literacy rate higher than 99 percent.

That's a government statistic, but I'd guess it's pretty accurate. I've never met a Japanese adult who couldn't read and write. When I used to have trouble making sense out of the orthographic jungle that is a Japanese newspaper, I would occasionally ask some nearby Japanese person for assistance. I was usually too hung up to ask a serious business type, so I directed my queries to less imposing people: janitors, cleaning ladies, subway ticket punchers. I always found that they could read any word, in any of the four alphabets, without a moment's hesitation.

How can one language have four different alphabets? Here's how it works:

* The Japanese have an indigenous alphabet with 47 characters–that is, one character for each of the 47 distinct sounds used in the Japanese language. Since each of the characters represents a whole syllable (*ka, sa, ta, na,* etc.), this collection is sometimes called a syllabary. But it works the same as any other phonetic alphabet. This Japanese syllabary would make for a simple and efficient writing system, because every word is spelled exactly as it sounds; there are no silent letters, no letters that change pronunciation from one word to another. You could write every word in Japanese with these 47 letters. But that would be too simple.

* In addition to that one 47-letter alphabet, there's a second, completely different Japanese alphabet; this one uses 47 different letters to represent those same 47 sounds. It, too, is used regularly in books, magazines, and so forth. The main purpose of this second syllabary is to write words that come from foreign languages–such as "ham-ba-gah" or "hotto doggu"–but it is also widely used to write plain old Japanese words as well. That makes things somewhat less simple. But it gets more complicated than that.

* The Japanese also use Roman letters for many purposes, so students have to learn our alphabet as well. You can write any Japanese word or name in Roman letters. That means there are at least three different ways–the first Japanese phonetic alphabet, the second Japanese phonetic alphabet, and the Roman alphabet–to write a Japanese word. But it gets more complicated than that.

♦ The primary Japanese "alphabet," imported by Buddhist priests from China in the sixth century A.D., are the Chinese characters. These constitute an alphabet that contains not 26, not 260, but well over 2,600 different letters. (Chinese characters are often known in the West as kanji; that's a Japanese word that means "Chinese character.") Unlike our Roman letters, and unlike the letters of the two Japanese syllabaries, the kanji have no phonetic value. That is, you can't just look at a character and know how to pronounce it. There's no way to sound them out. You have to memorize the pronunciation of every one of them–thousands of them. But it gets more complicated than that.

♦ Each one of those Chinese characters has two or more different pronunciations in Japanese. Take the character that means "horse," for example. The Japanese word for horse is *uma* (rhymes with a Bostonian's pronunciation of "rumor"). Naturally, then, the kanji for horse is pronounced *uma*. But not always. Every kanji has an alternative reading, representing the Japanese attempt to replicate the Chinese sound for that character. In the case of "horse," this comes out as *ba*. Or sometimes it comes out as *ma*. So when a student comes upon the character meaning "horse," she has to know by heart that it is pronounced either *uma, ba,* or *ma,* and she has to know by heart when each of the three readings is used.

While there's no way to tell how a particular character is pronounced just by looking at it, it is sometimes possible to discern the meaning of a character you've never seen before. All the Chinese characters started out about three thousand years ago as pictures. Some of these pictographs are straightforward, some complex. The character meaning "tree," for example, is a simple picture of a tree, with a trunk and four branches. That's an easy one to learn. And if you subsequently come upon a kanji that combines three of these "trees," that's the character for "forest." Most people have to put in year after year of hard work to learn all the characters, but some lucky ones–both Occidental and Oriental–seem to have an innate ability to break the code of the ancient Chinese wordsmiths, to know what characters mean with no study. The American poet Ezra Pound, was a master of this art form. The day Pound first came upon this kanji:

he knew immediately what it meant. "Any fool can see," he said, "that it's a horse." He was right, of course, because he was able see the ancient picture embedded in this kanji. The elements of the character, reading from top to bottom, show the horse's mane flying in the wind, the four flying hooves at the bottom, and a long tail hooking around behind the hooves. Any fool can see that it's a horse.

Unfortunately, a lot of people can't see it. And a lot of the kanji characters have evolved over the centuries and no longer look much like anything. What to do? A reader who doesn't know what a character means can always look it up in a dictionary. But this, too, takes on new dimensions of complexity.

In Western languages, a written word is a picture of the sound of that word. That is, the five letters that make up the English word "horse" don't have anything particularly horselike about them—there are no flying hooves in this English word—but the letters tell us the sound of the word. And from that, we can look it up in a dictionary. But the Chinese/Japanese character is a picture of a thing, not a sound. How then, do you find it in a dictionary? It's as if somebody gave you the symbol "&" and said, "look it up." Since there's nothing to sound out, how would you find it?

The Asians have developed two ways to do this. The simplest kanji dictionaries work by stroke count. You count up the number of brush strokes in the character you're looking at—for the kanji *uma,* or "horse," that comes to ten strokes—and open up the dictionary to the listing of ten-stroke characters. This method works, but it's inefficient; even the simplest kanji dictionary will have 120 or more ten-stroke characters, many of which look something like *uma.* So the better dictionaries break down each character into several parts, known as radicals. The reader then guesses which of the various radicals in the character is the controlling radical. This is fairly easy in the case of *uma*, which is such an important word that the whole ten-stroke character has traditionally been treated as a single radical. So all you have to do is open your dictionary to the section dealing with ten-stroke radicals, and look through the list until you see *uma*. It's a piece of cake.

This process is so complex and time-consuming that it quickly becomes clear that the only way to read the characters is to learn all of them—or at least, the most important of them—through rote memorization. The need for every student to memorize the meaning and pronunciation(s) of more than 2,000 different characters—merely to achieve basic literacy!—sits like a massive dead weight atop the Japanese education system. Every once in a while, accordingly, some reformer comes along urging that Japan dump this absurdly unwieldy system and write its language in Roman letters. Having spent the past two decades struggling with kanji, I sympathize. In Japan, though, the language reformers never get very far. The reasons are partly aesthetic. Those ancient characters are quite beautiful—that's why brush writing is still a major art form in all East Asian countries—and they reflect Japan's traditional Asian culture far better than the Western *A, B,* and *C.* But there are also practical objections to change.

For one thing, the characters make for a writing system that is incredibly succinct. You can convey a lot of idea with very few strokes of the pen. For example, let's take a look at the Japanese slogan *Datsu-ah, Nyu-oh,* a phrase as familiar in Japan as, say, "Remember the Alamo!" is in America. When the Japanese decided in the late nineteenth century to move beyond the old rice-paddy economic structure and emulate Western industrialism, the movement was encapsulated in that phrase, *Datsu-ah, Nyu-oh.* It means, "Abandon our Asian tradition and join the Western powers." It took me forty-nine letters to write that in English; in Japanese, it takes just four. (Now that Asia is ascendant in the world, incidentally, there are many people in Japan who want to end the country's close alliance with the United States and cozy up to the continent again. Their slogan is *Datsu-bei Nyu-ah,* or "Break away from America and join the Asian countries." This takes forty-three letters in English, four in Japanese.) For this reason, the use of kanji has always struck me as characteristically Asian: it takes a major up-front investment of time and effort to learn the system, but the long-term payoff is a lifetime of speed and efficiency. By investing the energy and the twelve years of schooling it takes to learn the characters, the nations that use Chinese kanji have a writing system that is faster, both to read and to write, than anybody else's.

For whatever reasons, Japan has decided to stick with its impossibly complicated writing system. It thus becomes the bounden duty of the teachers at Yodobashi No. 6, and every other Japanese school, to teach the reading and writing of several thousand characters before students leave the school system. Japan's Education Ministry, which acts as a single board of education for the whole country, has simplified the process (a little) by decreeing that a person needs to know "only" 1,945 different characters (plus the two Japanese alphabets and the Roman letters, of course) to be considered literate. The essential characters are divided by school year. Students learn 80 characters in first grade, 160 more the next year, 200 in third grade, and so on, until they finally reach number 1,945 in high school. People who go on to college or some specialty school will of course learn more than that, but virtually every Japanese achieves basic literacy.

To assure that all students keep pace, the Ministry of Education has created a schedule and routine that is followed year round in every classroom in Japan. The character for "horse" that Ezra Pound read so easily, for example, has been designated a second-grade character–that is, one that every student is to learn in second grade. That means every second-grader in every Japanese elementary school in every Japanese town is going to be learning "horse" at the same time. Sure enough, one morning when Erin Reid was in second grade at Yodobashi No. 6, Katayama-sensei wrote the character *uma* on the blackboard and told the kids that they were now to learn this new word. Some of the overachievers in the class already knew it, but everybody got down to work. They wrote *uma* over and over and over again in their notebooks, on the blackboard, on any piece of scratch paper that happened to be lying around. They wrote it with pens, pencils, crayons, Magic Markers, and traditional writing brushes. They wrote in the air with their fingers. Then Ms. Katayama told them to go home and write it another thirty times, asking their parents to check the accuracy. After a day or so, every student had written *uma* literally hundreds of times and committed it to memory forever—at which point, without further adieu, everybody moved on to the next character. With 2,000 of them to finish by high school, there was no time to dawdle.

One of the key points about learning to write "horse," or any other character, is that each stroke must be written in the correct order. Uma requires ten brush strokes; the order of strokes, which has not changed since the Chinese developed the character a couple of thousand years ago, is set forth as follows in any textbook of Chinese or Japanese:

That is, you start with that flying mane, next put in the hooked tail, and finally add the four flying hooves, from left to right. This is the right way to write *uma*. This is the only way to write *uma*. If some poor second-grader gets confused and writes the final four strokes from right to left, he is wrong. There's one way to do the thing correctly, and the students have to drill, drill, and drill again until they get it right.

Anybody can see—or perhaps I should say, any American parent, concerned about nurturing his child's natural creativity, can see—that devoting so much time and effort each school day to rote memorization and robotic repetition of antique procedures clearly has deleterious effects on the educational process. Since everyone is driven to learn the same characters in the same way in precise lockstep with everybody else, it seems obvious that it's going to be hard to get the kids to think independently or spontaneously when the class turns to other subjects. That's what I was thinking as I sat in the back of Katayama-sensei's classroom watching Erin Reid and her classmates being turned into automatons every time a new character had to be taught. The Japanese, however, seemed less concerned about the impact that assembly-line instruction might have on sensitive elementary-school minds. When I discussed the matter with Abe-sensei, the principal, she told me simply that this was the way they teach Japanese. The process has been successful, she said. The students are learning the characters right on schedule. So what's the problem?

But I was still confused, so I went home and took up the topic with my neighborhood Confucius, Matsuda-san. I told him how I had sat in the classroom at Yodobashi and watched the kids writing that day's new character over and over again, always making sure that each stroke was written in order, doing exactly what they were told to do. There was no spontaneity, I complained. There was no room, not a smidgin of room, for individuality. My neighbor responded politely, of course, but with a rather pointed question: How do American students learn the multiplication tables? Isn't that drill and memorization? Some things have to be memorized, Matsuda-san said; that's part of learning. Anyway, he went on, the constant drill is useful in more ways than one. It not only teaches the children to read and write but also helps them realize, day in and day out, that it's important to stick precisely to the rules.

As he had done so often in our quiet conversations, Matsuda-san had just pointed me to a crucial truth about education in Japan and other Confucian societies: the overlap between academic and moral education. There is no conception in East Asia that music and math belong in schools but moral values do not. Learning to do right is considered just as important as learning to add right. Every day at Yodobashi No. 6, the rules of life in a civil society were given at least as much attention as the rules of grammar or long division. Academic training and social training were blended in almost everything the students did.

The school made no bones about it. As in every Japanese school, the goals of Yodobashi No. 6 Elementary were posted on the walls all over the building. There was a school "mission," posted on the wall in the reception room. There was a set of goals for the year, posted in the teachers' office—a single room with a small desk for each teacher. In each classroom, there were goals posted for the year and the week. And many teachers wrote the goals for the day on the blackboard each morning before class. The interesting thing was that most of these goals said nothing much about academics. They were about building good citizens.

The overall mission of Yodobashi No. 6 was set forth in three phrases on the wall of the central entryway, where the kids took off their shoes each morning. "The Goals of Education," the sign read at the top, and it listed three of them: "A child who is energetic and friendly," "A child who warmly helps the whole group succeed," "A child who thinks carefully before acting."

These schoolwide goals were echoed in the classroom goals set forth on the walls of my girls' classes. Above the blackboard at the front of Katayama-sensei's second-grade classroom, there were two banners. "Let's work persistently until the job is done," said one. "Let's make a new friend at recess," said the other. These were written primarily in the Japanese phonetic letters, because second-graders hadn't learned enough characters yet to read the kanji for words like "persistently" or "friend." When Kate Reid was in sixth grade at Yodobashi, Yamanaka-sensei had three goals on the wall: "Let's not waste anything at lunchtime," "Let's work together on the road to junior high school," and "Let's remember the rules and follow them."

That last one was particularly important. As Matsuda-san pointed out to me, learning to follow rules—to respect authority—was a crucial part of daily education. Just as there is one right way to write the character for "horse," there was one right way to do just about everything at Yodobashi. There was one correct backpack to be worn, and one correct way to adjust its straps. There was one list of school supplies that everybody needed, and that list was sacrosanct. Each student was supposed to have three sharpened pencils in her desk—not four, not two—and there was a designated place inside the desk where the pencils were to be kept. The student leaders in each class went around the desks now and then to make sure these rules were followed.

When our children started at Yodobashi, Abe-sensei faxed us a sheet of directions on how to get to the school. She didn't just give us a map, though. She told us which buses and which trains to take, to the minute, and which car to ride on the train. (It's a little easier to do this sort of thing in Japan than some other countries, because the bus that is scheduled to leave at 8:17 will in fact leave at 8:17, every day.) She told us how the children should take their shoes off at the school's entryway, and how they should align their shoes (toes in, heels out) in the little shoe locker after they had put on the indoor slippers they were to wear inside. The school gave us directions on how our children's homework desk at home should be set up and equipped (including the number of pencils). For some reason—perhaps because Abe-sensei saw how I bristled when I happened upon that particular sheet of yellow paper—the school never subjected us to a home inspection, standard for all other Yodobashi families, to make sure we had complied.

Nothing was left to chance, because rules are too important to be left to chance.

It was while our kids were at Yodobashi that the Ministry of Education began its controversial initiative to phase out school on Saturday. On one Saturday morning each month, school was to be closed, and the kids were free to do what they wanted. Now, you might think the kids would get out their toys, tapes, or tricycles and find a way to fill the three free hours on their own. But that's not the way Japan works. No matter how controversial the new policy was, the one thing that everybody seemed to agree on was that a kid's Saturday morning is too important to be left to kids. For anything this serious, there have to be rules. The Education Ministry published a 225-page book designating appropriate activities for the monthly day off. School principals and PTA groups prepared detailed plans for their students—many of which involved schoolroom sessions suspiciously similar to the classes they were replacing. Most principals decreed that students had to wear their school uniforms on the free Saturdays, and most seemed determined to plan the first school-free morning down to the last second.

Reading the materials put out by Yodobashi, and reviewing the newspaper reports on what other schools were doing, I noticed that the various blueprints for Saturday off seemed to have two points in common. First, there were to be no couch potatoes. All the plans were based on the theory that kids would be up and about just as early on a school-free Saturday as on any other. Yodobashi, like most other schools, scheduled early-morning field trips, sports leagues, and other activities to keep kids busy. (The common American Saturday morning–lounging around watching cartoons on the tube–was never much of an option in Japan, partly because there is no special Saturday-morning television for children, and partly because most Japanese homes are too small to accommodate much lounging by anybody.) Second, there was to be no individualism. All the various plans involved spending the day off with others who would be spending it the same way. The most important point was, though, that even vacation was to be regimented. The school rules mattered, even when the kids were not in school.

In view of this inordinate emphasis on rules, and the regimented orderliness of Japanese life overall, it would be natural to assume that Japanese educators are control freaks and their students are subject to the strictest discipline if they do anything but sit quietly in their seats and study their brains out. Before I sent my kids to Yodobashi, I assumed exactly that. In fact, many times when I dropped by the classroom of one of my girls I was amazed at the disorder, the rowdiness, the sheer noise that confronted me. At fairly regular intervals– say, eight or ten times each school day–the teacher would assign some problem to solve or some job to do and just sit back while the students seemed to go wild.

In a fifth-grade classroom one day, three boys were standing on their desktops throwing books at each other. Girls were running around from one desk to another playing some kind of slapping game. Another kid was trying to lob a soccer ball into a trash can across the room. The most amazing thing of all was that Yamada-sensei was sitting calmly at his desk at the front of the room, grading papers or something, evidently oblivious to the bedlam breaking out in his classroom (and to the shell-shocked American parent shaking his head in disbelief at the back of the room).

After this went on for ten minutes or so, the teacher gave an almost imperceptible arm signal to one of the students—who was, it turned out, the designated class leader for the week. This boy walked up to the front and shouted "It's time!" Nobody could hear him at first, but he kept saying "It's time." And within thirty seconds or so, the disorderly mob was once again an orderly class, quietly looking up at Yamada-sensei to see what he wanted the class to do next. I learned later that this kind of temporary wildness in the classroom is specifically prescribed in the Education Ministry's Guidelines for Elementary Schools, so that the children can let off steam. The key point is that the teachers feel perfectly safe letting it happen, because they have complete confidence they can gain control again at any time.

I never entirely figured out how they do it. But one key factor, I concluded, is that keeping control in a Japanese classroom is not strictly the responsibility of the teacher. The students share responsibilities like that, and they consider this perfectly normal. Even in first grade, Japanese students have much greater responsibility for the daily activities of the classroom, and the school as a whole, than do their counterparts in Western countries. Unlike American teachers, for example, elementary school teachers in Japan do not have to dread that moment in the morning when they have to get the kids into their seats, quieted down, and ready to work. In a Japanese classroom, these preparations are not the job of the teacher. It is up to the student leaders—generally one boy and one girl, who hold the position for about a week—to do those things.

In Katayama-sensei's second-grade class, for example, two seven-year-olds would stand up in front of their noisy, giggling, squirming classmates at eight forty-five in the morning and urge them to straighten the rows of desks, to pick up all the hats, gloves, umbrellas, and butterfly nets strewn on the floor, and to get out the text and the notebook for the first subject of the day. Frequently, the two young leaders would make a quick inspection, to see to it that all their peers had the requisite number of pencils in the approved spot on the desk and had the correct book open to the proper page. When all was prepared, one of the leaders would pronounce the words "All rise." The students would stand and face the teacher. The leader would say, "Bow." The students would bow to the teacher and recite, "Good morning, Katayama-sensei." The leader would say, "Take your seats."

And only then would the teacher deign to rise from her desk and take over direction of the classroom.

Starting with the first grade, it was students—not the teacher, not parents—who were responsible for managing the permission slips and collecting the money for field trips. It was students, not teachers, who were responsible for the care and feeding of Yodobashi's farm animals, and for the maintenance and cleaning of that unicycle fleet. So much responsibility is left with students that Japanese schools rarely call in a substitute teacher. If the first-grade teacher is going to miss a day or two, she just provides a detailed plan for the day and lets the two student leaders direct studies. The teacher in the room next door pops in now and then to make sure things are okay. And this seems to work.

In Japanese schools, the students are the janitors; a certain amount of time is allocated each school day for the activity known as *oh-soji*, or "honorable cleaning." Kids wash blackboards, empty trash cans, clean toilets, and mop those shiny pine floors in the hallway. It isn't exactly fun, but it isn't exactly a chore, either. It is just something the students are expected to do, and they do it. Pushing a broom down the long hallway outside her classroom, my daughter Kate told her classmates during *oh-soji* one day that adults are hired to do this work in American schools. Nobody believed it. To the Japanese, "honorable cleaning" is a natural student responsibility, in the same way that keeping a neighborhood clean is the natural responsibility of the residents. One advantage of *oh-soji*, of course, is that it gives the students a built-in incentive to keep their school clean from the start. I once toured a high school in Nagoya with a group of visitors from a high school in Louisiana. The American principal, knowing something about teenagers, expressed surprise at the pristine state of walls, lockers, and toilet stalls. "Oh, they're not going to write anything on the walls," the Japanese principal replied. "If they do, they're going to be here that night until it's all cleaned off."

The student job I liked most to watch was *oh-shokuji*, or "honorable mealtime." At Yodobashi, as at other Japanese schools, lunch was served to the students in their classrooms—and all the work was done by fellow students. Each day at twelve-fifteen, the teacher would leave the room. The group assigned to "honorable mealtime" detail would put on clean white smocks and white chef's caps and scoot down the hallway to the school kitchen. They would come back laden with industrial-sized pots of rice, stew, salad, etc., and form a sort of makeshift cafeteria line at the front of the classroom. Each student ate at his desk, while the student Broadcast Committee played the latest rock songs over the PA system. When mealtime ended, the mealtime crew would haul the empty trays, pots, and utensils back to the kitchen. It was an adorable thing to watch, all these tiny creatures, six, eight, or ten years old, dishing up lunch from tall iron pots in their playtime chef's clothing. Except this wasn't playtime. The school wanted lunch, and it was the students' responsibility to see that it was served.

All these responsibilities are essential to maintaining the school's *wa*, the feeling of group harmony that is felt to be the sine qua non of a successful educational experience. Schooling in Japan, like everything else in Japan, is a group endeavor. The small group of four or five children is the basic unit of learning, in every subject, in every classroom. For Japanese educators, this methodology is a two-birds-with-one-stone kind of thing. Group learning is considered the preeminent strategy for academic topics, and, of course, the constant small-group interaction also teaches the children the essential Confucian skills of cooperative group membership.

The use of small groups, by the way, helps explain why Japanese and American educators have completely different theories on the subject of the teacher-to-student ratio. In the United States, a small class is the holy grail of educational administrators; in Japan, too few students in the classroom is considered a serious impediment to learning. On the average, Japanese schools have thirty-five to forty students per teacher; the ratio is largest in the lowest grades, and gets smaller as classes become more specialized in high school. When we started at Yodobashi No. 6, Abe-sensei actually apologized to me about the size of my daughters' classes. They were too small. Because of diminishing enrollment in central city schools like ours, Yodobashi had only twenty-five to thirty students per class. Even that number would be on the high end for many schools in the tonier American suburbs, but Abe-sensei felt it was much too low. A good elementary class needs forty to forty-five kids, she said, so the teacher can build a lot of groups and the various groups can work with each other.

In my daughters' classes, study groups were generally formed on the first day of school, or the second day at the latest. The proper architecture of such groups—the ratio of boys and girls, of boisterous kids and quiet ones, of leaders and followers—is a matter of extensive study in Japanese educational circles, and the Ministry of Education has put out enough guidelines on group making to keep any teacher reading for months. Naming the groups is also an art form. The standard Japanese word for a small group, *han* (rhymes with "Don"), is widely used, but in the more cosmopolitan private schools the fashionable term nowadays is the English word "group," which comes out "goo-roop-poo" in Japanese. Some teachers eschew fancy nomenclature and simply assign the kids to Han 1, Han 2, or Goorooppoo A, Goorooppoo B, and so on. But most teachers, particularly at the elementary level, come up with fancier labels. At Yodobashi, some classrooms had Lions, Tigers, Dinosaurs, and Pandas; others went with the names of Japanese baseball teams: Giants, Swallows, Carp, Blue Wave. My favorite was Erin Reid's fourth-grade class at Yodobashi, where the thirty students were divided into five *han*, each named after a Disney movie. There was Beauty and the Beast, Cinderella, Lion King, Alla-jeen (Aladdin), and Erin's *han*, which was called Kuma no Pooh-san, or Pooh-san the Bear.

Each *han* had a leader, a duty that rotated weekly. The Japanese word for leader is *cho*, so the *han* leader was known as the *han-cho*, a word that U.S. occupation soldiers brought home to America in the early 1950s in the form of "I gotta check it with the head honcho." (Many Japanese groups also have a subordinate role, for a person who carries out directions from the *han-cho*. This person is known as the *tan-to*, pronounced like Tonto, who was the Lone Ranger's *tan-to*.) For almost all academic endeavors—math, science, language, geography, history—the *han-cho* had a big role. The teacher would present a problem: What foreign country would you like to live in? And if you were there, what language would you speak, what foods would you eat, what church or temple might you go to, etc., etc.? Then the various *hans* would gather for noisy, animated discussions, with the teacher stopping by each group's table now and then to listen in. Eventually, the results would be presented, with each honcho coming to the front and describing his group's answers. It might be that Erin Reid's favorite foreign country was Ireland. But if the members of

Pooh-san the Bear decided on Hong Kong (where one girl's mother had recently had a shopping fling), that became Erin's choice as well. This was the rule of the *han*.

Getting along harmoniously within the "goorooppoo" was a key lesson to be learned in school, just as important as any academic subject. The training in membership began at home, before the kids ever got to a school, but it continued apace in the classroom. Japanese teachers have some notoriously brutal expressions for driving home the importance of fitting in with the others. Perhaps the best-known catch phrase in Japan is *"Deru kui wa utarareru,"* a sentence that rolls softly over the tongue because of all the *r* sounds in the passive verb at the end, but is not so gentle in meaning: "The nail that sticks up gets hammered down." Nobody in Japan likes a *deru kui*, a protuding nail. I give many speeches in Japan. At the point in my scintillating lecture when I can see the audience falling asleep, I can usually shock them back to attention by veering off into the importance of individualism. "My mother always told me to stand up for myself, you know, to be a *deru kui*," I say, and then relish the look of astonishment on those Japanese faces. They always knew Americans were weird—but really, everybody knows what happens to a *deru kui*.

I never heard a teacher say "The nail that sticks up gets hammered down" at Yodobashi No. 6, presumably because all the students already knew that rule. But I heard many other formulations of that central message. "You don't want to be the one that everybody laughs at" was a familiar pattern. That charming Katayama-sensei, who taught my daughter Erin in second grade, had a more chilling variation. "I noticed that Shinjuku Ward sent some workers over the other day to trim the hedges around our 'pu-ray hahbbu,' " she said. "They were looking for any young branch that grew up faster than the rest of the bush. And if any branch was sticking out, they took their big, sharp clippers and cut it right off."

Guilt by association was another common classroom tool. One morning when the sixth-graders in my daughter Kate's class were divided into their *han*, working on some problem with compound fractions, a little monster named Ryutaro was so noisy and obstreperous that even a Japanese teacher couldn't remain above the fray. "It's too bad that Ryutaro won't work productively with the rest of the Orange

Group," Yamanaka-sensei said curtly. "That means the Orange Group won't get its work done, and nobody in the group will have recess today." Ryutaro had a responsibility to work with his group, but the whole *han* also had a responsibility to see to it that Ryutaro did so.

It had to be confusing for our girls, who learned American-style lessons about individualism at home (Be yourself! Set your own standard! Just say no!) and Asian-style lessons about harmony and group solidarity at school (Fit in with the others! Don't stick out! Find a way to say yes!). And yet, Kate and Erin both loved their time at Yodobashi No. 6, loved the teachers and the students and the *han* and the roosters and that fleet of unicycles and even *oh-soji*. The principal was true to her word, and there was never the slightest hint of *taibatsu* or *ijime* while our daughters were at the school. And so we rated Yodobashi Dai-Roku Shogakko as a complete success. Our kids learned some Japanese, some math and science, some music.

And they also learned, along the way, the Confucian lessons considered just as essential: working hard, following rules, respecting authority, taking responsibility, and getting along with the group. These moral lessons, in fact, are so important to Japan—and to every other Confucian society—that they don't stop when school ends. In East Asia, they keep teaching you this stuff forever.

SIX

Continuing Education

IT WAS THE MORNING OF APRIL 1.

That date explained the sea of earnest, eager young faces in the audience, the somber ranks of white-haired executives on the stage, the huge blue-and-white felt banner on the wall reading "Nippon Denki K.K." (which is to say, Nippon Electronic Corporation, an industrial giant known around the world as NEC), and the overall aura of great expectations in the air as the corporate band launched into the familiar opening chords and 1,400 young people in dark blue business suits rose as one to gush forth a spirited and surprisingly harmonic rendition of a peppy, upbeat song, a song that would be, for the next three or four decades, *their* song:

> To build a culture of communication
> Shall be our destin-eeee,
> Nippon, Nippon, Nippon Den-keee!

That song, the "Nippon Denki Corporate Anthem," has been changed only slightly since 1889, when Alexander Graham Bell provided the money to start a Japanese counterpart of his Western Electric Company. Today, Western Electric is no more, and the Bell System is history, but NEC ranks as one of the world's largest and richest makers of electric and electronic equipment, a company with the wealth and stature of an IBM or a Microsoft. To start work there—or, rather, "to become a member of the Nippon Denki family," as the company's president, Tadahiro Sekimoto, put it in his speech that April 1—is an important and thrilling moment in the life of any Japanese person. That's why I saw all those eager young faces as I sat in the back of the ridiculously rococo Gold Ballroom at the Tanagawa Prince Hotel in Tokyo on the morning of April 1.

At NEC and hundreds of other companies all over Japan, April 1 is the day for the Nyu-Sha-Shiki, or Entering-the-Company Ceremony. About one million new graduates—kids who have finished high school or college about a month before this big day—start their working careers on April 1 every year. For NEC and most other big companies, it is the only day all year they will take in new employees. You can't just open the door on any old day and take in workers. Hiring somebody—inviting a person to share membership in the corporate group—is an important moment, not just for the company and the new worker, but for the society as a whole. Such things have to be done right, with ritual and ceremony that befit a defining moment. Confucius says in the first book of the Analects that joint observance of established rituals by all members of a group is crucial to building the feeling of harmonious relations that is required for the group to succeed. That applies whether it's the Nyu-Sha-Shiki at a Japanese company or the company picnic or the whole family gathering for Thanksgiving dinner in the United States. "Of all the things brought about by ritual," it says in the Analects, "harmony is the most valuable."

There was no shortfall of ritual at NEC. A few weeks before the ceremony started, each new employee had received a letter addressed "Dear New Member of the Company." It had directed them to wear a dark gray or blue business suit and to be in their seats—assigned seats, of course—thirty-five minutes before the ceremony. Most of the new "members" took these admonitions seriously, and just about all of the 1,400 new hires for NEC's Tokyo-area plants and offices were on ᵉᵉff

hand in the Gold Ballroom at 8:25 A.M., when roll was taken. Precise instructions were provided for the morning's events: when to stand, how to bow, when to applaud, etc. The group was ordered not to smoke, a fairly painful command for Japanese young people. The recruits then practiced singing "Nippon Denki Corporate Anthem" so there would be no errors during the actual ceremony.

The Nyu-Sha-Shiki began at precisely 9:00 A.M., and there was a perceptible ripple of pride, mixed with a little embarrassment, as the first of the white-haired corporate elders on the stage stepped to the microphone and wished a good morning to "my fellow company members." There followed a formal address from President Sekimoto, whose speech was nicely crystallized in its title: "Let's Build the Richness of Our Hearts Through Our Jobs." Then there were pep talks from a couple of board members, the head of the personnel section, and other in-house dignitaries. Then each new member was instructed to open the packet under his or her seat, wherein each employee found business cards (bearing the title "NEC corporate-member-in-training") and an NEC corporate lapel badge, exactly like the ones worn by the big shots on the stage. Next, one young woman from the entering class came forward as representative for all her peers to recite the New Company Members' Pledge, a short but high-minded declaration that "we will use all our strength and skill to improve daily life for all the world's people through electronics and communications." After that, President Sekimoto led the entire room in the recitation of the NEC corporate oath.

All the songs, speeches, and pledges marked a mutual oath of loyalty. The employees agreed, in essence, to be good corporate members—in short, to do what the company orders—and the company agreed to watch out for the employees in good times and bad, virtually guaranteeing that these workers will never face a layoff and will not be fired for anything short of outright crime. These are Confucian loyalties, of course, and they run both ways.

All the NEC recruits who joined the company that day would be paid about $1,500 per month, with yearly increases thereafter; the amount would be based strictly on seniority for at least the next ten years. That way, all the members of that day's starting class would remain on an equal basis. In addition to the pay, they would get housing–a single room with kitchen in a corporate dormitory cost $150 per month, about 90 percent less than market rent. They would get NEC corporate health insurance, with many routine medical services provided at the NEC health center. They would all wear their NEC lapel pins, vacation at NEC resorts, play on NEC sports teams, and join the NEC company union. They would all have accounts at Sumitomo Bank, because NEC is a member of the Sumitomo *keiretsu*, or corporate grouping; in fact, a pass book for an account that had already been opened in each new member's name at Sumitomo was included in that packet under the seat. In short, what happened in the Gold Ballroom that April 1 was that each of these people got a new job, but they got something more than that in the bargain.

"A job in Japan," wrote Edwin O. Reischauer, "is not merely a contractual arrangement for pay, but a means of identification with a larger entity–in other words, a satisfying sense of being part of something big and significant, [which] brings a sense of security and also pride in loyalty to the firm. Both managers and workers suffer no loss of identity but rather gain pride through their company, particularly if it is large and famous. Company songs are sung with enthusiasm, and company pins are proudly displayed in buttonholes."

For all of the new company members who started work that day, the first assignment was to be a two-month training course, covering the structure of NEC, the makeup of the global electronics and communications industry, and the rules of behavior that apply to employees. The packet under each chair contained a 320-page textbook, *The Business Manner*, published by the NEC Culture Center. This dealt with such matters as how to answer the phone politely, how to exchange name cards, how to serve tea, how and when to address corporate superiors. It's important to exchange respectful greetings when coming to work first thing in the morning, the manual observed, and to address corporate big shots politely if you meet them in a hallway or an elevator. "But when you see a superior in the bathroom, no greeting is necessary."

I got a real kick out of this book, particularly the section teaching the new members how to bow. Bowing is a symbol of respect in Japan, a way of expressing one's deference to others. It contributes to the *wa*, and thus it is too important to be left to chance. So the text lays out the rights and wrongs:

> This chart teaches new company employees the right way to bow: 30 degrees for greeting at a reception, 60 degrees as a "normal" bow, or 90 degrees when making an apology.
> Women should cross hands in front when bowing. Employees should not raise their heads or smile.

It isn't only NEC that makes a big deal out of April 1 in Japan. The whole country joins in to mark the august occasion of young people starting their economic careers. These new working people are given the collective title *shin-shakaijin*, or "new members of society." Retailers, bankers, and brokers mount special advertising campaigns every spring aimed at these "new members," with fancy booths set up, manned by attractive young people, to help the youngsters figure out what it means to have a bank account or a credit card. The department stores, acting on the theory that a kid just out of high school or college doesn't know how to dress for success, offer special package deals for new members. There's a *yon-ten setto*, or four-point set, offering a two-piece suit along with a shirt and a necktie guaranteed to match. For those even farther out of sync with fashion, there are five-point, six-point, or seven-point *setto*, which throw in shoes, socks, and a handkerchief certified not to clash with the other parts of the set.

Each year around the first of April, the Japanese TV networks all broadcast documentaries and dramas about the excitement and trauma of this new stage of life. I particularly remember a drama special one year in which Nishida Hikari, a cute, peppy young actress, was cast as a cute, peppy new corporate member at a big stationery company. The program showed our heroine attending the Nyu-Sha-Shiki on April 1, taking the pledge, and pinning on the company badge, after which she was assigned to a particular section of the firm and ordered to report to the section chief for work. The camera followed her as she wandered the seemingly endless corridors of the giant corporate headquarters and finally found the right office. She lingered outside in the hallway to take off her backpack—she wasn't a college girl anymore, after all—and straighten her new pin-striped blue suit. Then she bounded into the office and introduced herself: "Honorable sectionmates, I plan to work so hard for this section that I collapse from stress or a heart attack, so please welcome me as a member here." Everyone seemed to think this was a sufficiently self-effacing greeting, and they welcomed her with open arms. She was a member.

I met a woman who reminded me of Nishida Hikari that day I went to the NEC Nyu-Sha-Shiki—an earnest, nervous twenty-two-year-old who was seated next to me in the last row of seats in the Gold Ballroom. A few weeks earlier, no doubt, she had been hanging around some campus bar in jeans and a sweatshirt. But that day, she was freshly scrubbed and neatly tailored. Everything was so fresh and new, in fact, that the price tag was still hanging from the neat blue pin-striped skirt that matched her neat blue pin-striped blazer. I debated for a while but finally went ahead and told her about that dangling price tag. She was horrified. She ripped off the offending tag as if it were a carrier of bubonic plague, then turned to thank me profusely, over and over again, as if I had just saved her entire business career.

We got to chatting. In the course of conversation, this new NEC member-to-be asked me to describe my entering-the-company ceremony, back when I had joined *The Washington Post.* "What day do they do it over there?" she asked. Interesting question. I had no idea what date I had started at my company, and frankly couldn't remember anything that had happened on the first day, except that I had stood for a while at the edge of the newsroom until some sub-subeditor came up to say "There's your desk." That was my Nyu-Sha-Shiki at the Washington Post Company. The young woman seemed crushed. I had really let her down. Striving to salvage the moment, I quickly added the information that my company does in fact have a corporate song of its own—a truly great one, in fact: John Philip Sousa's "Washington Post March." Dah dah dah-dah DAH dah DAH dah DAH dah . . . That seemed to help a little, but she was still clearly crestfallen at the lack of ritual that marked an American's first day on the job.

And she had a point, I think. A society *should* make a collective fuss about a day so important in the lives of a million of its citizens. A society should sit back and take the time to make sure these young people understand the privileges and responsibilities that come with moving on to a new stage of life. Any society, as Confucius insisted, can benefit from the rituals and ceremonies that remind people that they live in a community with a shared moral and cultural tradition. For if there is a collective moral voice in a corporation, a school, a neighborhood, or a nation, it makes sense to be sure that newcomers hear that voice and understand it. The whole point of ceremonies like the Nyu-Sha-Shiki is to tell the members what is expected of them. Then a company, a school, or a community will rely on the members' basic human decency to make them live up to expectations, without the need for reprimand or punishment. That's how Confucius saw it twenty-five centuries ago, and that's the way things still work today, most of the time, in East Asian societies.

THE IDEA OF CONVEYING tradition and morality through ritual and ceremony is firmly established in East Asia. Asians love ceremonies and seem to hold them on the flimsiest of excuses. There are entering-the-school, entering-the-company, entering-the-flower-arrangement-club, or entering-the-something-else ceremonies going on all the time. Then there are the last-day-of-school, last-day-of-the-corporate-fiscal-year, last-day-of-Tanaka-san's-term-as-club-treasurer ceremonies. When a young sumo wrestler enters a training stable to begin his career, the event is marked by an elaborate celebration with Shinto priests, sacred salt, and ceremonial toasts of hot sake. When a not-so-young sumo wrestler retires from the sport, this weighty event requires even greater recognition, in the form of an elaborate ceremony that runs about six hours.

The New Year holiday–both the Western-style January 1 version and the Chinese-style lunar new year, which comes about two months later–is a rich occasion for ceremonies designed to charge people up for the new beginning and to remind them that the old values still matter. On January 4, the day that Japan returns to work after the New Year holiday, there are ceremonies at every school, company, store, temple, and train station. In fact, January 4, usually a cold and dismal winter's day in Japan, is one of the most colorful days of the Japanese year; everywhere you look, you see the brightly colored kimonos that young women are wearing for the first-day-of-business pep rally at the office. One March morning–it was the first day of the Chinese New Year festivities–in the Choa Chu Kang subway station in Singapore, I saw a horde of conductors, platform attendants, ticket takers, and sweeper-uppers in dark blue Mass Rapid Transit System uniforms, gathered in a big circle around the station chief. This hyperenergetic gentleman was leading a sort of pep rally to encourage all subway workers to put out their greatest effort during the busy holiday season. "We will serve the people of Singapore!" the head honcho was shouting. "We will guarantee their safe passage! On schedule! With no accidents! We will serve the people!" The assembled workers responded with a roar reminiscent of a football team charging out to win the Super Bowl.

When our daughters started at Yodobashi No. 6 Elementary School, the principal, Abe-sensei, held an all-school ceremony to mark the important occasion of these young foreign girls joining the Yodobashi community. The entire student body paraded into the gymnasium, with the student leaders of each class scurrying around in a desperate but futile effort to make sure the lines were straight and everybody was marching in step. The students sat Indian-style on the floor in their not-so-straight lines. They sang that peppy school song– the one about the nonexistent view of Mount Fuji–and then moved directly into another musical offering, a song in English called "Hello, My Friend," which they had all learned just so they could sing it to my daughters. Then the principal stood up and announced that some new students were joining Yodobashi that day: "Please let me introduce Keito-chahn"–that is, Dear Little Kate–"and Eh-reen-chahn," or Dear Little Erin. Dear Little Kate and Dear Little Erin stood meekly before their new schoolmates, who erupted into a vigorous outburst of greetings and cheers. "Keito-chahn will be in fifth grade, second section," Abe-sensei continued, "and everyone in that class will be her friend. But her first friend will be Makiko." At that point, little Makiko, wearing a denim skirt and a sweatshirt that said "Let's Surfing Waikiki," took Kate Reid by the hand and led her out of the gym toward classroom 5-2. Another "first friend" was announced for Erin Reid, and she, too, was taken by the hand and led off to her second-grade classroom. As they walked out of the gym, the Yodobashi students launched into another heartfelt chorus of "Hello, My Friend."

It was, at least to the bemused American parents standing at the back of the gym, a completely charming–indeed, moving–event, the more so because we never expected the whole school to turn out to greet our daughters. At first, I thought this gathering was part of Abe-sensei's anti-*ijime* strategy, to make sure she could deliver on her promise that my girls would never be subjected to bullying. When I suggested this, the principal gave me that look of hers, the one that suggested I must have just stepped off the spaceship from Mars. The ceremony had nothing to do with *ijime*, she said. It was simply the natural thing to do. When new students came to Yodobashi No. 6, an all-school ceremony had to be held to mark this important moment in the life of the community. Any fool knew that.

Of the countless ceremonies held regularly in Japan, my favorite was Seijin-shiki, the Coming-of-Age Ceremony, held annually on January 15. On that date each year, all the Japanese who will turn twenty during the year are toasted and honored in official ceremonies during which they are officially recognized as adult citizens of Japan, with all the rights and all the many responsibilities appurtenant thereto. This is considered so important that January 15 is a national holiday in Japan–Seijin no Hi, or Coming-of-Age Day. Every city, town, and rural hamlet in the country–about 3,200 jurisdictions in all–gathers its newly minted adults into the town hall or school auditorium for a combination reunion/party/lecture. The Coming-of-Age Ceremony is one of the chief means of inculcating the national sense of responsibility that helps make the country polite, civil, and safe.

Given the importance that Asian societies assign to concepts like honoring rules and recognizing a personal responsibility to advance the good of the group, it's not terribly surprising that Japan would take this opportunity to teach the lesson to impressionable young people on the threshold of adult life. What is surprising is that most of the young people actually show up.

Attendance at the Seijin-shiki is voluntary. Since schools, colleges, and offices are all closed for the holiday, January 15 is a perfect time for twenty-year-olds to hit the ski slopes or head out to the races, where they are, as of that day, old enough to place a bet, smoke cigarettes, and buy a drink legally. (Actually, the legal drinking age is not that much of a milestone for young Japanese, because there are vending machines everywhere selling beer, wine, sake, scotch, and bourbon. They offer ubiquitous opportunities for teen drinking. The machines all bear a sticker that reads as follows: "We respectfully request that honorable customers under the age of twenty demonstrate reserve about purchasing alcoholic beverages." But when you walk past these machines, it is often obvious that some thirsty teenagers fail to demonstrate the necessary reserve.) In fact though, most of the new adults show up at the local town hall for the ceremony. About two million people turn twenty each year in Japan, and roughly 70 percent of them take their seats on January 15 at the local Seijin-shiki.

I used to show up, too, every January 15, just to watch how the new members were inducted into Japanese society. It was, not surprisingly, our neighbor Matsuda-san—a man who spent a lot of time trying to inculcate that feeling of membership in me—who first told me about the Coming-of-Age Ceremony. "They don't have anything like this in America, do they?" he said. "You ought to go over there on the morning of the fifteenth." And I did—partly to see what happens at a Coming-of-Age Ceremony, and partly to try to figure out why any teenager would voluntarily attend such an event.

The gathering for new *seijin* from our section of Tokyo, Shibuya Ward, was held in the Shibuya Public Auditorium, another of those lavish glass-and-chrome public facilities built in the 1980s, when the country seemed to have more money than it knew what to do with. There's a sunken plaza outside the Shibuya Public Auditorium, with a ghastly statue of twisted beams and stained glass in the center and a big stone plaque explaining how the people of Shibuya Ward had built this handsome structure to enhance the common good. When I arrived, the plaza was swarming with thousands of twenty-to-be's, flirting, smoking, soaking up the bright winter sun, and showing off their new clothes. The crowd was split just about evenly between boys and girls, but the females stole the show. They were dressed, almost to a woman, in lavishly embroidered kimonos of brilliant coloring: orange, lavender, crimson, dark green, pink, splattered with spectacularly ornate designs of wind-blown flowers or flying cranes or royal-blue rivers winding beneath purple mountain peaks. These marvelous garments were bound around the waists with dazzling obis, or sashes, of contrasting colors and equally intricate design. A few males wore traditional Japanese robes with handsome dark obi, but most stuck to the salaryman's uniform: crisp new pin-striped suits and dark neckties.

New clothes are a key part of Coming of Age. The Seijin-shiki is generally the first occasion in a young woman's life when she can wear a formal adult kimono. Most girls jump at the chance. After all, a halfway decent kimono, together with the necessary obi, sandals, hair ornaments, handbag, handkerchiefs, pins, and other assorted accoutrements, runs about $6,500 nowadays. (The men's business suits, in contrast, were probably priced under $500, even for those who chose the seven-point *setto*.) These prices, well beyond the reach of most twenty-year-olds, constitute one reason why so many kids show up for a formal ceremony on their day off. There's an implicit deal at work: Parents want their kids to attend Seijin-shiki, so they pay for the expensive outfits. The kids want the formal kimono or business suit, so they agree to attend the ceremony.

In the plaza outside the Public Auditorium, I met a happy, energetic young woman named Nagashima Taeko. Her kimono was stunning. It started out at the shoulders the color of heavy cream, then gradually morphed from a pale lime shade to a deep forest green at the waist. At about knee level, the green turned into a leafy grove of bamboo trees, with a sleek orange-and-black tiger stalking its prey amid the trees. This had cost $3,200, she said, plus another $1,000 or so for the pale green obi and $240 for tuition at the kimono academy where she learned how to wear it. Taeko told me she had gotten up at four that morning so that she and three friends could get to the hair salon before the ceremony began. Her parents had paid for it all. But Taeko said that wasn't the only reason she had decided to come.

"I grew up in Shibuya, but I'm working now as an O.L. in Yokohama," she said. As a busy office lady with a one-hour commute to and from Shibuya each day, she didn't have much time at home. "So the kids I knew when I was growing up here, you know, some of them are in college, some got jobs, I just don't get to see a lot of them any– Oh look! There's Kyoko! Kyoko-san! Your kimono is so cool!"

But the new clothes and the old friends weren't the only reason these young people had come. A calm but earnest secretarial-school student named Sekiguchi Yuka, wearing a deep-orange kimono with a white flower pattern, told me she thought the Seijin-shiki was something a Japanese nineteen-year-old just ought to attend. "Well, my parents told me to come," she said. "I didn't have anything better to do today anyway, and sometimes my parents' advice turns out to be pretty good. And they did buy me this kimono, which I obviously couldn't afford myself. So those were sort of the practical reasons. But also, you know, I did this to, like, carry out my duty. I'm an adult now, I can vote, I can buy sake and tobacco, so I felt some responsibility to be here."

Gradually, the new adults of Shibuya Ward shuffled inside, just about filling the 7,500 seats in the auditorium. They dug through the various "gifts"—mostly commercial come-ons, like demo CDs by new rock groups or appointment calendars bound in tasteful brown vinyl with "Asahi Beer Congratulates the New *Seijin*" stamped on top—that were stacked on each seat. Reading through the program for the day, many gasped out loud when they realized that the last item was to be a performance by the highly popular singing star Marcia. This young woman used the stage name Marcia to advertise the fact that she sang only American pop songs; Marcia was evidently the most American-sounding name she could think of. Before Marcia's performance, though, there were to be speeches—many, many speeches.

On the dot of 9:00 A.M., exactly as scheduled, a serious-looking official in a dark suit stood up on stage to get things going. He started off, in fairly standard fashion for a Japanese ceremony, by reading out loud every word of the program that the members of the audience held in their hands. There followed formal greetings and congratulations from this councilman and that ward official. The audience was whispering and jittery but offered polite applause for each. Eventually, the time came for the day's main speaker: the chairman of the Shibuya Ward School Board, one Omori Toshio, another serious-looking gentleman in a dark business suit.

Omori-san started off promisingly, offering a historical glimpse at the Coming-of-Age Ceremony that the audience found interesting—or at least, interesting enough to stop their chatter. "What we're doing today is really a carry-over from the *genpuku* ceremony back in the shogun days," he said. "As you all know, that was the ritual where the young apprentice samurai were officially deemed to be warriors, and they swore to put protection of the lord and the clan ahead of their own lives." No such dramatic pledge would be required today, Omori went on, for modern Japan is a peaceful, prosperous country that has eschewed violence. And yet—and yet, there were parallels. Those newly anointed samurai gained certain privileges, such as the right to wear the topknot of their rank and the right to carry swords and use them with impunity. But the privileges came with life-or-death responsibility—the duty of protecting the clan, and all Japan, from enemies. "It's the same thing today, isn't it?" he continued. "All these handsome young people seated before me, so full of potential, will acquire great privileges as of today—the right to vote, to buy property, to smoke tobacco and enjoy alcoholic beverages in moderation. But these privileges of adulthood come with serious responsibility—to obey the law, to protect the people and the environment of Shibuya Ward, to work hard to preserve the future of our country.

"I ask you to engrave in your hearts," Omori-san said solemnly, "an awareness of your duties to society and a desire to fulfill your responsibility."

The speaker had a role model he wanted to offer up for the new adults to emulate: their parents. "When the people in this room were born, nineteen or twenty years ago, Japan was still a second-class nation in the world, a little brother to America and the great industrial powers of Western Europe. We were a small island nation with no resources, still recovering from the wounds of a tragic war. Today, our country is respected around the world as an economic superpower. Even in our present recession, the Americans come to us every year to borrow billions of dollars to finance their government. Japan provides more foreign aid to the developing nations than any of the other wealthy countries. We have come a long, long way during your lifetime, and the credit clearly belongs to your parents and grandparents. Those generations provided the intelligence and hard work that earned our country respect. You should thank them when you go home tonight. And now that you have reached adulthood, we need to harness your youthful energy, your hard work, for the good of our whole society."

This peroration drew an impressive round of applause, although it wasn't clear whether this was because the seven thousand young people shared Omori-san's ideas about their heavy responsibilities, or because the kids could see from their programs that the end of the lecture cleared the way for the appearance of Marcia. As the dark-suited officials on the stage stepped away to make room for the massive drums and speakers to be used by Marcia's band, I sat in the back of the hall trying to remember what my community had done to mark my arrival at adulthood. I turned eighteen at a time when American teenagers were being sent to die in distant jungles, which perhaps explains why the only official recognition I received was a mimeographed postcard from the Selective Service System, the official name back then for the draft board. The card didn't bother to congratulate me on my new status in society, but warned me that I faced arrest and prosecution if I failed to register for the draft within the next thirty days. That was Seijin-shiki, American-style.

It would be romantic to the point of naïveté to suggest that all the nineteen-year-olds in Japan that day came storming out of the local Seijin-shiki armed with a new determination to work hard, obey the law, and devote themselves selflessly to the overall society. But some of them probably did react that way. And all of those who attended at least were made aware that the community had expectations for them—that the society had certain values and that the values were important, important enough for the whole country to take a holiday, and for the city to hold a ceremony, and for their parents to shell out big yen for the necessary outfits. The so-called Confucian values or Asian values on display at the Coming-of-Age Ceremony were no better than, and not much different from, the Judaeo-Christian values or Islamic values or humanistic values treasured in other parts of the world. But the Japanese, at least on January 15 every year, were doing a better job of emphasizing how much those values matter.

THESE RECURRING RITES and ceremonies are not the only tools Asian societies use to perpetuate community values. Just about anywhere you go in China, Japan, Korea, Singapore, Malaysia, Indonesia, Taiwan, Thailand, etc., you find moral instruction right before your eyes—often in letters (or characters) ten feet tall. Acting on what appears to be a pan-Asian conviction that there can't be too much of a good thing, these countries are constantly preaching values, morality, and good citizenship to their citizens in the form of slogans, posters, billboards, advertisements, and TV commercials. Thus it was that within three minutes of our arrival in Asia we saw a big banner in Narita Airport: "Enjoy Your Stay in Japan, but Please Observe the Rules." That message was in English, and presumably aimed at foreign visitors. But there's another one right above it in Japanese, targeted at the home folks: "We Can Become More International, but Still Honor the Rules of our Society." On the passenger trains run by KMT, the Malaysian national railroad, there are framed signs that say (in English, Malay, Tamil, and Chinese): "Have a Safe and Pleasant Journey, in the Spirit of a Caring Society." I remember a big sign on a bridge over the River Han in downtown Seoul (a fairly good place for it, because the traffic jams there are so hopeless people have a lot of time to contemplate its meaning) that urges motorists: "Join Together to Maintain Moral Values!"

In the subways of Singapore, you constantly confront the sayings of Confucius. These are not just on posters stuck to the wall, but rather are words set in the tiles of the wall, permanently, so that regular riders get the same dose of moral instruction at the same station every day.

Many of these signs hanging in public places in Asia are strictly practical in effect—"Turn off the gas at the first hint of an earthquake!" (in Chiba, Japan), "Support Zero Inflation—Spend Less, Save More!" (in Johor Bahru, Malaysia), "Fight Back Against Traffic—Ride the Bus" (in Jakarta), "Watch for Children Dashing into Traffic" (in Seoul), "AIDS is the enemy—a condom is a friend" (in Bangkok)—and those never surprised me much, since you see the same kind of health and safety notices on American streets. What was different in Asia, though, was that messages about morality, about good conduct, about simply being kind to others, were considered more important than fire safety alerts or traffic warnings. Somebody, at least, thought they were more important, because there are a lot more signs about moral values than about fire prevention or traffic safety.

Not far from our home in Subsection 3 there was a busy street with a pedestrian overpass so that schoolchildren wouldn't have to risk the traffic when crossing. This crossing (like almost every other highway overpass in Japan) was considered prime territory for signs and banners. But no commercial advertisements were allowed there. Rather, the local governmental entity, Shibuya Ward, used to hang giant banners (five feet high by thirty feet long) on that overpass for passing motorists to read. The message changed monthly, but the tone was almost always the same. It was a reminder to the people of Shibuya (and anybody else who happened to be driving through) to be good citizens. Whoever wrote these messages for the ward government had two favorite words that showed up time and again in the monthly banner: *egao,* a Japanese word for "smile," and "mah-nah," the Japanese version of the English word "manners." And so we used to look up as we drove past and see our local government urging us: "Drive with a smile and good manners," or "Teach the schoolchildren by the example of your good manners." "Your smile and your kindness brighten our neighborhood," the sign said one month, a reminder that gave way thirty days later to "Kindness in driving makes for a friendly Shibuya." My favorite—which also lasted just one month—was this class equalizer: "Good manners behind the wheel are better than a fancy car."

Good manners matter so much to the Japanese that the government has created a whole artistic genre to propagate them: the manner poster, or, in Japanese, "mah-nah pos-tah." From serious painters to well-known commercial illustrators to amateurs just starting on the craft, thousands of artists around the world have been commissioned to create posters encouraging citizens to show good manners toward their fellow men. The Manner Posters hang on public walls everywhere, but primarily in subway stations and bus stops. They change monthly or so, and they are just interesting enough that people take a second, as they alight from the crowded train, to see what particular act of courtesy the state is encouraging this month. Generally, there's a picture of some thoughtless act—for example, two men talking so loudly on the subway platform that nobody else can carry on a conversation—and a gentle nostrum at the bottom—"Talk quietly and respect the rights of others." As befits their location, many of these municipal lessons in good manners deal with public transit: "Please don't run when boarding the train—you might bump into somebody." "Please sit with your legs tightly together on the bus, to make more room on the seat for others." But others have broader applications: "If somebody seems lost, why not offer to help him?" or "If you find a wallet on the street, look around—you might see the owner looking for it" or "Please take care not to block the way of blind people."

To an American, there's something of a Mickey Mouse quality to these manner messages, as if the posters belong on the wall of a third-grade classroom rather than the public subway station. But in Japan, the Manner Posters are an accepted fact of daily life, and a popular one at that. Every once in a while, some museum or art gallery in Tokyo holds an exhibition of Manner Posters, and tens of thousands of people turn out to see their old favorites again. In the spring of 1997, when the Tokyo Municipal Subway System held a referendum to choose the most popular Manner Posters of the past two years, millions of people took the time to fill out ballots. So as not to hurt any artist's feelings, the complete results were not reported. But judging from the rather vague wording of the announced results, the big winner appeared to be a poster showing a frail old woman, carrying a cane, being helped onto the subway by a polite youngster. "If you're young and energetic, make way for the elderly," the caption says.

In addition to smiles and manners, many of these signs, banners, and posters emphasize another key word: "rules." The Japanese are people who love rules. I think this is partly because knowing what the rules are in any situation provides social security: If you never break a rule, you'll probably never stand out from the crowd. To be a rule breaker is, almost by definition, to be a nail that sticks out—and is sure, somewhere along the line, to be hammered down. And then there's the simple fact that the people of Japan, like their fellow Asians, tend to live in enormously crowded urban places, with neighbor constantly cheek by jowl with neighbor. In such conditions, sticking to the rules prevents the kind of outbursts that can turn to crime and violence.

In any case, a lot of the urgings to good behavior rely on the motive power of rules. Japan's Health Ministry puts up posters all over the place urging young people not to smoke. Nothing strange here. All over the world, including my own household, adults are warning teenagers about tobacco. When I try to warn my own kids against smoking, I use what seem to me to be practical arguments: Smoking is a filthy habit, once you start you can't quit, it ruins you for sports, and it will give you cancer and kill you. But the Japanese appeal is quite different. Health is not the issue, the rules are. "You can wear a man's suit before you're an adult," one of the standard posters says, "but you can't smoke a man's cigarette before you turn 20. THAT'S THE RULE." Another ad aimed at teenagers pictures an NBA basketball star wearing big springs on the soles of his shoes. "He could probably jump higher and score a lot if he wore these," the poster reads. "But nobody would stand for it. In sports, as in all life, there are rules. People under 20 can't smoke tobacco. THIS IS A RULE."

Looking at all these moral reminders on the walls, streets, and overpasses of Asian cities—reminders that you generally don't see, outside of a church or school, in the West—I used to wonder about the view of human nature reflected in this phenomenon. When I first came to Asia and saw all those signs about following rules, being a good neighbor, helping the elderly, and so forth, I thought that the Orient must have extremely low regard for mankind. The basic mind-set seemed to be that if you don't constantly remind people to be good, all hell will break loose. But the more I looked, the more it seemed that Asians were less fearful of their fellow man than we Americans are. We never saw a house with bars on the windows or one of those signs saying "This home protected by Security Shield Alarms"; we never saw the Club attached to the steering wheel of a car, or heard the angry blaring of a car alarm. Gradually, I changed my mind about Asians' view of human goodness. Here was a society that clearly believed people will be virtuous if you encourage them to; that's why so much time and money were put into the continuous effort to encourage good behavior. And that seemed to be a fairly confident view of mankind.

This basic confidence comes through in a lot of the public signs and notices in Japan. At Kinuta Park, in a residential neighborhood in southeast Tokyo, I was so struck by the sign at the park entrance that I pulled out a notebook and copied the full text. The sign didn't just come out and say, "No dogs. No alcohol. No dumping." Instead, it was a series of exhortations, with an explanation provided for each of its suggestions:

- To keep things clean for others using the park, let's leave our dogs home when we come here.

- To preserve the grass for people who want to sit outside, let's do our jogging on the designated paths and not cut corners.

- To protect others from injury, let's try not to bring any glass containers into the park.

- To make sure this is a park our community can be proud of, let's pack up our trash and take it home.

- To make the park a pleasant place for everybody, let's try not to do anything that might bother the other people who are here.

I was standing out on our narrow, narrow street in Shibuya Ward one day when my neighbor Matsuda-san weighed in on this point. Somebody who lived down the street was having trouble with parked cars blocking his driveway. He had posted a sign in front of his house to deal with this problem. And as I told Matsuda-san, the sign seemed classically Japanese to me. The owner of the house had a perfect right to tell people to keep his driveway clear, yet his sign had the tone of an abject apology: "We're sorry, but we must respectfully request that owners of honorable cars not connected to this household cooperate by refraining from parking in front of our humble driveway." I pointed out that this was rather convoluted, and that an American would make the same point more directly: "No parking in driveway."

"It's a difference of expectations, isn't it?" my silver-haired neighbor said. His point was that the signs in Japan, full of deference and emphasizing cooperation among neighbors, reflect a benign notion of human nature, the belief that if you encourage the good in people, if you appeal to their sense of virtue, they'll respond. In contrast, a society that has lower expectations—a community that assumes people will do the wrong thing unless it is expressly prohibited—relies on prohibition and punishment: "No Parking—Violators Will Be Towed."

For some reason, I wasn't surprised one bit when I later found essentially the same thing Matsuda-san had told me in one of my books about Confucius. Confucius felt that humans were basically good, and that they would do the right thing if they knew what it was. People are perfectible, the master said, through endless repetition of moral precepts. We've already quoted Confucius's great teaching on this point: "Guide them with edicts, keep them in line with punishment, and people may stay out of trouble but will have no sense of shame," he taught. "But if you guide them by your own virtue, and keep them in line with acts of decency, they will develop a sense of shame and control themselves." And I came to agree with Matsuda-san that this reflects a basically optimistic view of human nature: that people will do the right thing if they know it. You don't have to be Asian, or Confucian, to share that optimistic viewpoint. It has been repeated in every Western society as well. The scholar Amitai Etzioni, an American of Italian extraction and Roman Catholic upbringing, said essentially the same thing about 2,400 years after Confucius did: "We are each other's keepers in the moral sense, and we need to be able to tell each other that. . . . The more we feel comfortable doing that, the more we rely on the moral voice, the less we need to be tempted by government controls."

Although East Asian societies draw their ideas of virtue and responsibility from Confucian teachings, they don't always cite Confucius, or any other moral teacher, in their continuing efforts to promote moral behavior among the populace. Schoolchildren learn about Confucius. Years later, as adults, when they see a sign in the park saying "Let's try not to do anything that will bother the other people," they probably know that this is the kind of ethical rule the Confucian masters used to preach. But people don't go around quoting Confucius to each other. The moral teachings in signs and posters sometimes mention Confucius, but often they don't. The important thing is not the teacher but the teaching. The ancient lessons, the traditional rules of social behavior, are constantly reiterated.

Professor Robert J. Smith, an Asian scholar at Cornell, studied how the old rules and traditions are passed along in Oriental societies. A good deal of his research began with conversations, just talking to Japanese adults about their moral convictions. He found that the Confucian influence was undeniable, although a number of the people he interviewed didn't seem to think of their ideas as the product of Confucianism (or any other "ism," for that matter). Some were surprised when Smith told them that the ideals they clung to were Confucian ideals—a reaction, Smith noted dryly, that reminded him of "the students who, introduced to poetry for the first time, discover that unwittingly they have been writing prose all their lives." In an essay published in 1996, Professor Smith quoted from a letter written by a middle-aged Japanese woman about Confucius (whom she calls Koshi, which is the Japanese reading of the Chinese characters Kung Fu-tzu) and Confucianism (which she calls *jukyo,* or "the teaching of the master"):

> You asked me if I thought my family was in any way influenced by Confucianism. I know very little about Confucianism, so I borrowed a library book called "Koshi and The Analects." After reading it, I realized something for the first time. The thoughts and ideas of Koshi, who is the father of Confucianism, have entered into the fundamental ways of thinking in our daily life. This came as quite a surprise to me.
>
> In Japan today, Confucianism has nothing to do with religion, but rather is cultural and part of our basic education. For example, one of the famous sayings of Koshi is: "What you do not want done to yourself, do not do to others." We are conscious of this advice in our daily life, but in our family life as well. . . .
>
> Another of Koshi's sayings, "Look at the complexion of a man," has also influenced our family life, for we often say, "You can understand what I want to say, even if I don't say it." Anyway, I find that it is true that we have been influenced by Confucianism, even though we don't realize it. It can be said that *jukyo* has entered our ethical system.

In this woman's family, and all over East Asia, the traditional values are being passed on. Even if people don't know much about their society's traditions, even if people don't have any idea where the values came from, they are constantly reminded—at work, at school, waiting for a subway, driving down the street, turning on the television—that the ancient moral rules still apply. In Western societies, the job of transmitting moral norms is left largely to churches, families, educational organizations, and the like. In Asia, moral values are considered too important to be left to the private sector. The whole community, public and private, takes part in teaching values, and the teaching never stops.

You can see the results, in large ways and small, in the Confucian societies today. Those dramatically low crime rates, the low rates of divorce, unwed motherhood, broken homes, drug use, vandalism, etc., are testament to the fact that moral directives about obeying the law, honoring the family, and respecting fellow members of the community still have potent force in Asian societies. In our daily life in Asia, our family saw the results in the safe, clean streets and the civil, courteous tone of daily life. We could see the lingering power of the old moral directives in smaller segments of life as well—things like the success of smokeless cigarettes and the outcry against public kissing.

American tobacco companies introduced several new cigarette brands in the early 1990s which were designed to deal with the problem of second-hand smoke and the annoyance a cigarette causes for nearby nonsmokers. One innovation, sold under the label "Salem Preferred," used special chemicals in the cigarette paper to make the tobacco produce less smoke, and make the smoke smell less like tobacco. Another idea was R. J. Reynolds's inventive but doomed "smokeless" cigarette, "Eclipse," which used a chemical heat plug to heat up the tobacco and create a sense of smoking with no need to light a match. In the United States, both products were sorry flops; smokers found it was hard to suck any flavor out of them, and the flavor was pretty bad when they succeeded.

But the tobacco firms' investment was not a complete loss. They shipped the technology across the Pacific. In the Asian countries (particularly Japan, where people love both tobacco and technology) both the low-smoke and the "smokeless" varieties have become big market hits, selling under labels like "Pianissimo," "Frontier Pure," and "Airs." The head of R. J. Reynolds's Japan operation explained that these new cigarettes caught on because they "appeal to traditional values in Japanese society, such as a focus on harmony and respect for others." Even when they step out on the corner for a smoke, in other words, people feel the need to "try not to do anything that might bother the other people."

While we were living in Tokyo, in the mid-nineties, we observed one of the stranger manifestations of the lingering strength of traditional values in modern Asian societies. Japan went into a mild panic over kissing.

A few trendy magazines in Japan, followed in short order by the mainstream newspapers, the TV newsmagazines, and eventually the entire nation, decided that members of the younger generation–high school and college kids, plus young working people–were actually kissing each other in public. Yes, you read it right: A guy and a gal in their twenties, returning to her apartment after a date, would actually exchange a good-night kiss right out there on the sidewalk. Or at least, that's what the media reported. Duly alerted, our family started looking for evidence of this shocking behavior, but it was hard to find. Seeing a kiss in public is not an everyday thing in Japan. It's not even an every-week thing. But now and then, particularly late at night, we might catch a glimpse of a smooching couple on the doorstep, or the train platform, or in a corner booth at a downtown restaurant. This was officially declared to be shocking. A well-known social critic, Aso Chiaki, wrote a long exposé of the new trend–"it's disgusting," she concluded–in *Shukan Yomiuri,* a generally serious newsmagazine. She reported that others had reported to her that there were instances of outright necking on the trains. Nobody I know ever saw that.

In a homogeneous nation where everybody gets excited about the same thing at the same time, this alleged trend became serious media fodder. Among other things, it became a running subplot on one of Japan's great TV soap operas, *Tokyo University Story.* Despite the name, this is a high school drama; it is essentially an Asian version of the American hit show *Beverly Hills 90210,* although it presents a vastly more innocent picture of high school life. Unlike the students of *90210,* whose problems tend to revolve around drug deals, cheating on tests, and which high school junior is sleeping with whom, the basic tension of the Japanese melodrama is whether two seniors–the attractive mini-skirted Haruka and her handsome boyfriend, Mura-kami—can study hard enough to pass the entrance exam for Tokyo University, Japan's most prestigious college.

Right in the middle of the national kissing-in-public scare, young Haruka let herself get so aroused in one episode of the show that she permitted Murakami to kiss her, in a public park! There followed a long period of suspense and anguish, focusing on Haruka's fear that Murakami might tell the guys in school what had happened, thus destroying her reputation. As it turned out, Murakami's lips were sealed, which made Haruka love him all the more. (And, yes, both did eventually pass the test for Tokyo U.)

Two things about this "trend," and the reaction to it, were baffling. In the first place, I'm still not convinced that it was ever real. Our family, as noted, had trouble spotting a public kiss even when we were looking for it. In my role as a journalist, I asked a lot of people about this phenomenon and rarely found anybody who had kissed in public (or would admit to it). The Shiseido cosmetics company, which is Japan's largest seller of lipstick, and thus would appear to have a professional interest in kissing, public or private, commissioned an opinion poll. Of four hundred Japanese men surveyed, 71 percent had never kissed a woman, wife or otherwise, in a public place. Of the 29 percent who admitted to kissing at train stations, airports, or street corners, more than half said they were embarrassed about it and probably wouldn't do it again.

The other disconcerting point about the kissing-in-public issue was that kissing seemed decidedly tame compared to the stuff anybody could find in some of the raunchier Japanese magazines or even late-night television. One of the Japan network shows that ran after midnight each Saturday—the time period when Japanese TV gets down and dirty—was all about kissing, in fact. It was called *Mizugi de Kissu Me,* or *Kiss Me in a Bathing Suit,* and it featured pretty young women, some wearing only half a bathing suit, who would kiss men while the audience hooted and shouted. Real life was even wilder than these TV offerings. Japan, after all, has ubiquitous, if illegal, prostitution and a thriving pornography business. Even in relatively mainstream publications, pictures of naked women are so common that United Airlines had to ban some Japanese newsmagazines from its planes because of passenger complaints. Japanese video-rental stores offer rack after rack of "adult" films, including countless videos purporting to show high school girls stripping out of their sailor-suit school uniforms. There are stores where men can buy used lingerie packaged with a photo of the high school girl who reputedly wore it. That's something that really qualifies as disgusting, but for some reason, it was the innocent public kiss that drew a storm of angry reaction.

Obviously, this kind of demonstration of affection is not supposed to be carried out where others can see it. The Japanese are extremely decorous on this point. When you greet an old friend, business partner, spouse, or lover, you're supposed to do it with a polite bow. In 1991, when Saddam Hussein released several dozen Japanese people he had been holding as hostages in Iraq, I went to the airport to watch the joyful homecoming. The pattern was the same for each of the former prisoners: A man would step onto the tarmac, his business associates, wife, and children would step out to welcome him home, and then everybody would bow. There were no hugs, no handshakes, no bodily contact, and certainly no kisses to welcome these people home after a month's captivity in a distant jail. Since the homecoming was taking place at an airport, full of passengers and reporters like me who had come out to watch, restraint was required.

The problem with kissing in public, according to its many critics, was that it demonstrated a lack of restraint—a lack of shame. And if people no longer restrain themselves in public, even in something as simple as kissing, the whole society may soon go to pot. Confucius knew this, of course: "Guide them with edicts, keep them in line with punishment, and people may stay out of trouble but will have no sense of shame." The kissing-in-public crisis demonstrated that the ordinary people of Japan knew it, too.

A housewife named Tsutsumi Shizue was one of many people who wrote letters to the editor on the kissing crisis to the *Yomiuri Shimbun,* Japan's biggest daily newspaper. "These young people have lost their sense of shame," her letter said. "Without shame, there is no sense of restraint. If we lose that, we're no different from animals." The other problem was that the kissing couples didn't seem to care whether their public display of affection bothered anybody else. The social critic Aso Chiaki complained: "These people never give a thought to how others feel, the people who have to see them kiss."

I'm pleased to report that the so-called trend for kissing in public died away about as quickly it blossomed. Today, you still won't see many kisses in Japan, unless you tune in to *Kiss Me in a Bathing Suit* late some Saturday night. The interesting thing was the way the whole society seemed to agree that kissing in public had overstepped some unstated social limit, and that this was not to be tolerated.

Whether it's a stolen kiss or some more serious transgression, people in East Asian societies know what the rules are—even the unwritten rules—and feel obliged to follow them. Which means that all those ceremonies, signs, banners, posters, ads, and exhortations that color daily life in Asian countries are doing the job they are supposed to do. The public has developed the sense of shame that Confucius cared so much about. But there are other forces at work in Asian societies that strengthen the general sense of civility. Along with that sense of shame, there is also a sense of belonging, a broad consensus that maintaining social order is in everybody's interest.

Each citizen has been made to feel that he is a stakeholder in the overall economy and social structure. And to a large extent, this feeling is accurate. As the nations of East Asia have grown prosperous over the years, they have done an excellent job of spreading that prosperity to every member of society. This is a significant social achievement—one that we ran into the day we went swimming at an indoor beach.

SEVEN

The Secret Weapon

Is this beach perfect, or what?

Beneath a brilliant and cloudless sky of royal blue, I am lolling around on a spotless coral-pink beachfront, watching our younger children gambol in the shorebreak. Farther out, the older kids are surfing, wave after perfectly tubular wave. Above us, a gentle breeze tosses the palm fronds, and above the breeze we hear the gentle call of sea birds: *Pyah! Pyah!* The lapping surf, the soothing breeze, and the call of the birds lull me into a long, easy nap. I finally wake in early evening—just in time to see deep purple twilight descending on the horizon as the first stars of evening twinkle to life above the waves.

It's perfect, all right. And what's more, this beach in Kawasaki, Japan, stays perfect every single day—the same clear weather, gentle breeze, and seventy-two-degree temperature, all summer long and all winter as well, 365 days per year. And that's exactly how things were designed by the creator of this beach: not Mother Nature, but rather NKK Steel Corporation, one of the world's biggest steelmakers. NKK spent tens of millions of dollars, in fact, to make sure this beach was perfect. And just to make sure that nothing would go wrong, the company then put its beach indoors—inside a mammoth steel structure called Wild Blue Yokohama. The indoor beach quickly became the hottest new thing in Japanese theme parks, and Wild Blue Yokohama has been a smashing success, even though its name is wildly wrong. It's not in Yokohama (although Kawasaki is just a few miles north of that port city). It's not blue. And it's definitely not wild, or natural, in any way. The beach, the breeze, the breakers, the bird calls, the purple twilight, those stars twinkling in the artificial night—they're all man-made.

They're so well made that this ocean resort with a roof overhead draws more than eight hundred thousand beachgoers every year. They pay twenty dollars just to get into the place; then they shell out far more to rent beach chairs, surfboards, rubber rafts, goggles, and other beach paraphernalia. Why? Well, if my family is any guide, Wild Blue Yokohama succeeds because everybody has fun there. The water is predictably warm and clean. Those perfect small waves roll out in assembly-line fashion every few seconds, and every half hour—after a warning on the PA system that "surf's up!"—there are a few minutes of much higher waves, specifically designed for serious surfers. There's also a man-made river, which roars around the periphery with a rushing current for swimmers to play in. There are man-made waterfalls and a man-made jungle where kids can swing out, Tarzan-style, on man-made vines to plop down into a warm lagoon. Our kids loved the place, and my wife and I enjoyed it, too. We would pay forty dollars to rent two lounge chairs, sit on the artificial beach, and watch the children play in the man-made ocean.

Sometimes, sitting there under the simulated sunbeams, I used to wonder why it was that the Japanese felt the need to build this fake seashore out of plastic and fiberglass beneath that huge steel roof. Japan is a narrow island country with thousands of real beaches, some of them as alluring as the best Hawaii has to offer. More than 90 percent of the Japanese people live within one hour's journey of a beach. There are a couple of real-life beaches—although they are nowhere near as pristine as this indoor spot—right in Kawasaki, maybe ten minutes' walk from Wild Blue Yokohama. What is it in the

Japanese psyche, I kept asking myself, that drives them to build a place like this? And who was the genius who had inspired this idea?

The answer was deliciously complex. It wasn't just that somebody got the idea to put an ocean indoors and erected a big steel building with a wave machine inside. Rather, Wild Blue Yokohama came about because of various intersecting aspects of international trade relations, because of changes in global markets, and because of Japan's traditional and thoroughly Confucian respect for mutual loyalties between companies and their workers. Still, if the question is, who is the man most responsible for this indoor beach in Kawasaki, Japan, the best answer would be: Ronald Reagan.

Our story at this point zooms backward to 1985, when Reagan was the U.S. president and James A. Baker was his Treasury secretary. It was the height of Japan's postwar economic miracle. The notorious "Japanese juggernaut" was approaching full speed, and all over the world consumers were lining up to buy Japanese-made cars, cameras, computers, color TVs, and the like. Every industrial democracy suddenly found itself running a large balance-of-trade deficit with Japan—which is to say that Japanese companies sold a lot more stuff to France, England, the United States, and other countries than those countries could sell to Japan. This caused political problems for most of the Western governments, but the criticism was particularly sharp in the United States. By buying more and more imported goods and exporting less themselves, Americans had run up the world's largest deficit in foreign trade. Reagan, after all, was famous for his speeches about "making America great again" and rebuilding national strength. But now his political opponents and the press kept pointing to the trade statistics; if our country is so great, they would say, how come it leads the world in red ink in the balance-of-trade ledger?

There were, in fact, countless reasons for the situation, but in political terms, a simple explanation—a scapegoat—was needed. Japan was the obvious choice. Japan had a balance of trade surplus with the United States of around $40 billion in 1984, which was half of the total U.S. trade deficit. So Reagan and Baker decided to point the finger at Japanese industry. And once Japan was identified as the problem, Reagan needed a solution.

On September 22, 1985, James Baker gathered his fellow finance ministers from Japan, the United Kingdom, France, and Germany at the Plaza Hotel in New York and made a stunning proposal: The U.S. government and the Federal Reserve banking system would cooperate to weaken the U.S. currency against the yen. The idea was that if American dollars could buy less, Americans would import less from Japan; and if the yen could buy more, the Japanese would buy more American (and British, and French, and German) goods. This would even out the trade statistics, in theory, and the Reagan administration would no longer face those embarrassing questions about why the U.S. economy was so deeply in the red on export-import markets.

The assembled finance ministers all agreed to this American plan, and the so-called Plaza Accords were put into effect. Almost immediately, the dollar started losing value against the yen on currency markets. Before that session at the Plaza, it cost 252 yen to buy one dollar. By early the next year, a dollar was worth only 200 yen. By late 1987, the exchange rate was down to 125 yen to the dollar—which meant the U.S. greenback had lost half its value. The slide continued until the dollar reached its nadir in the summer of 1995, ten years after the Plaza Accords. Now a Japanese buyer could get a U.S. dollar—or, more important, a dollar's worth of U.S. goods—for just 87 yen. Thereafter, the U.S. currency began to regain some of its strength, but never got much above 125 yen to the dollar. In other words, a dollar could buy only half as much as it could have bought when Reagan decided to slash its value in 1985.

International currency transactions are confusing, to say the least. The eyes-glaze-over factor is strong when people start talking about fluctuations in the yen-dollar exchange rate. The results of the Plaza Accords, though, can be stated in plain English: This initiative by the American government made the American people poorer. With weaker dollars, Americans had less money vis-à-vis Japan; meanwhile, the Japanese people became richer. They could buy more. To understand why, let's look at two consumers: Ms. Hannah Hampton of Toledo, U.S.A., and Ms. Hamada Hanako, of Tokyo, Japan.

Let's say, for example, that Hannah Hampton had saved up her money so she could buy a Toyota Camry, made in Japan. She had saved $10,000, which was enough to buy the car in the summer of 1985. Just six months later, though, the same car would cost $13,000.

To buy that Camry, Ms. Hampton would have to use all her savings and borrow another $3,000. The car was the same, and the price (in yen) was the same. And Ms. Hampton had the same amount of money. But now her money wouldn't buy the car. Thanks to the Plaza Accords, this American consumer was poorer than she had been six months earlier.

Across the Pacific, meanwhile, Hamada Hanako had been saving her money to buy a one-week vacation in Hawaii. In the summer of 1985, the tour package cost $2,500, or 630,000 yen, which is exactly the amount Hamada-san had in her savings account. By the end of 1985, however, the same $2,500 tour cost just 500,000 yen. Nothing about the tour had been changed; it was just that Hamada-san's yen were now worth a lot more money, in dollar terms. When she took her savings out of the bank, she could pay for the entire tour package and still have an additional $500 to buy a DKNY suit, a Coach bag, a box of Godiva chocolates, and a Mariah Carey CD in the shops of Waikiki. Thanks to the Plaza Accords, this Japanese consumer was richer than she had been six months earlier.

Why would the U.S. government deliberately make its own citizens poorer? The economic theory underlying this policy, as the Reagan administration explained it, was that it might increase sales of American-made products, both in the United States and in Japan. If Hannah Hampton suddenly found that she didn't have enough money to buy that Toyota, she might have changed her mind and bought a Ford or Chevrolet instead. And since Hamada Hanako had money left over after her big purchase, she could spend the remainder on American-made clothes, handbags, candy, and popular music.

In fact, things never worked out the way the theory had suggested. Americans did not significantly reduce their purchases of Japanese cars, cassette players, or computer chips. They just paid more for the same goods. The real reason for the decision to weaken the dollar was political: the hope that the currency changes would eventually show up in the trade statistics and make the U.S. balance of trade deficit look smaller. In fact, this didn't happen either. Even after the dollar was weakened, the balance-of-trade statistics got worse and worse for the American side. By the mid-1990s, the U.S. trade deficit with Japan was running more than $50 billion per year, which was far worse than it had been before that session at the Plaza in September of 1985.

Still, the Plaza Accords had a brutal impact on some Japanese companies. Firms in Japan that were dependent on export sales, and faced foreign competition in their markets, suddenly found that the price of their product on world markets was much higher. Even if they could turn out the same car, camera, or widget at the same price in yen, the price in dollars was suddenly much higher. (Most international sales are denominated in dollars.) So if Minolta, for example, had a camera that sold for 25,000 yen, it would have cost about $100 in, say, Chicago in the summer of 1985. After the Plaza Accords, the same camera cost $200 or more. At that point, some customers would presumably switch to a Kodak or Polaroid camera, which would cost less.

The Japanese firms hit hardest by the currency manipulation were those making big industrial products that could be made anywhere. There were a lot of products that nobody was able to make as well as Japanese companies: industrial robots, computer display screens, home video players, giant color printing presses. But a Japanese company making a fairly fungible product—steel ingots, say, or RAM chips, or extension cords—suddenly found itself trying to sell the same product as its competitor at a much higher price. Japanese exporters of such goods were now billing their customers in meager dollars while paying their costs—labor, equipment, electricity, etc.—in the mighty yen.

In the West, there are fairly standard ways to deal with this kind of crunch. If costs are going up and earnings are flat or falling, one normal form of response from management is to cut labor costs—or, to use the coldly efficient term favored by contemporary managers, to "downsize." If costs are high, you lay off some workers. If this doesn't improve the bottom line, you lay off some more. If the economy turns around, or the company succeeds in some new market, these people may be rehired later, of course. But it is accepted industrial truth that for the short term, at least, some workers will have to go.

One reason the Plaza Accords were so painful in Japan is that this "normal" corporate response was simply not an option for major Japanese manufacturers. As a rule, Japanese companies don't downsize. To lay off workers–to make employees pay the price of corporate setbacks–would undermine central principles of the way Japan is organized. It would impair the overall harmony of the nation. It would destroy the group commitment, the sense of family, that is a crucial element of the corporate atmosphere in any Japanese company. It would set workers against one another. It would, in short, violate the *wa*.

In the 1980s, when Western experts on business and management began looking for the keys to Japan's postwar miracle, one factor that was constantly cited was "lifetime employment," the system under which a person who enters employment at a company is guaranteed to hold a job there for life, regardless of changing markets or other economic circumstances. Much was made of this "unique" Japanese practice. It could be costly, particularly in tough economic times, but it also had some clear business benefits. A company that never laid anybody off was assured of a trained, experienced workforce with a strong institutional memory for ideas that had worked in the past. And a company that was loyal to its workers in hard times could count on the employees to return the favor when the chips were down. The reason Japanese employees rarely go on strike, or desert a company to join a competitor, is that they feel a loyalty to the firm–a loyalty that many Western workers will never know.

That's what the textbooks said, at least. In fact, there is less to "lifetime employment" than meets the eye.

For one thing, "lifetime employment" is not unique to Japan. In most Western countries, the same system is in practice in government agencies, where the idea of a permanent corps of civil service workers with guaranteed jobs is considered a necessary protection against the whims of politicians, and in the military and most educational institutions. For another, even in Japan, guaranteed employment is formally practiced only by the government and the largest corporations. The promise of lifetime employment actually applies to fewer than one-third of Japanese men, and fewer than 10 percent of women.

But there is something stronger than a formal system of guaranteed employment that protects workers in their jobs in Japan. There is a collective agreement, a national consensus, that full employment is useful both to corporations and to the society as a whole.

One natural result is that almost all Japanese schools, businesses, and agencies have more workers than a comparable company would have in the West. The "escalator girl"–the young woman in a blue uniform and white gloves who is employed to wipe clean the handrail all day long on the escalator of the big department stores–is a famous example of the kind of featherbedding that is a national pasttime of Japanese business. In our neighborhood in Shibuya-ku, I used to go down the street now and then to a book store so narrow that it had space for just two long shelves with a skinny aisle in between. The store was so small that there was only room enough for one person to be inside it at a time. When a customer came in to browse, the clerk had to step outside onto the street to make room. And yet this tiny postage stamp of a shop always had two employees at work–one the cashier, at a cash register out on the street, and the other helping customers find books and wrapping their purchases.

The second natural result of the commitment to keep everybody at work is that Japanese employees don't get laid off. Whether the boss is the national Ministry of Health or Matsushita Electronics or just a fruit stand on the corner in some small town, the sense is strong that it is simply wrong to let a worker go–no matter how bad the bottom line may look. Businesses big and small are expected to ride out the weak years without making employees bear the cost. In the mid-1990s, after three years of losses, the respected electronics firm Pioneer told thirty-five middle managers that they would have to "retire" as part of a broader cost-cutting drive. The Japanese media immediately spotted this forced "retirement" as a layoff, and the fate of those thirty-five Pioneer executives became a national cause célèbre. In the end, the thirty-five employees kept their jobs, and the corporate president was forced to resign in disgrace.

During the seven straight years of recession that lashed Japan's economy in the nineties, there were virtually no mass layoffs of the type familiar in the West. In 1989, at the peak of a boom economy, Japan's unemployment rate was 2.9 percent. In 1998, with the country mired in deep recession and a banking crisis, Japan's unemployment rate hit 4.1 percent–a shocker by Japanese standards, but comfortably low for any Western country. (At the same time, by comparison, the U.S. unemployment rate was 4.5 percent, a level that

economists referred to as "full employment.") The increase in unemployed people came almost totally from new graduates entering the
workforce who could not find work; there were remarkably few
workers anywhere in Japan who lost their jobs because of the economic doldrums.

Why? I think one reason is that workers are fairly scarce in Japan;
once a company finds and trains an employee, it is not inclined to let
the person go. This need to hold on to proven workers is heightened
by Japan's exclusive attitude (a less polite term would be "racist attitude") toward outsiders. The Japanese don't want a lot of foreigners
coming in and taking jobs in their labor force, even though the country faces a labor shortage in the near future. So it's important to keep,
and to coddle, any Japanese employees already on the corporate
rolls.

A more significant explanation for the low rate of unemployment,
even in recession, is that the Japanese have made a national calculation of comparative costs. They have decided that the social costs associated with large-scale unemployment would be greater than the
costs required to keep people at work. "There are always costs involved in unemployment," the economist Takeuchi Hiroshi, the chief
forecaster for the Long-Term Credit Bank of Japan, explained to me
once. "The only question is who bears the expense. In your country,
it's usually the worker first, and then the government, and then the
society as a whole because you have all those people on the street
without a job. In Japan, the company is expected to bear the costs, because that's better for society as a whole."

This policy explains why Japan, despite its emergence as a global
financial and industrial power, always rates fairly low on global com-
parisons of productivity. My economics text defines "productivity" as
"the relative efficiency of economic activity–that is, the amount of
products or services produced compared to the amount of goods and
labor used to produce it." This means that a company or country that
turns out a lot of product with few people working to produce it has a
high rate of productivity. Japan has low productivity, in people terms,
because it generally has more people working on any given job than
you would see in another country. In purely industrial terms, low productivity is a Bad Thing; it increases direct costs. But for Japan, low

productivity is the secret weapon. It's a key reason why the society remains civil, stable, and safe. Other countries have to spend far more money, time, and energy combating crime, drugs, and family decay than Japan spends. So economists may find, when measuring the direct cost of producing a new car, case of beer, microchip, or whatever, that Japan has low productivity. But Japan has also reduced the indirect costs that stem from the rigors of high-productivity societies.

The policy of keeping everybody employed is of course reflected in price tags. Prices for almost all goods and services (even at discount outlets) are high in Japan—considerably more than the same product would cost in the United States. Those prices include not only the cost of the item, but also the social benefit of full employment. It's a surcharge most Japanese people are willing to pay.

While we were living in Shibuya, one of my daughters turned ten years old and was ready for a new bicycle. I consulted a friend of mine back in Colorado who owns a bike shop. He recommended a Trek 860 bike. It cost $400 in his shop. "It was made in Taiwan, and a lot of the parts come from Japan," he said. "So you can probably get it even cheaper over there." We eventually found exactly the same bike in a big Tokyo store called Tokyu Hands—a store where the bike salesmen, in suits and neckties, almost always outnumbered the customers, and the repair experts wore white gloves while assembling the bikes in the back room. But my friend guessed wrong: it wasn't cheaper in Japan. In Tokyo, that $400 Trek cost a little over $500—25 percent more than I would have paid for the identical item in the United States. I wasn't happy with this padded price, but with my daughter's birthday looming I had no choice but to pay. Before I left the store, it occurred to me that I had better protect this costly item, so I asked the salesman to sell me a lock. "A lock?" he said. "Oh, that's no problem. I'll give you a lock for free." And so he had one of the guys with the white gloves mount a simple little lock on the front wheel—something that any determined bike thief could probably pull off with his bare hands.

In fact, my daughter almost never used that little lock, and didn't have to. We never lost the bike, either. But I gained something from the transaction. I gained an understanding of those high prices in Japan. Yes, you pay like mad for a bicycle in the store, with all sorts of extraneous salespeople and auxiliaries scurrying around. But once you leave the store with your bike, you know that there is probably nobody out on the street who would steal it. I didn't have to buy one of the forty-dollar U-locks that you always see on good bicycles in Western countries. I didn't have to pay for insurance on that bike, and I never really had to worry if somebody was going to swipe it. (Of course bikes get stolen in Japan, but not very often.) So, yes, I had paid a lot for that bicycle—but I had bought more than a bicycle.

In addition to this economic calculation, there's a cultural basis for keeping workers on the job. The group orientation of Japanese society dictates than any employee becomes a member of a group. In some cases, the corporate "group" extends to hundreds of thousands of people around the world, as it will for those young people I met at NEC Corporation's Nyu-Sha-Shiki; in others, it may be limited to the two employees of a tiny bookshop in Shibuya-ku. Group membership creates loyalties that flow up and down. In any group, as Confucius himself taught so long ago, the requirements of loyalty must be honored, and the collective harmony must be preserved. It is hard to lay off anybody without violating these cultural "musts," so Japanese companies, and in fact the whole society, take extraordinary steps to avoid downsizing anybody.

The wage structure, for example, has been designed specifically to let companies absorb bad times without cutting the workforce. All Japanese employees are routinely given a base pay (weekly or monthly) and then an additional bonus amount. In a normal year, the total bonus over a year's time may total four or five months' pay. On top of that, Japanese companies of every size routinely provide overtime pay. On top of that, Japanese employers often pay the employee for various expenses connected with the job: commuter tickets on the train, office clothing, lunch and snacks. When conditions turn sour, then, a company can take several steps to cut labor costs without laying anybody off. First, the subsidized lunch and other such benefits are eliminated. Next, overtime pay is slashed. After that, the bonus gets cut. Some economists estimate that a Japanese employer can cut direct labor costs by 30 percent or more without laying off a single worker.

Employees tend to be kept on the job even if there is no job for them to do. If a manufacturing firm has excessive capacity, for example, the factory workers might be shifted to painting the walls or cutting the grass outside. Assembly-line workers are sent to training programs that can go on for months—which not only keeps them employed, but makes them better workers when the economy turns around and they are needed in the factory again. The ruinous Kobe earthquake of 1985 killed six thousand people, destroyed large sections of that charming city, and ruined several massive sake breweries. (Kobe is a capital of sake-brewing because it is famous for pure spring water.) The major sake factories were off-line for a year or more, but no worker was laid off from any of them. People received their full pay to help with the clean-up and then wait for the factories to be rebuilt. When I asked an executive at Hakushika, Kobe's biggest sake maker, about this policy, he told me it was the only possible response: "The earthquake was a big enough shock to our people. Of course we couldn't deliver another shock by laying off the workers."

One day in 1995 I traveled to the Japanese factory town of Toyota City, just west of Nagoya, a town that is home to the headquarters offices and many assembly plants of the big automaker. I had come to see the newest generation of industrial robots welding various sections of cars together. If you've been to an auto factory in the past ten years or so, you know that these welding machines (they're known as robots, although they don't look anything like the humanoid robots of the science-fiction movies) put on a spectacular sound-and-light show all day long on the assembly line. As the two parts to be joined pass the appropriate point in the line, a long, metal pointer—that's the robot—swings out and sticks an arc-welding tool along the seam. There's a sudden explosion—BLAM!—and a shower of multicolored sparks sprays out over the factory floor. Then the arm swings back, ready to weld the next seam, with another burst of fireworks, twenty seconds later. With proper programming and careful human adjustment, these machines can make a perfect connection time after time, without rest.

On that trip in 1995, I was taken to Toyota Plant 9, where I saw many talented robots and got some great photos of flying sparks. And yet the engineers from Toyota kept apologizing to me. I ignored this at first—Japanese people are always apologizing for something—but gradually I began to realize that there was a fascinating tale embedded in those apologies.

Toyota, I learned, had recently opened a new assembly plant in southern Japan, and most of the work from Plant 9 had been shifted to that new, more efficient operation. Many of the workers at the plant had moved, with their families, to the site of the new factory. But some four hundred workers had stayed behind in Toyota City. And there was no work for them.

Consternation! The company appointed a project team to study the problem and figure out what should happen to the four hundred employees who now had nothing to do. Eventually, a solution emerged. A new Toyota model, a car that had never been produced before, would be assigned to Plant 9. The old factory hands could go right back to work, in their old plant, assembling this new car. It was a neat resolution—until the inevitable flaw appeared: The new model was to be produced in such limited numbers that only about two hundred workers would be needed to man the plant and maintain the industrial robots. So Toyota's planners once again got out their blueprints and calculators, and came up with yet another twist. Originally, this new model had been designed so that 95 percent of the welded connections on the car could be made by those welding machines. The production engineers switched things around so that only 60 percent of the welds would be done by machines. That created welding jobs for another two hundred human workers—and now everybody was satisfied.

And that's why my guides from Toyota kept apologizing to me all day. I had come to see robots, and they had inadvertently taken me to a factory that had fewer robots making welds than any other Toyota plant. In fact, I had found something more interesting than robotics: a car company that would deliberately sacrifice production efficiencies just to keep its people on the job. How could they afford to do this? I asked. Could they still produce cars at a competitive price?

"Well, I guess we were lucky," explained Takahashi Hiroshi, the Toyota engineer who took me around. "The car we are building in this plant has turned out to be very, very popular with customers. So the project is a huge success." The car they were making was the Toyota RAV-4, or Recreational Active Vehicle 4, an adorable jelly bean of a four-wheel-drive car that looked like a Ken-and-Barbie version of a Ford Explorer. The name is a pun in Japanese, because the acronym RAV is pronounced "lah-bu," which is the same way the

Japanese pronounce the English word "love." Anyway, the RAV-4 created a new car category—the small-car version of a sport-utility vehicle—and has been a runaway hit both in Japan and the United States.
Plant 9, even with all those humans doing the welding, became one of
the most successful of all Toyota production facilities.

But of course, this happy ending had a fairly large element of luck
to it. I asked Takahashi-san what would have happened if the new
model had been a flop. Would Toyota have found something else for
those four hundred workers to do? Or would the company eventually
have decided to downsize them? The answer was delivered with no
hesitation. "Oh we would of course keep them on the job, as a matter
of principle," Takahashi-san said. "The word 'downsizing' is not part
of our vocabulary here."

Companies in Japan often do the same kind of thing in the management suites. Executives with no work to do may be dispatched to a
junior-level job at a subsidiary company. Others may be sent out selling products door-to-door. Still others may find themselves joining the
wretched *mado-giwa zoku,* the "window sitters," who are given seats
near the wall or window—the worst spot to be in a Japanese office,
since it is the farthest from the section chief at the front of the room.
Obviously, none of these prospects is enticing for a person who considers himself an executive. Some people quit rather than face such ig-
nominy. But even window sitters still have a steady income, plus that
corporate badge on the lapel and all the respect and stature that comes
with it. Even being a window sitter is probably better than getting
downsized.

Business doesn't bear all the cost of carrying these unneeded
workers. Japan's unemployment insurance program has been designed to spread the burden without causing stress for workers. In the
United States, a worker can't receive unemployment benefits until
she has officially lost her job. Only after she has been thrown out on
the street can she take her discharge papers and line up with all the
other ex-workers in some dismal government office. In Japan, in contrast, benefits can be paid by the government to the company, not the
employee. The business keeps the worker on its payroll, but uses the
government money to offset the salary. This Japanese worker is essentially on the public dole, just like the person receiving unemploy-

ment checks in America. But the Japanese worker never knows it. She retains the respect, the stature, and the self-esteem that come from having a job. She avoids the pain and stress of being laid off. And the employer gets to retain the services of an experienced and loyal worker without the disruption of severance and rehiring. As a result, the social costs of unemployment are significantly mitigated.

For all these reasons, Japan as a country, and the Japanese people as individual customers and consumers, have made a commitment to keep people employed. Downsizing is not generally an option—not even in response to a business cataclysm as severe as the Plaza Accords. Which brings us back to that indoor beach.

ONE OF THE JAPANESE industrial giants that was knocked for a loop in September of 1985 by the new, stronger yen was NKK Steel. Various parts of the company suffered to different degrees, but the blow perhaps fell hardest on NKK's Marine Engineering Division, which had a huge shipyard in Kawasaki. Among other products, NKK's shipyard turned out icebreakers, those heavy-hulled steel giants that smash through shipping lanes each spring to clear the ice floes and open the seas for commercial transit. NKK was, in fact, the Rolls-Royce of icebreakers. Its ships were state-of-the-art in design, in materials, in reliable performance under difficult conditions.

This wasn't just an accident. For one thing, NKK's shipyard had a team of veteran workers, many with twenty years' experience or more—well-paid, well-trained, and proud of their products. For another, NKK devoted more money and manpower to research and engineering than any other builder of icebreakers. It maintained laboratories where engineers studied icebergs, glaciers, and sheet ice so that they could devise the best designs for smashing same. It had computer-controlled welding machines that could join two sheets of metal so smoothly it was hard to find the seam. It had big test tanks—bigger than a house—where new models of icebreaker design could be subjected to new ordeals of wind, wave, and snow.

Still, the leap in the strength of the yen after 1985 looked like a devastating blow to Japan's leading producer of icebreakers. After a burst of orders in the early 1980s, global demand for new icebreakers was declining. Since icebreakers were almost always priced in dollars, NKK's ships suddenly cost buyers about twice as much as they had before. That is, a shipping company that went to, say, Norway to buy its new icebreakers found that it could buy two Norwegian-built ships for the price of one in Japan. Even with its reputation of advanced testing and design, NKK couldn't compete against a 100 percent price advantage. There wasn't enough distinction between different makes of icebreaker for NKK to make its ships competitive at the higher price.

NKK's shipbuilding arm, like other Japanese exporters, could try to make up the difference by cutting costs. Indeed, the parent company did some of that, selling the company baseball team and merging some manufacturing operations. But the major cost factor was labor. And for a Japanese firm like NKK Steel, there could be no labor reductions. Slowly, reluctantly, the corporate brass concluded that there was no way a Japanese firm could be competitive in the global icebreaker business any longer. NKK's Marine Engineering division would have to find some other product to sell.

At a meeting of the division's eighty marine engineers, top management announced that the division would be given ten years to find some new product that would restore it to profitability. Nobody would be laid off in the interim, but workers were expected to find a way to channel their shipbuilding skills into other ventures. Financing was not much of a problem, because NKK, like most Japanese firms, maintained cash reserves just to meet such emergencies. The parent company, and its various banks, would absorb losses and provide investment capital as needed while the division figured out what to do next.

But what can a shipyard sell, if it can't sell ships? Everybody at the shipyard, from the division director to the lowliest dock sweeper, was put to work pondering that question. The engineers began by looking at the kinds of skills their unit had developed over the decades. The first and most obvious skill the shipyard had was welding. Building a ship involves welding large steel plates as seamlessly as possible, and NKK had perfected various computer-aided tricks to enhance high-performance welding. So the company began looking for other products that required large welded steel boxes resistant to weather and tides.

The division's first new product was a fish farm—a large steel box that could be lowered into a river or bay to serve as a hatchery for commercial fish-farming operations. As it turned out, the fish-hatchery business is so low-tech that NKK's finely honed computerized welding skills amounted to overkill; there was nothing NKK could provide that existing fish farm makers weren't already producing.

From this experience, the engineers concluded that they needed to find a big welded product that encompassed high technology. At a brainstorming session, somebody suggested limousines—those long, long stretch limousines with an engine in front, a long rectangular box in the middle for driver and passengers, and the trunk and rear axle assembly at the back. The theory was that NKK could buy somebody else's limousine, saw it in half, weld a long passenger section between front and back, and remarket the product as an even longer limousine. As it turned out, the NKK limousines did have some of the finest, smoothest welding ever seen in the auto industry. Still, it was almost impossible to compete, because limousines from established automobile companies like Honda and Toyota somehow turned out to have better handling and suspension than the cars built by an icebreaker company.

A series of such false starts made for rough going at NKK. In the first three years after the Plaza Accords, the Marine Engineering Division lost about $15 million in its struggle to find something to sell. And yet every employee was still on the job.

Those initial failures prompted a reevaluation of the particular skills NKK's shipyard could bring to new markets. Welding—even the world's finest welding—clearly was not enough. What did the division have that nobody else did? One obvious answer was those huge test tanks, where model icebreakers were subjected to ice, snow, and driving waves. The machinery that made waves in those tanks was in fact proprietary NKK technology, developed by engineers on the spot to meet specific test needs. After years of tinkering, they had developed machinery that could produce perfect waves, one after another, of almost any size. These man-made whitecaps could wash across the surface of the tank at perfectly regular intervals, or in random bursts, like the ocean running before a fickle wind. Gradually, the engineers came to realize that making waves could be their meal ticket. Unable to sell ships, the Marine Engineering Division would sell waves instead.

There are some countries in the world where it might not be instantly obvious that there is a market for man-made waves that replicate the rolling sea. But the application of this technology was a little more obvious in Japan, because Japan is a country that is wild about theme parks simulating natural experiences.

There are indoor golf courses in Japan, for example. You stand in a bedroom-sized enclosure and swat a real ball with real clubs toward a computer-controlled screen that moves down the course of your choice, automatically following the flight of your shot. These virtual golf games come complete with virtual wind and virtual sound. When I played the simulated Pebble Beach course at one of these operations, the sound system produced virtual splashes—in stereo, yet—whenever the computer decided that I had driven my ball into the sea.

At other amusement centers you can play a similar game of simulated ice hockey, smashing a real puck with a real stick toward a movie screen, where a simulated goalie moves to block your shot. There are indoor cliffs where you don technical rock-climbing gear and scale man-made rock faces. At an amusement park called Tokyo Roof, I once went indoor sky-diving: Decked out in a flight suit, padded gloves, and an oversized crash helmet, I leaped off the edge of a narrow platform into a twenty-foot abyss—and found myself suspended safely in midair by the eighty-miles-per-hour blast of wind from an industrial-strength fan set into the floor far below.

Looking at all these other simulated-nature theme parks, the NKK engineers hit on their inspiration: They would use their wave-making skills to build a simulated ocean. Japanese surfers, after all, were willing to travel far and wait days or weeks for the perfect wave. A man-made beach could provide predictably perfect waves hour after hour, day after day. Since the Marine Engineering Division had already been contracted to do some construction and pipe-laying at more traditional (that is, outdoors) water parks in Japan, there were people on staff who knew what kind of attractions a man-made beach should be expected to offer. To set their project apart from other water parks and beach resorts in Japan, the NKK folks decided to use their vaunted welding skills to build a massive steel box–that is, to put their beach resort indoors.

In 1991, the Marine Engineering Division entered and won a companywide competition to find the best use for the chunk of real estate in Kawasaki that had been the home of the NKK baseball team. Then they went to work around the clock for a year, and in 1992 the indoor beach, Wild Blue Yokohama, opened to the public. It had an artificial ocean big enough to hold several hundred swimmers and a few dozen surfers at the same time. It had an artificial rain forest, with cool lagoons and rushing waterfalls. It had a small nest of water-slides–a required item at any water park in Japan–and a series of hot tubs of varying sizes. It had that big man-made river circling the building, and a lighting system that could create purple twilight and twinkling stars each evening. It didn't have any natural light, even on a sunny day, because a local zoning ordinance in the city of Kawasaki prohibited the necessary skylights. Of course, the folks who wrote that zoning law had never contemplated that it might be applied to an indoor beach resort, but this was irrelevant. In Japan, rules are rules.

Wild Blue Yokohama was popular almost from the start. It wasn't terribly surprising that people would line up to get to a warm, indoors, beachlike setting in the depths of winter. The surprise was that people lined up at Wild Blue's ticket window in the summer months as well. In fact, about 40 percent of the resort's customers today come during the summer months–particularly in August, when Japanese schoolkids get three weeks' vacation. The place was clever, different, and just plain fun.

It was not, however, profitable–although NKK now says that Wild Blue is just about breaking even each year. The problem was that the "resort" wasn't big enough. The building covered an entire city block, but was still too small to take in enough paying guests to cover the enormous fixed costs. Yet the concept was promising enough to encourage NKK's brass to try again. This time, the shipyard engineers took their wave-making machines to the city of Miyazaki, on Japan's southern island of Kyushu, and opened an indoor resort called Ocean Dome. This leviathan is four times as big as Wild Blue–bigger, in fact, than most football or baseball stadiums. It boasts the world's largest retractable roof, which produces huge savings in cooling and lighting bills during the summer. Its beach is real sand–six hundred tons of real sand. In addition to the artificial ocean, it has a dozen or more separate pools, and seventeen restaurants. It has become popular not only as a family "resort" but also as a dating spot for working singles–so popular that people line up hours before opening time to pay eighty dollars for a full day's admission. Although it is now under different ownership, the place has continued to thrive despite Japan's long 1990s recession.

Emboldened by their success at building a man-made seashore, the engineers went back to the drawing board to create a man-made mountain as well. In addition to those wave-making machines, after all, NKK also had snow-making and ice-making machinery for its test tanks. That is, this was a company that knew how to produce man-made snowstorms, inside a building. Was there a market for snowstorms? In Japan, there was. It was another new variety of amusement park: the indoor ski area.

There actually were half a dozen indoor ski areas in Japan in 1992, when NKK and Mitsui Real Estate started thinking about building a new ski resort. But the existing indoor resorts used a fake snow made of resin pebbles; you could slide over the stuff on a pair of skis, but it wasn't really skiing. NKK engineers took the concept to new heights. Next to a sprawling shopping center called LaLaPort in the Tokyo suburb of Funabashi, they built the biggest indoor ski resort in history and filled it with real snow, or at least man-made real snow. The place is called LalaPort SkiDome SSAWS, but everybody just calls it SSAWS, which is pronounced "zou-su" and is an acronym for "Ski Summer, Autumn, Winter, Spring." SSAWS is a twenty-five-story metal box, one end of which is propped up on 240-foot steel stilts. This created an indoor slope 1,500 feet long. Industrial-strength refrigeration units cool the whole structure to a temperature in the mid-thirties, and hundreds of NKK's patented snow-making nozzles in the ceiling deposit a fairly powdery snow to an average depth of about twelve inches on the slope. SSAWS is easy to spot, towering over the flat stretches of suburb, and easy to get to, if you happen to be in Tokyo. You just take the train headed for Tokyo Disneyland–countless signs point the way in the Tokyo train and subway stations–and ride four stops past the Magic Kingdom to the station called Minami Funabashi, or South Funabashi.

The indoor ski hill is one broad run, about one hundred yards wide, with two high-speed quad chairlifts, one on each side. Once at the top, you have to make a choice: one half of the slope is fairly steep, and rated an "advanced" run. This side of the hill is steep enough and snowy enough to develop actual moguls. The other half is a more gradual beginner run. A single run takes about forty seconds to get down, and the chair back up takes three minutes or so. The man-made snow is pretty close to the real thing—wet, cold, and slippery—but there's not enough of it. When you fall at SSAWS you can definitely feel the concrete slope underneath that foot of snow.

Except for the novelty of skiing in the middle of summer half an hour from downtown, I found SSAWS to be pretty boring. But our kids loved the place, particularly in the summer, and kept dragging us back. And we kept going, despite lift tickets that cost about forty-five dollars for adults and thirty-five dollars for children. My kids obviously weren't the only people who fell in love with SSAWS. The place took off almost from the first day and has been a profitable venture, despite what must be the world's largest refrigeration bill. Even better, from NKK's standpoint, the idea of indoor skiing caught on with a rather surprising group of people—tourists from Hong Kong, Singapore, and other nations of Southeast Asia. Now the Marine Engineering Division is taking its snow-making capability to new indoor resorts in those countries. For the one in Hong Kong, they didn't even have to worry about putting in a ski slope; people pay just for the pleasure of walking inside and playing in snow.

In September of 1995, on the tenth anniversary of the Plaza Accords, the dollar was weaker than ever—it could buy less than half as much in global markets as the 1985 dollar. But NKK's Marine Engineering Division was no longer in crisis. The company had turned away from the icebreaker business and found new ways to be profitable; in fact, the division had more employees in 1995 than it had had a decade earlier. The original effort had been simply to avoid downsizing, but by holding onto its people, and taking advantage of their skills, the company had managed to upsize instead.

The innovation and entrepreneurship that helped NKK reinvent itself are not unique to NKK, or to Japanese companies, or to East Asia. The same kind of risk-taking and ingenuity is rampant in the United States and is a major reason why the American economy had such a spectacular decade in the 1990s. But the plot that played out at NKK would probably not have happened in the same way in America. A U.S. company facing the loss of its global market would most likely have "downsized," laying off most workers and struggling to rebuild. Some of the unemployed workers might then have formed a new company to launch new business ventures, and the net result would have been roughly the same as in Japan: workers finding new markets for their old skills. But in Japan, because of the basic loyalty any group must show to its members, the happy result was achieved with no layoffs, and thus with far less social tension and upheaval.

In other East Asian countries as well, businesses, like all other groups, are expected to show a high level of loyalty toward their employees. These nations have also created wage structures and government programs—many of them based on the Japanese model—designed to let companies adapt to changes in local or global markets without resorting to layoffs. They have made serious, national commitments to full employment, partly because of economic calculations and partly because their cultural heritage demands it.

We Americans celebrate our system, and with good reason—it has worked. We've built the richest society in history. Accordingly, the repeating pattern of boom and bust, of market setbacks followed by layoffs followed by new start-ups, is accepted as a painful but necessary aspect of the business cycle. The Harvard economist Joseph Schumpeter is still an object of veneration in the business schools for his famous comment that capitalism is a continuing process of "creative destruction." But there are side effects. The destruction of jobs, careers, and companies, no matter how creative in the long run, leaves people lost along the way. Most victims will pick themselves up, dust themselves off, and start all over again. But it is inevitable that some whose careers are creatively destroyed will stumble into marital discord, poverty, crime, drug abuse, and other social ills. This is the price of the system, a price that is reflected, of course, in America's rates of crime, divorce, drug use, etc. (Schumpeter himself wrote that capitalism will eventually disintegrate, because societies will no longer be willing to pay the social price.) Today's East Asians are capitalists, all right, but they've made it clear they don't want to pay the price of recurring destruction. And so they are searching for methods—like the ones just discussed at Toyota and NKK Steel—to practice capitalism without sacrificing the overall goal of social har-mony.

The effort to do that–to meld world-class capitalism with a tradi-tional culture that emphasizes harmonious group relations and avoidance of confrontation–has been labeled "Confucian capitalism." It shows up in those low unemployment rates (which don't go up much even during recession), in the feeling of "family" that is delib-erately cultivated and nurtured in Asian corporations, in the tendency to engage in long-term shared ventures based on personal relations rather than a signed contract, and the vigorous effort to resolve busi-ness disputes through meetings and negotiations rather than the liti-gation that Confucius himself warned against. Perhaps the most striking sign, though, of how much Asian cultural patterns have influ-enced the Asian form of capitalism is the level of economic equality in Asian nations during the past two decades of explosive growth.

Economists who study newly industrializing economies have gen-erally found a familiar pattern in fast-growing countries: the rich get richer. But in the high-performing Asian economies, the results have been quite different. "Contrary to the conventional wisdom," notes a 1996 study by The Brookings Institution in Washington, "in East Asia rapid economic growth has been associated with relatively low, and declining, levels of income in equality. . . . Though economic growth need not necessarily reduce poverty, the experience of the HPAEs suggests that growth can alleviate poverty." To put it simply, every-body got richer. There is a handful of new billionaires in Asia–and there are hundreds of millions of new members of the middle class. At the dawn of the Asian century, East Asia has brought more people from poverty to middle-class status in a shorter period of time than any other region in history. China, which had nearly a billion resi-dents close to subsistence level two decades ago (and still has hun-dreds of millions of poor people), now has the biggest middle class on earth.

There are several tools that development experts use to measure income equality. The best-known and most widely used is the so-called GINI ("growth and income inequality") coefficient. The eight Asian high-performers rank better than every other developing coun-try by this measure–in other words, they have managed to distribute the total of all national income more evenly than other developing na-

tions have. Another gauge of equality is called "comparing the quin-
tiles"–that is, measuring how much wealth the richest 20 percent of
the population has, and comparing that to the wealth of the bottom
20 percent. By this standard, too, East Asia has a more equal distribution of wealth than any other developing region. At a time when the
Western developed nations have generally seen increased inequality–
that is, the richest 20 percent controlling more and more of the
country's wealth–East Asia has been moving toward a more even distribution–a shared prosperity across the board.

The countries of Asia have used various mechanisms to reduce income disparities. The wage structure and employment system described above tend to keep everyone in a job, not only in the boom
years but also when the economies face bank failures, currency
crises, and flat growth. As the overall economies have been industrializing, governments have also put considerable investment into rural
development, so that the lives of country people can improve along
with those of workers in the cities. Wage levels, in Confucian style,
generally depend on age rather than position; thus people in Asian
countries tend to be about as rich as others their age. The standard
Western disparity of wealth between city and suburb, between one
neighborhood and another doesn't really exist in Asian countries.
When I was a reporter in Japan, one of my bosses, visiting from
Washington, asked me to take him to "Tokyo's richest neighborhood."
I had to tell him that, outside of the Imperial Palace, there really isn't
such a place. Most neighborhoods are pretty much like most others.
(He didn't believe me, of course, and probably still wonders how he
could have made a dumb klutz like me his Tokyo Bureau chief.)

Further, the difference between what average workers earn and
what their bosses earn seems to be vastly smaller in Asian countries.
This is a little hard to measure, because most Asian companies don't
report corporate compensation the way public companies in Western
countries do. But various organizations have done studies in Japan,
the richest Asian nation, and it's clear that Japanese companies maintain much greater parity between the pay at the top level and at the
bottom.

Business Week magazine, which does an annual study of chief executives' pay, reports that the average American chief executive at the

end of 1990s makes about 157 times as much as the average American factory worker. In Japan, the gap is much smaller: the CEO earns a little less than 30 times what he pays his factory hands. American chief executives' average annual pay is more than 100 times what an average American teacher earns; in Japan, the ratio is just 20:1. The corporate jets, the country homes, the $100 million stock option packages that American business leaders now consider de rigueur are considered shocking in Japan. To pay that much to one "member" of a company would undermine the sense of family, the group harmony, that is essential to any corporate entity in that group-oriented society.

These mechanisms have not eliminated all disparities of wealth in East Asia. But they have made everyone feel more equal. In opinion surveys in Japan, more than 90 percent of the population defines itself as "middle class." In Korea, the figure is just as high. (In the United States, in contrast, about 60 percent call themselves "middle class," with the rest divided between upper and lower and variations on the two.)

After the chain of currency crises that struck Thailand, Malaysia, Indonesia, and South Korea in the summer and fall of 1997, there was a fairly bitter clash between the values of Western-style "creative destruction" and the gentler employment practices of East Asia. The International Monetary Fund, an organization that was set up by the rich countries of the West and Japan specifically to deal with the currency crises in second- and third-world countries (and thus to make sure that these countries would be able to repay the loans they receive from the West and Japan), moved into the affected Asian countries and began imposing Western standards of "efficiency." The IMF ordered, in effect, that the Asians impose Western-style management rules—which meant sweeping layoffs and corporate blood-letting on a massive scale. The Asians tried to resist. They argued that Western practices like downsizing and restructuring would inevitably bring with them Western social problems like crime, family breakdown, and drug abuse. In the Western press, this was reported as dogged and mindless resistance to the inevitable. The Asians, in contrast, saw themselves fighting to maintain a system that had worked.

The result of all these efforts at "shared prosperity" is that people in East Asian countries–virtually all the people–get the feeling that they have a personal stake in the well-being of the overall society. If their country gets richer, all the citizens–not just the select few in the prime minister's office or the executive suite–will get richer along with it. If the state as a whole is safe and civil, all the citizens will be safer and more secure. In essence, this is a modern version of Confucius's teaching that life's central loyalties run both ways. Individuals have an obligation to mold a harmonious society, and the society has an equal obligation to take care of each of its individual members.

In the United States, a certain underclass of (primarily) young people has evidently decided that they have no personal stake in the larger society. On a strictly individual basis, there's a certain perverse logic to this point of view. Since society has essentially ignored these kids, they've concluded that their best bet is to reach out and grab what they can. "In our toughest neighborhoods, on our meanest streets," says a close observer of contemporary American trends, Bill Clinton, "we have seen a stunning and simultaneous breakdown of community, family, and work. . . . We must give people, especially our young people, something to say 'Yes' to."

Across East Asia today, two billion people are saying "Yes" to a social and cultural system that gives them a personal interest in enhancing the good of the community. At the same time, it must be said that the people of Asia also know which social system they are saying "No" to. For they have been taught–by their governments, their schools, their politicians, and their mass media–that Asia must steadfastly avoid the social problems they think they see across the Pacific. The one thing they don't want to do, the one mistake they definitely don't want to make, is to build a society in the image of contemporary America. For the "America" that is portrayed in contemporary Asian pop culture is a country that no American would ever want to live in.

EIGHT

"Too Much Freedom"

WITH HIS NICELY TAILORED PIN-STRIPED SUIT, his gleaming black wingtips, the butter-soft brown leather attaché in his hand, and the distinguished traces of silver in his jet-black hair, the Japanese banker was the picture of success as he strolled down Madison Avenue in midtown Manhattan. He was evidently thinking about some business deal as he walked, for suddenly he bumped right into a young man coming along in the opposite direction. The impact caused the young American to drop a bag he was carrying, and a bottle of wine smashed to the sidewalk.

The American was livid. He pulled himself up to full height, towering over the Japanese visitor, and screamed angrily in the banker's face: "You idiot! Why can't you watch where you're going? Now look what you did—you smashed my Lafite-Rothschild! That's a two-hundred-and-fifty-dollar bottle of wine, buster. We were going to have it tonight! And you broke it!" Stunned, embarrassed, and not a little frightened, the Japanese banker backed away, but the angry young man was right on top of him. "It was your fault, pal," he shouted. "It's two hundred and fifty bucks! What are you going to do about it?"

Unable to think of any English phrase he knew to handle this situation, the shaking Japanese visitor quickly pulled out three hundred-dollar bills and handed them over, bowing feverishly and apologizing over and over for his carelessness. To the banker's enormous relief, the young man pocketed the bills and stalked off, without another word. Of course, there was no reason for the American to hang around, because his scam had worked. That sidewalk collision was no accident, and the spilled wine was no Rothschild. It was $2.99 rotgut, purchased specifically for the purpose of shaking down a rich Japanese tourist on the New York streets.

The "bottle man" had claimed another hapless victim.

I have walked Madison Avenue countless times and never encountered the bottle man myself, but then, I don't look like an easily intimidated Asian tourist. I first heard about the bottle man in Tokyo, in the classroom of Kazama Hiroko, a consultant who makes her living teaching Japanese travelers how to protect themselves against the many perils awaiting any Asian visitor to the United States (and particularly any Asian who looks as if he might be rich). "We Japanese are completely lacking in the techniques required to survive in New York," Kazama said at the seminar I attended. The tightly clutched handbag, the wallet stuffed into an inside pocket, the quick look around before stepping into an alley—all of those basic urban skills, Kazama pointed out, are alien to the Japanese, who are accustomed to safety and security on any street at any time of day or night. "It's not like home," she insisted. "Once you arrive in America, you have to be on guard at all times. The pickpockets, the flimflam artists, the muggers—they are professionals."

Kazama had countless lessons as hair-raising as the tale of the bottle man—some from her own experience, she said, but most drawn from the Japanese mass media, where stories of peril in America have long been a staple. There was the notorious case of the Nissan executive arriving at Kennedy Airport on his first trip to the United States. Exhausted from jet lag and confused by the rush and hustle of New York, the Japanese visitor was delighted when he met a polite

American who seemed to know his way around. The young man explained that New York cab drivers get angry, and sometimes violent, if a customer uses large bills to pay the fare. He thoughtfully offered to help the Japanese visitor find change. Gratefully, the executive handed over four $100 bills to be changed. He never saw the polite young American again.

Of course, the Japanese don't have to sign up for one of Kazama's $200 seminars to hear horror stories about America. Like the rest of East Asia, Japan has an intense, ongoing love-hate relationship with the colossus across the Pacific. There is general admiration for America's youthful vigor, its flair for invention, its constant willingness to try new ideas. In Japan as in other Asian countries, the United States is valued and respected as the region's largest market and, for the past half century, its military defender. But in terms of civility and public safety, America can be a terrifying place for Asians. The popular culture milks these terrors for all they are worth.

Most adults in East Asia could name the U.S. president and his wife. Certainly, there are far more Asians who could name Bill and Hillary Clinton than there are Americans who could name, say, the prime minister of Japan or the first lady of South Korea. And of course, the great names of Hollywood and the music world are widely familiar—Schwartzenegger, Cruise, Mariah Carey, Madonna. Beyond that, though, the best-known Americans in Asia are those whose stories tend to confirm all the worst stereotypes of a dangerous, decadent society: O. J. Simpson, Lorena Bobbit, Timothy McVeigh, the Unabomber. Murder, mayhem, drug abuse, sexual harassment, racial intolerance—that's what Asians know about America, because that is the side of America that the media and the politicians like to dwell on.

In America, politicians of every stripe describe their country as the light of the world: "the shining city on a hill" (Ronald Reagan), "the last, best hope for man on earth" (George Bush), "the dream of free men and women everywhere" (Bill Clinton). In East Asia, though, this shining city is just as often depicted as a dark swamp of drugs, downsizing, dirty slums, and daily violence that has become so routine people adjust their lives around it rather than putting a stop to it. The United States depicted in Asian media is a country where every third person you pass on the street is either unemployed, on drugs, packing a loaded pistol, planning a scam, or looking for a lawyer to beat the rap for killing his wife's teenaged lesbian lover.

This image pops up everywhere. My family used to watch the weekly Japanese sitcom *Double Kitchen*, about a smart young office lady named Tomoko who has just married a junior executive in her company. Since the young couple couldn't possibly afford to buy a house in Tokyo, they move in with the groom's parents–a standard pattern for Japanese newlyweds. This causes countless cross-family and cross-generational crises, all of which tend to come to a head when both Tomoko and her mother-in-law are making dinner (hence *Double Kitchen*). The program seemed to be realistic, and it was usually funny, so we almost never missed it.

One year on January 1, the biggest television-watching day of the year in Japan, the network put on a special two-hour version of the show: "Double Kitchen Goes Hawaiian." In this episode, the entire household–the young couple, the groom's parents, and his assorted siblings–took a trip to Hawaii for the New Year's holiday. It turned out to be an eventful vacation. Since there's no tipping in Japan, the family naturally forgot to tip the bellman when they arrived at their hotel in Waikiki; the bellman, a huge black man, was depicted as ranting, raving, and terrorizing the whole group until our heroine Tomoko figured out what was wrong and paid him twenty dollars. The next morning, the family awoke to find two armed burglars in their suite. The day after that, Tomoko was pawed on the street by a drunken American groper. On the last day of the vacation, the mother-in-law was handcuffed and hauled away to jail because she had accidentally wandered onto a corner where the Honolulu police were setting up a drug bust. Just your typical American holiday.

It isn't only TV, either. While in Japan, I became a huge fan of *mahnga*, the ubiquitous comic-book magazines that sell tens of millions of copies every week. It seems to be conventional wisdom in the United States that Japan's "adult comic books" are routinely "adult" in the sense of being filthy, but this is not accurate. There are some filthy *mahnga*–so bad that stores won't carry them, and you have to buy them at vending machines. But the vast majority of Japanese comics are family fare. Some are funny, and some are serious novels–serial novels, really, like the one-chapter-per-month novels that Dickens and Thackeray used to write for Victorian magazines. I was particularly taken with the enormously popular weekly comic *Section Chief Shima*, about a junior executive named Shima Kosaku, who works for a giant electronics firm and fights a never-ending battle for truth, profits, and the Japanese way.

In one extended episode, Section Chief Shima is dispatched to America to oversee his company's acquisition of a giant Hollywood movie studio (just like the acquisitions Sony and Matsushita had made in real life). One thing that deeply concerns the young executive is the possibility of a U.S. backlash if an Asian company buys a famous American firm (just like the reaction to the Sony and Matsushita purchases in real life). But an American-based executive tells Shima he need not worry: "The government won't be a problem, because we've already put a half-dozen ex-congressmen on the payroll, and they are lobbying for us." This exchange didn't bother me excessively, because it's probably what big companies actually do when they plan an acquisition. But it was disturbing to see what happened to Section Chief Shima personally during his stay in Los Angeles. When he sets out to see the beach, his rented Ford breaks down. When he tries to negotiate his business deal, an employee of the U.S. branch of his company sells corporate secrets to a competitor. When he walks outside his hotel, he's mugged on the sidewalk. Just your typical American business trip.

Our family grew increasingly angry at this depiction of a dirty, dangerous, dishonest America, partly because we found it hard to avoid, anywhere in Asia. Even those ingenious Japanese amusement parks picked up on the theme. One day when school was off for some holiday, I took a couple of our kids on a journey north of Tokyo to a theme park called Tobu World Square. The Tobu railroad company, which runs the lines linking Tokyo with Nikko National Park, Japan's equivalent of Yellowstone, was looking for a way to boost its ridership during the winter months, when few people ventured up to mountainous Nikko. And so, on some vacant land it owned near the park, the company built a model of the world—or at least, models of many of the world's most famous wonders, all about one-tenth actual size. Buckingham Palace is there, complete with models of the Beefeater guards. There are models of St. Peter's Basilica, the Eiffel Tower, the Great Wall of China, the Sphinx and the pyramids, and Tokyo's central train station.

Among the wonders of the world depicted in reduced scale at Tobu World Square is an attractive model of lower Manhattan. The creators replicated the Statue of Liberty, Ellis Island, Battery Park, the two towering World Trade Center buildings, and busy, bustling Wall Street. On the streets of New York you could see businessmen racing to the stock market, cabbies picking up fares, women walking their dogs, kids jumping the curbs on skateboards, vendors selling hot dogs and pretzels–a pleasant and fairly accurate doll-sized picture of a day in the life of that great American metropolis. But as I was pointing out these elements of American life to my kids, I noticed something else– something we hadn't seen in the park's models of London, Paris, or Tokyo. Down on the New York street, two armed desperadoes were shown racing out of a bank, with stolen cash dropping from the bags over their shoulders. Policemen were firing at the robbers, terrified pedestrians were racing for shelter, and a bank guard was lying on the sidewalk in a pool of blood. Just your typical working day in New York City.

PERHAPS WE SHOULD HAVE been pleased to have these constant opportunities to see ourselves as others see us–to know what mental image people had in mind when we told them we came from the United States of America. In fact, though, it was infuriating to confront this badly distorted picture of our country. I frequently got the chance to appear on Japanese TV talk shows, where the United States–its politics, its problems, its social structure–was among the most popular topics. I regularly blasted the mass media for conveying such a dark and dire image. "You guys on Japanese TV always show the rapes and robberies," I would say, "but you never show Boy Scouts cleaning the parks, or church groups making box lunches for the elderly, or business people taking time out to volunteer in the schools. Those are all parts of American life, too." Generally, the host of the show would nod solemnly and agree with me that the media were doing a great disservice; then he'd turn to some other guest and start talking about the Rodney King case, or Jon Benet Ramsey.

I think it is fair to say that one reason for this recurrent need to run down the United States is jealousy. It's true that the Asian century is coming, but the fact is that the American century is not quite over yet. For now, the United States remains the dominant military, political, and financial power on Earth. When an Asian country faces a currency crisis, more often than not it still has to come running to Washington for emergency help. For contemporary Asians, who are eager to be recognized as "just as good" as any Western nation, pointing out American social problems may be a way to equal things out. America has a stronger army, the Asians tell each other, but we have safer streets. (This chip-on-the-shoulder attitude is not unknown in Europe, too. In the summer of 1997, when the world's richest nations held their annual G-7 summit in Denver, the visiting heads of state quickly grew tired of hearing Bill Clinton declare—as he did over and over again that week—that the United States had the world's healthiest economy. Clinton was telling the truth, but nonetheless, it grated. On the last day of the summit, British prime minister Tony Blair summed up his feelings about America in the *Financial Times:* "They kept telling us that the American system was the best—and then they would warn us that we'd better not go outside the hotel after dark.") Because the stereotype of the United States as the land of drugs and crime is so strong in East Asia, the countries regularly use "America" or "American values" as a ready scapegoat to rationalize their own social problems. The argument is that dangerous ideas from the wild-and-woolly West seep into pristine Asian cultures, and the rot spreads. (For this reason, Singapore refers to its regulations seeking to limit use of the Internet as "anti-pollution" measures.) This provides a convenient explanation when something goes wrong: It was America's fault.

I spent some time in South Korea during a period when the entire country was shocked and horrified by the crimes of a twenty-three-year-old college student named Park Han-sang. Never much of a student, the young man had been dissolute on campus and run up gambling debts in excess of twenty thousand dollars. He pleaded with his father, a prosperous pharmacist, to send the money, but the parents refused. So young Park attacked his parents in their sleep, stabbed and slashed their bodies, and then burned the house down to destroy the evidence. When he was caught—a nurse treating him for

burns found his hair soaked with his parents' blood—the case became
the chief topic of national conversation for months. "Such a violent
crime proves that filial piety is completely lost," said a despairing professor at Sungkyunkwan University, the Korean college that special-
izes in Confucian ethics. "It represents the end of our society's value
system."

And why did this young Korean, a graduate of Korean schools that
had taught him Confucian ideals of respecting elders, become a parent killer? The mass media had a ready answer for that one: He had
gone to college in the United States, at Fresno Pacific. There he became enamored of what he evidently thought was the American college scene—guns, knives, drugs, and gambling. He even had a plastic
surgeon round out his eyes to make himself look more American. He
had been infected, in short, with American values—no wonder the boy
became a killer! "Park's case shows vividly," the *Korea Times* said in
an editorial, "how dangerous going abroad for study is for young people who are immature." The media also decided that the means of the
murder—death by stabbing, followed by a large fire—was something
Park had learned from watching a Hollywood murder movie on the
plane after his parents had ordered him to return home from school.

It wasn't just Park Han-sang, either. The Korean press followed
this sensational story with a series of reports on the so-called parachute kids—young Koreans who had "parachuted" out of the highly
disciplined, workaholic Korean lifestyle to take up lives of panhan-
dling and drug-dealing in Los Angeles and other American cities.
Here was further proof (as if any were needed) that traditional
Confucian ethics were being undermined by the contagious bad
habits of the West. This uproar did not die down until about a year after the Park case, when the newspapers came upon a gang of self-
styled Buddhists in Seoul who had decided that their religion
required them to murder all the rich people they could find. After
each killing, the group would meet before a Buddhist altar and eat the
powdered bones of their victims—a practice evidently followed by
some ancient Korean religious sects. Somehow, the media were never
able to blame these bizarre habits on America.

It's a little presumptuous for me, an American journalist, to criticize the Asian media for concentrating on the dark side of American

life. After all, we in the American mass media also dwell endlessly on horror stories about the United States; one reason the Asian media jump so hard on this type of news is that they are simply following the lead of American print and broadcast journalists. When some particularly horrible mass murder, or bombing, or celebrity trial launches the American media into full-scale wretched-excess mode–something that seems to happen two or three times a year nowadays–the rest of the world's newspapers, magazines, and trash TV shows tend to follow the story as well. In Asia, naturally enough, the American horror stories that get the most extensive play are those involving Asians, particularly those sad cases when some Asian immigrant, student, or tourist is attacked or murdered in the United States.

One of the most influential news events of the 1990s in terms of molding the image of the United States among Asians took place on a cool October evening in Baton Rouge, Louisiana. A sixteen-year-old Japanese foreign-exchange student named Hattori Yoshihiro was heading to a Halloween party with a group of his American classmates. Yoshi's costume was a fancy white tuxedo; he was supposed to be John Travolta in *Saturday Night Fever*. The boy walked up to the door of an ordinary suburban home, a home decorated with skeletons, pumpkins, and similar Halloween paraphernalia.

According to trial testimony, a woman came to the door and was frightened by the teenager on her front step. She screamed for her husband, a butcher named Rodney Peairs; he raced to help, taking the precaution of picking up one of his guns along the way. Peairs stood in the doorway, pointed the gun at the smiling sixteen-year-old, and barked the word "Freeze!" We'll never know whether or not young Hattori understood what this command was supposed to mean. To a Japanese teenager who had lived in America for just two months, the English word "freeze" would probably suggest something having to do with ice and snow. In any case, the Japanese boy took another step forward. Peairs blasted him at point-blank range with a .44 magnum pistol, a gun powerful enough to kill an adult bear at a hundred yards. The Japanese boy died almost instantly. He still had a smile on his face; right to the end, he evidently thought all this was some kind of playful American Halloween tradition.

To the American news media, Hattori's death was just another death—one of about 16,000 deaths by gunfire that take place in the United States every year. That's about 44 such cases every day—far more than a daily newspaper or broadcast news show has room for. Young Hattori's killing made the Baton Rouge newspaper the next day, but it wasn't reported anywhere else. Lousiana's governor called the shooting "just one of those unfortunate things." The Associated Press didn't even bother to send the story to its clients outside Louisiana, on the grounds that nobody would consider this sad case to be a newsworthy event.

But it was newsworthy, of course, in Japan. I can still remember, vividly remember, the tone of disbelief and horror in the voice of Chikushi Tetsuya, Japan's equivalent of Tom Brokaw, when he announced the death of this cheerful teenager on the nightly news. "In America, this is called freedom," Chikushi said, his smooth announcer's voice suddenly shaking and broken. "Guns everywhere— this is called freedom. It's more like cancer." The newspapers and magazines picked up the cry: A completely innocent, unarmed boy could be shot to death in a suburban front yard, and Americans called it "an unfortunate thing." This was a horrendous tragedy—and Americans couldn't recognize that. "In America, shooting children is not even very unusual," the newscaster Chikushi said. The fatal shooting quickly became the top news item throughout East Asia. Gradually, the intense reaction overseas made the Baton Rouge case a news item in the United States as well. The four big American TV networks, which had completely ignored this routine killing when it happened, started giving it saturation coverage because of the response it had triggered in Asia.

Japan's initial state of amazement at the killing turned to anger and disgust a few months later when a jury in Baton Rouge acquitted Peairs of all charges in the case. Peairs himself expressed deep sadness about the boy's death, but insisted he had done the right thing. Jurors who were interviewed after the verdict said that they thought Peairs was a decent man who had done what any husband or father would do. That idea—that killing an unarmed teenager was a normal and responsible act—was denounced everywhere in Japan. The magazine *Shukan Post*'s editorial was titled "America: Six Children Shot Dead Every Day." It said, "That the man who shot a sixteen-year-old boy dead was not a gangster or a thief, but just an ordinary citizen—that is the most frightening thing about the whole case." Many Japanese, predictably, used the case for larger broadsides against America's social shortcomings. "With their economic weakness in the world and the tension between the races, Americans spend their lives full of anger and fear," opined Sotei Rinjiro, a Tokyo professor. "And they actually believe that their guns will protect them."

Another court case that made an almost equally forceful mark on both the Asian and American psyche involved another high school student—this time, an American teenager living in Asia. Michael Fay was an eighteen-year-old whose parents were divorced; his father worked in the United States and the boy lived with his mother and her new husband in a comfortable apartment in Singapore. There was a spate of vandalism in the upscale neighborhood where Fay lived, and Singapore police tracked it down to a group of students from the Singapore American School. Those formally accused included two Malaysians, one Chinese from Hong Kong, and two Americans, one of whom was Michael Fay. After nine days of police questioning, Michael Fay signed a confession to charges of spray-painting cars, throwing eggs at cars, and other acts. After police found several stolen street signs in his bedroom, he confessed as well to possessing stolen goods. Fay's parents flew in a British lawyer to defend him. Recognizing, though, that he would be convicted (almost everybody accused of a crime in Singapore is convicted), Fay pleaded guilty in court. The sentence for his various acts of vandalism was a $2,200 fine, four months in jail—and six lashes on the buttocks with a rattan cane.

The U.S. government and many American commentators denounced the sentence—at least, the caning aspect of it—as "brutal" and "torture." "Caning is an excessive penalty for a youthful nonviolent offender who pleaded guilty to reparable crimes against public property," protested the U.S. Embassy in Singapore. President Clinton personally asked Singapore to suspend the physical punishment. Singapore, an island state of three million people, found itself supporting a harsh and seemingly untenable position in a highly visible argument with the most powerful nation on Earth.

And then something remarkable happened. All over Asia, government officials and editorial writers began siding with Singapore against the United States. It wasn't that everybody favored caning; many Asian commentators were clearly sqeamish about the penalty Singapore had in mind for Michael Fay. The point was, rather, that the United States had long ago lost the moral authority to lecture other nations about crime and punishment. "It is rather mysterious," said a column in Japan's *Yomiuri Shimbun,* "that a country with 25,000 murders each year and one million of its citizens locked in jail for long terms would try to convince other nations to follow its advice on matters of crime." A column in the Seoul newspaper *Korea Times* compared Singapore to Los Angeles. Los Angeles has about twice the population of Singapore, but the American city had twenty times as many murders and thirty-eight times as many robberies. Who should be advising whom, the paper asked, on crime problems?

And then something even more remarkable happened. The American people, or at least a majority of them, seemed to be siding with Singapore as well. Opinion surveys showed that the American people, by a healthy margin, approved of what Singapore was doing to its young vandal. Even in Michael Fay's hometown in Ohio, the *Dayton Daily News* reported that people supported the caning by a ratio of two to one. Talk show hosts began wondering why America didn't cane its own youthful vandals. A conservative white Republican state legislator in Arizona and a liberal black Democratic city alderman in St. Louis both introduced legislation to authorize caning for young offenders in their jurisdictions. Clinton stood his ground in calling the punishment excessive, but the American people were clearly on a different wavelength.

All of which emboldened Singapore to use the Fay case as the vehicle for yet another round of its Asia-good, America-bad campaign. Singapore's justice minister defended his island nation's system of criminal law on the grounds that it served to "ensure that violent crime not spread to the same extent as it has in the United States." When an American columnist complained that the practice of lashing vandals was the product of "institutionalized racism practiced by Chinese leaders," Singapore's ambassador to the United States pointed out in reply that caning had been introduced to Singapore, and regularly employed, by its British colonial rulers. When Fay's father complained that the American boy has been singled out for harsh treatment, Singapore pointed out that Fay's codefendant from Hong Kong was sentenced to twice as many lashes. In a final brush-off, Singapore announced that, out of "respect" for the U.S. president, it would reduce Michael Fay's sentence–from six lashes to four.

On a warm April day in the courtyard of Singapore's Queenstown Remand Prison, Michael Fay received his painful, bloody punishment. He returned to Ohio shortly afterwards to contemplate various book and movie offers (none of which has yet come to fruition). In TV interviews back home, the young American took a stiff-upper-lip attitude toward the whole affair. He didn't insist on his innocence, and he refused to dwell on his punishment. He fairly quickly disappeared from public view. But the incident, and the reactions it provoked both in Asia and the United States, only served to strengthen the East Asians' conviction that they are doing the right thing about crime, while the United States has gone badly wrong.

THERE'S NO QUESTION that a lot of the America-bashing in East Asia can be traced to politics, or jealousy, or lingering anti-Western resentment dating back to the colonial era (which is, as we've noted, not very long ago in Asian countries). In the same way that American presidents–and heads of state everywhere, for that matter–tend to use foreign affairs as a means to change the subject when domestic conditions are criticized, so Asian leaders use the United States as their favorite target of convenience. If Western critics point out (accurately) that Asian nations have corrupt politicians and a sycophantic press, if Western governments complain (accurately) that the autocratic regimes in China, Singapore, and Indonesia routinely violate the human rights of their citizens–in those difficult moments, it is much easier for the powers that be to lash out at some American shortcoming than to face up to their own domestic problems. The Malaysian president, Mahathir; China's president, Jiang Zemin; and Singapore's strongman, Lee Kuan Yew, are past masters of the art of ducking the question by bringing up social problems in the United States. Each year the United States issues a "Human Rights Report," a thick volume documenting abuses of basic rights on a country-by-country basis. For the past few years, the government of China has responded by issuing a "Human Rights Report" of its own, citing prison conditions, racially motivated crimes, and pockets of poverty in the United States.

There is also a strong sense in Asia that the United States is often guilty of glaring hypocrisy in its efforts to change the way other countries do things. The American government criticizes China and North Korea for selling weapons to terrorist states in the Middle East. To which a North Korean diplomat, Kim Ming-ho, replies: "The United States is the world's largest seller of weaponry. It earns thousands of times more money selling guns, warships, and fighter planes than we do. We are called an evil nation, we are subjected to international trade boycotts, for doing the same thing America always does." Much the same reaction greets American complaints about human rights violations in Asia. Kimura Taro, a commentator for Japan's Fuji-TV network, mangled his metaphor a little but still made the point fairly clearly: "People who live in glass houses full of assault weapons and violent crimes should not throw the stone of human rights violations at others." But it would be a serious error to write off all criticism of the West as the product of envy or political manipulation. Many Asian critics of American ways are thoughtful people who find much to admire in Western civilization. Many of them, well-trained in the teachings of Confucius and Mencius, are deeply committed to democracy but disturbed by the social detritus they observe in America and other established democratic countries. Many of the Asians who comment on American society are conducting a serious argument about the right way, and the wrong way, to run a country. Americans (and Europeans, for that matter) who care about democracy and want to see it flourish really can't afford to ignore what these observers across the Pacific have to say. After all, as Confucius himself said, "If the government is wrong, and nobody dares say so—that's the one thing the could ruin a country."

One of the most outspoken critics of Western ways is the bright, amiable Singaporean diplomat we met in the first chapter of this book, Kishore Mahbubani. Mahbubani is a disciple of Lee Kuan Yew and no doubt shares the strongman's political interest in insisting that neat authoritarian rule is preferable to often disorderly democracy. But I would say, as a friend of Mahbubani's, that he is also a serious student of government and society. He has lived in two U.S. cities and deserves to be heard when he talks about the problems he perceives in America. He overstates his case, but many Americans seem to agree that there is a kernel of truth in what he has to say.

"In most Asian eyes," Mahbubani has written, "the evidence of real social decay in the United States is clear and palpable. Since 1960, the U.S. population has grown by 41 percent. In the same period, there has been a 560 percent increase in violent crimes, a 419 percent increase in illegitimate births, a 400 percent increase in divorce rates, a 300 percent increase in children living in single-parent homes, a more than 200 percent increase in teenage suicide rates, and a drop of almost 80 points in Scholastic Aptitude Test scores. A recent report by the United Nations Development Program also ranks the United States number one among industrialized countries in intentional homicides, reported rapes, and percentage of prisoners."

Mahbubani wrote that stinging indictment in 1994. Some of the indicators he cited—the number of violent crimes, the rates of teen suicide—have improved a bit since the mid-1990s. Further, there are laudable explanations for some of his unpleasant data. A key reason the average SAT score has gone down, for example, is that a much broader cross-section of the population is now taking the test and heading to college. Overall, however, Mahbubani has the trend lines about right. Few people who are old enough to remember life in the United States in 1960 would deny that American streets are less safe, and the American family unit is less stable, than it was at the end of the 1950s.

Like many Asians who have spent time in the United States, Mahbubani was particularly struck by the way Americans have come to live with crime, to accept it as a normal element of daily existence. He saw the bars on the windows, the Club on the steering wheels of parked cars, the free-ride programs at American universities to spare women the risk of walking across campus at night, and downtown streets virtually empty at night because people were afraid to venture outside after dark. And this, he argues, contradicts Americans' fundamental belief that they live in a free country.

This is a point that Asians continually make about the United States, and to a lesser extent about Western Europe as well. The coun-

tries that place the most stock on individual freedom have created societies where people are *politically* free but more or less prisoners in
their daily life. Mahbubani is hardly the only Asian observer saying
this, but he has said it perhaps more vividly than others. Here's the
argument:

> Today, many Americans who live in cities, or now even sub-
> urbs, live in little fortresses and leave their homes at night
> with some fear. Nothing can deprive people of their freedom
> more effectively than the fear of losing their own lives. It en-
> velops their minds and confines them to narrow spaces where
> they can be free of fear. Despite America's vast territory, each
> citizen is living and working within increasingly narrow con-
> fines to protect his or her personal well-being. . . . To any
> Asian, it is obvious that this is an enormous reduction of free-
> dom.
>
> A clear American paradox is that a society that places such
> a high premium on freedom has effectively reduced the physi-
> cal freedom of most Americans, especially those who live in
> large cities. They live in heavily fortified homes, think twice
> before taking an evening stroll around their neighborhoods,
> and feel increasingly threatened by random violence when
> they are outside. The have to carefully map out routes for
> travel, even in their cars, to ensure they make no wrong turn
> in Miami, New York, or Chicago.

I heard this same indictment time and again from Asian intellectu-
als and business or political leaders: The United States has let crime,
divorce, and deviant behavior go too far, the argument runs. By lifting
the rights of the individual onto a pedestal, America has reduced the
collective good of the overall society to a low priority. In the name of
freedom, individuals have been permitted to run amok, undermining
the freedom of the community as a whole. Naturally, our friend
Mahbubani has addressed this point as well: "American society has
swung too much in one direction: liberating the individual while im-
prisoning society. . . . What is striking is the Americans' failure to ask
fundamental questions such as: 'Is there too much freedom in
American society?' "

Not long ago, in Tokyo, I heard Malaysia's president Mahathir give a speech about the American form of democracy. It was a scathing, deliberately nasty attack, so one-sided and insulting that the U.S. ambassador, Walter F. Mondale, got up midway through and walked out of the room. I was tempted to do the same, but I was there as a reporter, and I thought it might be useful to tell American readers what others have to say about us. Here is some of what this Asian leader said:

> Democracies are only beginning to learn that too much freedom is dangerous. But they are not yet ready to do anything about it.
>
> The rights of the citizens are so honored that they can form armed militia with the expressed intention of overthrowing the Government by violence. Since all they have done is to wear uniforms and carry arms, including machine guns, in countries where there is no dress code and everyone has a right to carry arms, they cannot be considered as breaching the law....
>
> Whether the West admits it or not, David Koresh and the Jones cult were the products of the Western form of democracy. So also is the recent bombing in Oklahoma. The Michigan Militia Corps has as yet done no real harm. But you can bet that sooner or later they will be using those guns which they democratically own.
>
> Liberal democracy may be good for religious deviationists and cultists. The innocent victims may not think so. They have a right to their lives, too.
>
> For Asians, the community, the majority comes first. The individual and the minority must have their rights, but not at the unreasonable expense of the majority. The individuals and the minority must conform to the mores of society. A little deviation may be allowed, but unrestrained exhibition of personal freedom which disturbs the peace or threatens to undermine society is not what Asians expect from democracy.

We could go on at much greater length here quoting East Asians who are disturbed or appalled by what they see as "too much freedom" in the Western democracies in general and the United States in particular. The Asians themselves are likely to continue this line of criticism–partly because they believe what they are saying, and partly because they keep finding some Americans who agree with them on one point or another. Years after the Michael Fay caning incident, Lee Kuan Yew is still bragging to audiences all over the world about those polls showing that most Americans favored the flogging of the convicted American vandal. Mahathir finds himself featured on the Christian channels on American cable television when he complains that "abolition of religious instruction in [public] schools, while allowing absolute freedom of beliefs, has resulted in a loss of direction and the emergence of numerous cults, some of which are violent." The same man's criticism of the freedom to own guns resonates with a whole different group of Americans.

Moreover, there's a familiar ring to much of the Asian criticism. Western societies are full of anguished voices expressing deep concern about violence, drug use, and the breakdown of traditional families. Contrary to Mahbubani's assertion, many Americans do, in fact, "ask fundamental questions such as: 'Is there too much freedom in American society?'" In the United States, the question is generally stated in slightly different terms: What is the relationship between individual freedom and personal responsibility? At what point do my rights as a person give way to my duties as a citizen?

Still, the dark and dismal picture of American society that is commonplace today throughout East Asia has convinced many people there that the United States, despite its vibrant economy, is a decaying society caught in a downward spiral. Today's prosperous and confident Asians are arguing that America and other Western nations need to become more Asian. This idea is not strictly the creation of America's critics, either.

Kim Dae Jung, the Confucian scholar who led South Korea to democracy in the 1980s, is clearly not one of those given to denouncing the United States. (Indeed, it was only last-minute intervention from Washington that saved Kim's life when the Korean dictator gave him a death sentence for agitating against the regime in 1974.) But Kim, too, wants to see America change along Asian lines. "Instead of making Western culture the scapegoat," he wrote, "it is more appropriate to look at how the traditional strengths of Asian society can provide for a better democracy.... For the past several hundred years, the world has been dominated by Greek and Judaeo-Christian ideas and traditions. Now is the time for the world to turn to China, India, and the rest of Asia for another revolution in ideas."

In short, Kim Dae Jung and other neo-Confucianists in contemporary Asia are convinced that the United States is a sick society that needs to be treated with a healthy dose of the Asian way. But is there really an Asian way?

N I N E

Atogaki: What's Wrong with the Thesis of This Book

ATOGAKI IS A JAPANESE WORD made from the two characters meaning "after" and "written," and thus it is linguistically just about an exact counterpart of the English term "afterword." An *atogaki*, like an afterword, is a section near the end of a book where the author can restate the basic point, wrap up loose ends, slip in a few snide remarks about competing books, and so forth. But many Japanese authors include an *atogaki* for quite different purposes: They use the section, sometimes with remarkable honesty, to set forth the various flaws, fallacies, logical lapses, and factual lacunae in the book they've just written. It is not at all surprising that a serious book dealing with fairly complex ideas and historical processes will have some problems of this nature; a truly seamless argument is probably as rare as a truly cloudless sky. It is kind of surprising, though, that the author comes right out and identifies the problems.

I have always found it admirable that Japanese authors are willing to lay out the deficiencies in their own work for all to see. As the architect and builder of a book, the author is probably better able than anybody else to point out the places where the foundation is cracked, or where two joints in the frame don't meet as neatly as the blueprints say they should. But the normal tendency–completely understandable–is to patch over these rough places with a bit of verbal spackle and a coat of rhetorical paint and hope that everybody is so impressed with the overall grandeur of the structure that they don't notice the weak spots. At least, I always thought that was the normal human tendency of writers everywhere, until I began to find those sections at the back of Japanese books where the author explicitly laid out "What's Wrong with the Thesis of This Book."

Why do they do it? The first few times I came across an *atogaki* taking this honest approach, I decided that this must reflect some deep facet of the Japanese psyche–that self-effacing, constantly apologetic stance that I found in my next-door neighbor, Matsuda-san. As I've tried to show in these pages, Matsuda-san is a man of strong opinions, strongly held, but he invariably presents them in the gentlest, most courteous manner imaginable. And this is a fairly common Japanese trait.

But there were some shortcomings with this explanation of the *atogaki* phenomenon. For one thing, some Japanese authors who took the trouble to add a chapter on "What's Wrong with This Book" turned out to be fairly arrogant, unyielding figures when I met them, or saw them interviewed on TV. For another, some Westerners are just as inclined to let the audience know that they have fallen short. The young Princeton scholar Andrew Wiles is a good example. In 1993, Wiles suddenly became the most famous mathematician on Earth (if you don't believe it, name another) when he announced that he had found a solution to the most notorious conundrum in mathematics, Fermat's Last Theorem. Despite 350 years of effort by the world's greatest theorists, nobody had been able to provide a proof; but Andrew Wiles did it. Quick reviews by other mathematicians showed that his equations checked out, and Wiles became the toast of the mathematical world. And then, six months later, he issued a sort of *atogaki* to his historical achievement: He announced that the proof had a flaw. It was the intellectually honest thing to do, and I hope that any mathematician would have done the same–and, as is so often the case with people who choose the ethical path, his story has a happy ending. After nearly a year of intense thinking, he was able to eliminate the flaw, publish his miraculous proof, and take his place, unsullied, in the mathematical pantheon. This suggests another reason for the *atogaki:* Someone who cares more about getting at the truth than about selling her own theories will presumably be inclined to set forth the problems in those theories in the hope that others might produce even better theories.

Wiles has since said that he was "devastated" when he had to announce that his proof was faulty. But he also had a basic conviction that this famous problem was in his grasp; he knew his overall approach was right, so it couldn't really hurt to reveal that there was a small glitch in the works. In the same way, I've come to conclude that those Japanese authors who provide an *atogaki* are demonstrating not deference or apology but rather a fundamental toughness. In that sense, an *atogaki* is a display of confidence. Convinced that the house they have erected is structurally sound overall, the authors don't mind letting people know about particular parts that may need replacement or repair.

READERS WHO HAVE COME this far along in this book will have noticed by now that it has a thesis. The idea is not quite simple enough to fit on a bumper sticker, but it can be set forth fairly succinctly, as follows:

At the dawn of the new century, a fundamental shift in the allocation of global wealth, power, and influence is imminent. The people of East Asia, after five hundred years of fiscal and political domination by the West, are determined to stand as equals of Europe and the United States in setting the course of the world. They are demanding respect and a place at the table. They feel they've earned both, because of two Asian "miracles" spun out over the past three decades. The first is the economic miracle, which has made East Asian countries among the most prosperous on Earth—but that's not the topic of this book. This book is about East Asia's social miracle—how the Asians have built modern industrial societies characterized by the safest streets, the best schools, and the most stable families in the world. It's about how they manage to maintain minimal rates of violent crime, property crime, and drug use, along with egalitarian distribution of wealth and opportunity and a sense of civility and harmony that you can feel when you walk down the street in Tokyo, Taipei, Bangkok, Beijing, Seoul, Singapore, Kuala Lumpur, and other Asian cities. To find out how they've done it, our family traveled all over East Asia, and I spent a lot of time asking Asians to tell me their secret formula. The answer I got was that the Asians achieved their social miracle primarily by holding to a set of ethical values—what they call Confucian values or Asian values or, sometimes, the Asian way.

That's a fairly far-reaching thesis. I think it's correct, and important, which is why I've written a book about it. But the thesis naturally involves a number of generalizations and assumptions that are open to question and challenge. So in this *atogaki*, I'll entertain the questions and deal with the challenges.

The first and most sweeping assumption underlying the thesis of this book is that a place called Asia actually exists. Of course we can all spin a globe or open an atlas and a find a massive chunk of the earth called Asia. But that's a geographer's construct—a block of land that has to be differentiated from the other blocks. Geographic names and borders are human creations, but lines on a map do tend to create their own reality. This point is made nicely in the old New England joke about the farmer who worked a rocky stretch of land in western New Hampshire, right on the bank of the Connecticut River, which forms the border between New Hampshire and Vermont. The great flood of eighty-seven was so forceful in that region that the river was thrown out of its banks and cut a new channel about four hundred yards east of its old course. The farmer suddenly found himself on the west bank—that is, on the Vermont side of the border. The new Vermonter thought about it for a minute and then decided that this was a change for the better. "I never could stand those New Hampshire winters," he said.

The deeper question is how closely the lines on the map coincide with the facts of real life. In Asia, this question has a history.

The very notion that there is a single unified region called Asia is a European invention. Humans have been talking about Asia for about 2,400 years, but for more than 2,000 of those years only Europeans ever used the word.

The ancient Greeks coined the word "Asia." Herodotus, in his his-

tories, written in the fifth century B.C., used the term "Asia" for all
lands east of Greece, and that usage seems to have been common
among the Greeks and their successors, the Romans. Ancient and
medieval maps depicted Asia as a huge, amorphous blob of a continent stretching vaguely eastward. For the Greeks, Asia ended at the
tip of the Indian peninsula; by the end of the Roman era, though,
traders coming along the Silk Road had learned that the East reached
much farther than that. The maps included in Marco Polo's *The
Description of the World* (1298) offered a surprisingly accurate addition to Western knowledge, and the early waves of exploration around
the horn of Africa and the tip of India provided increased awareness.
Abraham Ortelius's stunning world map of 1575, titled "*Typus orbis
terrarum*," depicts a detailed picture of the full continent, from the
Red Sea to the islands of Japan and the Philippines; in contrast,
Ortelius's map of North America (named "America, or India Nova") is
a nondescript hunk of land, and his South America (which has no
name) ends around mid-Brazil.

The names used for this vast land reflected the European point of
view. The Greek word *Asia* was probably derived from the Assyrian
word *asu*, meaning "east." ("Europe," in turn, may come from the
Assyrian word for "west," *ereb*.) The terms "Orient" and "Oriental"
stem from the Latin gerund *oriens*, or "rising"—Europeans see the sun
rising from that direction. (*Occidens*, in turn, is the Latin word for
"setting.") The term "the Levant," used for the eastern end of the
Mediterranean, also means "place where the sun rises." The distinctions between "Near East" and "Far East" obviously reflect the
European perspective. These were terms adopted by the British military because the "Far East" was farther from England than India; the
"Near East" (which became the "Middle East" under the British command structure in World War II), was nearer to Britain.

Some leaders of contemporary Asia have worked themselves into a
state of advanced indignation over the arrogance of the Europeans in
lumping all those living eastward into a single classification. Here's
what Ogura Kazuo, the Japanese diplomat I quoted in Chapter 2, has
to say about the Western invention of "Asia":

The concept of "Asia" was originally manufactured in the West,
and over the course of history it has been laden with negative

values. It has stood, for example, as a symbol of despotism and subservience to authority, contrasting with Europe's liberty and equality. For a while it represented the source of serious military threats to Europe. . . . It was also sometimes a synonym for the barbarian forces ranged against the enlightened civilization of the West, as can be seen in the "Yellow Peril" thinking that reared its head in response to Japan's emergence.

In other words, "Asia" was a nuisance, an enemy, and a rival to the order and civilization of Europe. . . . All in all, "Asia" is a concept that the Europeans and Americans have manufactured to suit themselves.

Ogura-san has a point here. Until the last century or so, the people called Asians would have reacted with amazement and disdain if you had told them that all the millions from the green meadows at the foot of Mount Fuji to the sandy base of the pyramids, with their varied collection of languages, creeds, and races, were somehow the same group of people. Even in the considerably smaller region of East Asia, it would have been rather shocking to suggest that Siam and Singapore had much in common.

Still, it seems a little strange for a Japanese government official like Ogura to be complaining about "Asia" as a Western invention. The Japanese were the first Asians to pick up on the idea of a place called Asia, and they acted on the concept with disastrous consequences. During their swift and successful transition from isolated feudal state to modern industrialized nation near the end of the nineteenth century, the Japanese firmly embraced many Western inventions and ideas, including the idea of the East, or Asia. As the richest, most advanced, and mightiest country in the region, the Japanese began talking—first among themselves, then more openly—about a place called Asia. Since Asians were one people, the Japanese decided, they should be ruled by one divine ruler. And Japan had just the ruler in mind to assume the role: the emperor of Japan, the lineal descendant of the Sun Goddess. And so the Japanese borrowed the Western invention of Asia to serve as the justification for forty years of conquest on the continent.

The intellectual godfather of Japan's "noble endeavor" to unify Asia and free it from Western control was an unlikely advocate. Okakura Kakuzo, who later moved to America and changed his name to Tenshin Okakura, was an artist, an archaeologist, and an incurable aesthete who argued strenuously all his life that the fine arts were the salvation of the world. In 1886, when the new Japanese government was sending emissaries around the world to study and bring home state-of-the-art Western ideas on education, transportation, electric illumination, military organization, and the like, the young Okakura was dispatched, as a member of the Imperial Arts Commission, to study contemporary art in Europe and America. The government's goal was to wean Japanese painters and musicians away from traditional Japanese forms to adopt Western-style oil painting and symphonic composition. But Okakura decided on his travels that Japanese and other Oriental arts were superior to anything the West had to offer. And upon his return to Japan, he began a lifelong crusade to convince the world–first in Asia, and then in America, where he served for decades as curator of the Boston Museum–that there was such a thing as "Asian art," and that it was the finest.

Along the way, Okakura also became an advocate for the newly emerging idea of a single Asia, united under Japanese rule. He took a turn-of-the-century Japanese political slogan, *Dobun Doshu* (literally, "One Culture, One People"), and converted it into a famous English declaration: "Asia is one!" He expanded on the idea in lavish rhetoric in his book *The Ideals of the East*, written in Boston in the year 1903–4. Not burdened with excessive humility, Okakura noted on the title page that "this book is written in English by a native of Japan." And in his florid English, Okakura firmly adopted the Western idea that there is a place called Asia, stretching from the Indian subcontinent to the Pacific coast of Japan.

Asia is one! The Himalayas divide, only to accentuate, two mighty civilizations, the Chinese, with its communism of Confucius, and the Indian, with its individualism of the Vedas. But not even the snowy barriers can interrupt for one moment that broad expanse of love for the Ultimate and Universal, which is the common thought-inheritance of every Asiatic race, enabling them to produce all the great religions of the world, and distinguishing them from those maritime peoples of the Mediterranean and the Baltic, who love to dwell on the Particular and to search out the means, not the end, of life.

For if Asia be one, it is also true that the Asiatic races form a single mighty web. We forget, in an age of classification, that types are after all but shining points of distinctness in an ocean of approximations, false gods deliberately set up to be worshipped for the sake of mental convenience . . .

It has been, however, the great privilege of Japan to realize this unity-in-complexity with a special clearness. The unique blessing of unbroken sovereignty, the proud self-reliance of an unconquered race, and the insular isolation which protected ancestral ideas and instincts . . . made Japan the real repository of the trust of Asiatic thought and culture.

By the time that book appeared, Japan's Imperial Army had already set out to establish, at bayonet point, that Japan would be the "real repository . . . of Asiatic thought and culture." The people of Korea, China, Manchuria, Taiwan, the Philippines, and Southeast Asia, who would eventually fall before the advancing Japanese, obviously didn't share the notion that Japan had a holy mission to unify Asia, but they didn't have the means to resist. It has been more than fifty years since Japan surrendered at the end of World War II and gave up the notion of a "Greater East Asian Co-Prosperity Sphere." And to this day, many of the countries that were involuntarily unified celebrate August 15 as a national holiday, their day of deliverance from "unity-in-complexity."

How pleased Tenshin Okakura would be today to know that many East Asian leaders have adopted his Pan-Asian mind-set. Today it is Chinese, Malaysians, Koreans, Taiwanese, Singaporeans, who are singing the virtues of the Asian way, while Japan seems to be deeply confused as to whether it wants to throw in its lot with the newly rich and confident Asians or rely instead on the alliance with the United States and Europe that has served it so well over the past half century.

To accept the assumption that there is an Asia—and thus an Asian way—you have to overlook some significant differences in language,

religion, history, and governmental structure. The Pan-Asian argument works best for the countries that have been identified as part of
the "kanji culture" or the "chopstick culture" (see Appendix: Defining
"East Asia")–those nations that look to China as their great cultural
teacher and still use Chinese characters, to a greater or lesser degree,
in their writing systems. That group would include Japan, China,
Taiwan, Korea, and Singapore. Thailand, Malaysia, and Indonesia fit
the mold to some extent–primarily because of the influence of the
"overseas Chinese" who have emigrated to those countries–but
Malaysia and Indonesia are predominantly Muslim countries, with
weaker connections to East Asian religions and/or Confucian teachings.

Even within the ambit of traditional Chinese culture, there are
some evident differences from one Asian country to the next. A trav-
eler who goes from the thoroughly "Asian" and Confucian city-state of
Singapore to the equally "Asian" and Confucian nation of South Korea
might well wonder how deep the cultural attachments really are.

Singapore, with a leadership that has made the study of Confucius
a top national priority, is a tidy, industrious, self-righteous, and thoroughly intolerant place controlled by a small clique under the aegis of
Lee Kuan Yew, who has been the effective ruler for three decades. Lee
notes, accurately, that Confucius was most concerned about the "ethical basis of society," and he is determined to keep Singapore in line
with his definition of "ethical."

Thus police watch with binoculars from the rooftops of Singapore
to catch people committing "crimes" such as chewing gum or litter-
ing. It is against the law to drive across the causeway to Malaysia with
less than half a tank of gas (an ordinance that has little to do with
ethics but a lot to do with assuring that people don't fill up in Malaysia
and avoid the sky-high Singapore gas tax); to make sure people are
following this rule, the police regularly stop northbound cars on the
causeway and impose a five-hundred-dollar fine on anybody whose
gas gauge is too low. Parents of schoolchildren deemed to be over-
weight receive letters ordering them to change the family menus. The
government tells people how much of their money to save. As we saw
in the previous chapter, people convicted of scratching cars or spray-
painting graffiti on walls are sentenced to the lash.

Almost nobody in Singapore complains about this—at least, not publicly. The reason is that Lee's ruling party has been quick to haul its critics into court on charges of "libel" or "disturbing public order." One opposition politician was tried and convicted because he denied the ruling party's charge that he was a racist. No Singapore-based news outlet would dare criticize the party; foreign papers that do so (including the *International Herald Tribune,* partly owned by my company, The Washington Post) are hit with multimillion-dollar libel judgments. No publisher or media outlet in Singapore would dare to reprint the paragraph you are reading right now, because it would probably draw libel fines running to tens of thousands of dollars.

If this is the Asian way, most people lucky enough to live under some other way would probably be just as happy to do without it. But this is not the only Asian way of life, and it is not the only modern implementation of Confucian teachings. As we saw in Chapter 4, many contemporary Confucians insist that Lee and other autocrats masquerading as neo-Confucians have corrupted the master's teachings to create a high-minded rationale for maintaining personal power.

An hour's flight away, South Korea is evidence that a Confucian society need not take on the authoritarian spic-and-span face of Singapore. A bulwark of Confucian culture for centuries, a country where the master's works have always been, and still are, required reading in all schools, South Korea is a dirty, smelly, noisy, rambunctious nation where people not only chew gum and litter on the streets but eat, bathe, and urinate there as well. Dissent and democracy are thriving in South Korea, where the newspapers routinely savage the politicians, where citizens by the thousands take to the streets to oppose government policy, where free press and free speech are generally protected—all in the name of Confucian principles. One of the most daring democrats in the world—Kim Dae Jung, who was assaulted, jailed, kidnapped, and very nearly killed because he dared oppose the military dictators who ran his country—is a devoted student of Confucianism. Today he is the democratically elected president of South Korea.

Here, then, is the first thing that may be wrong with the thesis of this book about the Confucian way, or the Asian way. Can the Asian way or Asian values really exist, when the whole concept of Asia is an outsider's invention, and the "way" seems to run in many different directions? I'd say yes.

For all the differences and disagreements, there are certain basics about Asian culture that transcend geography. Just as a billion and a half people in that part of the world share some physical features—straight black hair, oval or almond-shaped eyes with dark black pupils, a shorter and lighter frame than that of the average Westerner—they also share a worldview. They continue to adhere to certain principles of life that were taught by Confucius and his disciples: concern for the group, close family ties, a deep commitment to education, and a sense of shame that acts as a guard against wrongful conduct. They value social harmony and cultivate a sense of loyalty that restrains the tendency toward "creative destruction" in capitalist economies. And this common inheritance helps explain why the two postwar "miracles"—the economic success and the admirable social indicators—have become, to a large degree, Pan-Asian phenomena.

SOME OBSERVERS of East Asia's social miracle—the safe and stable communities, the relative infrequency of violence, the educational achievement, the strong sense of respect for the life and property of other people—suggest that the explanation is simpler than the one offered by many Asian leaders. The argument runs roughly like this: The peace and harmony of Asian societies aren't the result of some antique set of ethical rules. Asians get along with each other because they are racially homogeneous. So it's easier for them to build a cohesive, civil society than it is for a multiracial society like those found in the Americas or Western Europe.

This explanation would tend to undermine the thesis of this book if it were accurate. And to some degree it is. Some of the nations of East Asia are extremely homogeneous; just about every Korean, for example, comes from centuries of Korean stock. There has never been much immigration into the peninsula, and foreigners who visit the country or live there for a while tend to feel like the outsiders they surely are. Japan's population is slightly more varied than Korea's; among other things, there are more than a million ethnic Koreans living in Japan, and a smaller number of descendants of aboriginal tribes who lived on the islands before the ancestors of today's Japanese majority came across the land bridge from northern Asia. Japan, too, tends to turn a cold and unwelcoming face toward those who are different. Indeed, anybody who cannot claim endless generations of Japanese ancestry tends to be branded as a *gaijin,* or outsider. When a young Japanese woman gets engaged, it is still common for her parents to hire a private investigator to make sure that her groom-to-be is not "tainted" with Korean or Chinese blood. In one of the most notorious incidents of Japanese racism, whole familes of ethnic Koreans were murdered by angry mobs following the great Tokyo earthquake of 1923 because of rumors that *gaijin* had somehow caused the natural disaster. Obviously, the Confucian ethic failed to preserve national harmony in that case.

In fact, though, racial homogeneity simply doesn't work as an explanation of the strong sense of community found in Asian societies. For one thing, it's simply not true that homogeneous societies are always harmonious. There have been countless instances where people have been driven to attack and slaughter members of their own race and nationality. Stalin killed millions of his fellow Russians. Mao Zedong let millions, perhaps tens of millions, of his Han Chinese brothers die. The same applies to individual acts of violence. In America today, most black murder victims are killed by blacks, and most white victims by whites.

Moreover, not all Asian countries have homogeneous populations. China, a sprawling nation forged by centuries of conquest, is one of the most diverse nations on earth in terms of race, religion, and language; there are well over one hundred million citizens of China (in the Moslem provinces of central Asia) who have never been to a Buddhist temple and don't even speak Chinese. Singapore is a mix of ethnic Chinese, Malays, Indians, and white Europeans living right on top of one another in a crowded island metropolis. Malaysia is a similar racial potpourri, with a majority of Malays living quite peacefully alongside Chinese, Indians, and a million or so members of indigenous tribal groups. My son, the budding linguist, used to love watching television in Malaysia because every program turned into a language lesson. A sitcom broadcast in the Malay language, for example, would have subtitles in Chinese, English, and Tamil (an Indian language).

And yet these racially mixed societies share the same positive social attributes as the homogeneous countries of Asia–safe streets, strong families, successful schools. If anything, the characteristic Asian emphasis on mutual loyalties and the overall good of society seems to help maintain harmony among the various races. Japan's crime rates are just as low among the minorities as among the ethnic Japanese, and the country today has no evidence of racially motivated crimes.

Malaysia has instituted one of the strongest affirmative action programs in the world, with almost none of the rancor and interracial bitterness that affirmative action has sparked in the United States. The effort is accepted because it is perceived to enhance overall stability and equality. As such, it makes an interesting study in social values.

During the centuries when the British controlled the Malay peninsula, they applied the principle of divide and conquer, deliberately stirring up ethnic rivalries to prevent the colonials from uniting in opposition to British rule. The Chinese were encouraged to change themselves from coolies into capitalists, and by the time of independence they were the dominant financial magnates of Malaysia. Many Indians were successful in small businesses and the professions. The Malays, mainly restricted to farm villages or manual labor in the cities, were the poorest of the races. In the 1960s, after Britain's Malay Federation became the independent nation of Malaysia, these disparities spurred resentment on all sides and prompted some outbreaks of racial rioting.

The result was the New Economic Policy, a "benign discrimination" plan designed by the government in 1970 to help the Malays and the indigenous tribal peoples gain economic equality. It set rigid quotas, limiting Chinese and Indian access to high schools, colleges, public jobs, and bank loans to make way for the Malays. Overall, the program achieved its goals. Today disparities of income have been sharply decreased, and Malays have a much greater involvement in business and finance than ever before. The stringent quota system has been relaxed somewhat, but special assistance for underprivileged groups is still a fact of life in Malaysia. In sharp contrast to the American experience with affirmative action, though, this program has been widely accepted and sparks little or no controversy.

It's hardly surprising that the Malays would approve of this policy. After all, they're the beneficiaries of the affirmative preferences. What did surprise me was that the other racial groups, too, support the plan because of the way it has created a more harmonious society. I have met some Chinese—but not many—who are bitter about the quotas. But the most heartfelt defense of affirmative action I've ever heard came from a Malaysian of Chinese ancestry, a slender, friendly politician named T. K. Koh, the chief minister (that is, the governor) of the Malaysian state of Penang.

"Look, the New Economic Policy wasn't perfect," Chief Minister Koh told me in the easy, Americanized English he learned as an undergraduate at Princeton. "I've been really critical of some specific cases when Chinese people got blatantly unfair treatment. But the situation we had before, where the distribution of wealth was so skewed—it couldn't last. It made for an inherently unstable society. To be a successful, peaceful nation, we needed more harmony among all the citizens of Malaysia. This is something any Chinese can understand. It's our tradition, and, yes, you can call it the Confucian tradition. We had to eliminate the racial resentment and build an overall sense of membership in a society where all the races could do well."

ANOTHER POTENTIAL PROBLEM with the underlying thesis of this book—and one that is harder to argue away—is the fact that Asian societies, for all their emphasis on harmony and respect for the law, are tainted with shocking levels of corruption in government and big business. Anyone who picks up a newspaper can read how relatives of government officials always seem to land the construction contract for some new bridge in East Asia, or how the site picked for a new international airport often tends to be on land owned by the family of the prime minister. To some extent, these habits are simply extensions of, or distortions of, traditional values. The Confucian emphasis on the family unit, for example, has led to a long tradition of family business dealings in Asian societies. And those who attain positions of governmental or industrial power often go out of their way to provide connections and sweetheart deals to family members. Just about every major industry in Indonesia, for example, was controlled until

1998 by some relative of the former president Suharto. This looks a lot more like a case of crony favoritism than a healthy respect for family values.

Industrial and governmental corruption have become so much a part of business-as-usual in Asian countries that I got tired of reading about it and watching it on TV. Almost every night on the evening news you see the familiar footage of some businessman in a pin-striped suit, hiding his face from the camera behind a hand or a coat, being hauled away in a police car on charges of bribery or price fixing or tax evasion. These are not just middling bureaucrats, either. Corruption goes right to the top. In South Korea, two of the nation's last four presidents were sent to prison for receiving massive corporate payoffs, as was the son of yet another president.

After a while, I didn't even pay attention to these recurrent scandals unless there was something particularly striking or bizarre about the case. One that I do remember vividly involved the governor of Japan's Niigata Prefecture, who received some $4 million in bribes from construction companies in return for highway contracts. The governor couldn't figure out what to do with all this money; the cash was too bulky to leave around the office, but taking it to the bank would naturally arouse suspicion. As a temporary solution, the governor decided to store the money in an oversized coin locker down the street at Niigata's train station. The locker fee was about four dollars per day, so the governor had one of his staffers run down to the station every morning to put in the coins. The problem was that the governor was too cheap to provide the four dollars himself. Eventually, the staffer got angry that he had to pay for this coin locker every morning out of his own pocket. So the angry young man went down to the prosecutor's office and spilled the beans on his boss. I remember the case because of the wonderful headline in the *Nikkan Spohtsu* newspaper when the whole scam was revealed: "Can you lend me $4 again today? I've only got $4 million."

Some critical observers of Asian values argue that corruption in high places is an inevitable feature of Confucian societies. Their reasoning seems to be that Confucianism puts a high priority on loyalty to the ruler and respect for one's superiors, and thus people are expected to put up with their corporate or governmental superiors, no matter how corrupt. (And of course, the corrupt bosses do their best to convey this view of Confucian duty.) Another theory is that as long as Asian governments provide their people with safe streets, good schools, and growing economies, people are willing to tolerate a little personal corruption at the top.

In fact, corruption in high places is a total perversion of true Confucianism. The Master Kung consistently argued that a leader must rule by example, and that ethics flowed downhill like water; only if there was virtue in high places could a nation be virtuous. "To govern is to be straight," he said in Book 12 of the Analects. "If you steer straight," he told the ruler Chi Kang, "who would dare not to go straight?" As we saw in Chapter 4, when the same Chi Kang complained about all the thieves in his province, Confucius cut to the heart of the matter: "If you yourself, Chi Kang, were not on the take, nobody would be trying to steal from you."

Far from tolerating corruption in the governing class, a real Confucian would denounce it, demanding the highest conceivable ethical standards from those in the highest positions. "The mandate of Heaven," after all, "is not immutable." Since a ruler must continually earn the right to hold his exalted position, a corrupt governor forfeits his right to rule. That's why those two ex-presidents of South Korea went to jail, and why I kept watching those news items about Japanese prosecutors nailing yet another politician on the take.

Still, the extent of governmental and corporate crime in East Asian countries makes it harder to sustain the argument that there is some Asian value structure that explains the low rates of crime in those nations. And yet, other indicators of healthy societies—the minimal rates of violent crime, theft, drug use, family breakdown, and out-of-wedlock births—remain strong in the East Asian world. It's hard to come up with an explanation that reconciles the sharp distinction between an honest, decent general population and corrupt leaders. Perhaps the only way to resolve this apparent contradiction is to note the obvious: No matter how pervasive its value structure, Confucian Asia has still not found a way to cure all the ills of human nature. "Even an aristocrat," Confucius himself observed, "may not always achieve the state of benevolence."

TEN

Our Own Miracle

WE HAVE, THEN, A MYSTERY TO RESOLVE.

Judging from some standard social indicators–crime rates, family stability, educational achievement–East Asians have done a better job than most of the Western democracies in recent decades of building stable and civil communities. They've done it (as the Asians argue, and I agree) by teaching and implementing a core set of cultural values. This would all make sense, of course, if Eastern cultural values were different from those in the West.

In fact, though–as I've pointed out here and there along the way– the basic cultural values of East and West are not different. What the Asians have learned from Confucius and other great teachers of the Eastern tradition is essentially the same as what Americans and Europeans have learned from Socrates and the Judaeo-Christian teachers of the Western tradition. The basic precepts are the same in both hemispheres; they differ in nuance but not in substance.

Which raises an important question: Why are these rules of ethical conduct working so well for them, and not as well for us? And what should we do to make things better on our side of the world?

Thoughtful people from both West and East have contemplated this mystery in recent years. As we saw in Chapter 8, some Asians have concluded that cultural values are not universal—that the so-called Asian way differs sharply from the Western way.

Some American observers have been saying the same thing. With the Cold War ended and the Asian century about to begin, Americans in the 1990s began to take stock of the new world order and America's place in it. Countless reports, studies, and books were published, examining these issues from every conceivable angle. Of all these papers, two in particular caught the public eye. First, a Washington policy analyst, Francis Fukuyama, published an essay called "The End of History"—which, despite that wonderfully intriguing title, actually dealt with the end of the Cold War. Then Samuel Huntington, a political scientist at Harvard, produced an essay called "The Clash of Civilizations," which dealt with the kind of war, or at least competition, that would take place in the future. Both of these thoughtful and provocative studies prompted widespread discussion and debate. Both were eventually turned into books.

And both, I think, were wrong about Asia.

Fukuyama's *The End of History*—to simplify the book fairly drastically—did not really say that history is over. Rather, it said that the aspect of history dealing with man's eternal search for the best form of government had come to an end. With the victory of the Western democratic alliance in the Cold War, Fukuyama said, the world had decided that American-style, individualistic democracy is the optimum form of national organization. Democracy had already triumphed, after all, in North America, much of South America, most of Europe, parts of Africa, and much of South and East Asia. All that remained was for the rest of the world to develop its own local variations on the basic U.S. blueprint.

Huntington's *The Clash of Civilizations*—to simplify the book fairly drastically—said that the end of the Cold War did not mean the end of the struggle to find the best form of social and political organization. For him, the world was headed toward a period of greater struggle and more confrontation, not less, with the nations dividing into cul-

tural and racial blocs. Huntington identified eight different "civilizations": Western, Confucian, Japanese, Islamic, Hindu, Slavic-Orthodox,
Latin American, and African. He predicted that conflicts among these
civilizations will inevitably increase. (As evidence of the kind of political and philosophical conflict to be expected in the future, he quoted
many of the same voices I cited in Chapter 8–East Asians expressing
their disgust with American values.) His prescription, for the United
States and Europe, was that the Judaeo-Christians had better all band
tightly together and make a last stand for "Western values" in the face
of the new "cultural assertiveness" from prosperous and confident
East Asians.

It would be hard to find two more different predictions of the
world's future, and yet on one salient point, Fukuyama and Huntington agree. They both see Asia as an "other"–if not an enemy of the
Western democratic tradition, then at least something strikingly different. They both see a fundamental gap between East and West, between the Confucian culture of East Asia and the Judaeo-Christian
culture of Europe and North America. For Fukuyama, this gap won't
be closed unless the Asians move closer and closer to the American
system of social organization. For Huntington, the gap probably won't
be closed at all, which is why he urges the Western nations to hunker
down together in a defensive posture.

We've heard all this before, of course. As everybody knows,
". . . East is East, and West is West, and never the twain shall meet."
(Nobody ever quotes the next lines of Kipling's ballad, where he
makes exactly the opposite point: "But there is neither East nor West,
Border, nor Breed, nor Birth / When two strong men stand face to
face, though they come from the ends of the earth.")

The experience of my own thoroughly Western family during our
years of living and traveling in the East, however, suggested something quite different from what Fukuyama and Huntington said.
When I stood face to face with my neighbor Matsuda Tadao in the
grimy gray concrete neighborhoods of Subsection 3, I didn't feel that
there was a impassable border between us. What was most surprising
was how much we had in common.

Most of the things that Matsuda-san talked to me about–the responsibilities of membership, the duty of loyalty to your family and to

the various other groups in your life, the need to avoid causing trouble for the neighbors—were ethical principles I already knew. For him, those principles could be traced back to Confucius and the other great teachers of the Orient. For me, they came from the Bible, the Greeks and Romans, and other key sources of the Western tradition. But we both knew the same core truths. There was very little culture clash between his civilization and mine.

Time and again in the course of this book we've seen cases where the great teachings of the East track precisely with the ideals that are considered elementary principles of Western civilization:

When Confucius was asked to provide "a single word that could serve as a guide to life," he answered with a word meaning "compassion" or "consideration," and went on to explain it this way: "Do not impose on others what you do not want for yourself." Five centuries later, when Jesus Christ was asked the same question, he gave the same answer: "In everything, do to others as you would have them do to you; for this is the law and the prophets."

Confucius said to the men of Lu: "Shall I teach you what knowledge is? When you know a thing, to recognize that you know it, and when you do not know a thing, to recognize that you do not know it. That is knowledge." A century later, Socrates said to the men of Athens, "I decided that I was wiser than the man who . . . thinks he knows something when he knows nothing. Because while I may not know anything, at least I never pretend that I do."

Confucius told a provincial ruler that he must teach virtue by example. "If you yourself desire what is good, the people will be good. The moral power of the gentleman is the wind; the moral power of the common people is the grass. The grass will always bend in the direction of the wind." Twenty-five centuries later, the American jurist Louis D. Brandeis said the same thing: "Our government is the great, the omnipresent teacher. For good or ill, it teaches the whole people by its example."

Confucius's disciple Mencius taught that the government must have "the mandate of heaven" to rule effectively, and that the mandate to rule can be bestowed only by the people being governed. "The consent of the people is the will of Heaven," Mencius wrote. Some 2,300 years later, Thomas Jefferson wrote the same thing: "Governments are instituted among men, deriving their just powers from the consent of the governed."

WHEN YOU MAKE A LIST, then, of the "Asian" values–hard work, honesty, thrift, a commitment to education–they sound remarkably similar to the values I was taught as a boy, far, far from Asia, growing up in the United States. This point came through to me vividly one day at the United States Embassy in Tokyo.

A group of senior executives from the Big Three Detroit auto companies–the firms known in Japan as the "Biggu Suree"–had traveled to Japan to dramatize their complaints about Japanese trade practices. They made a call on the U.S. ambassador to Japan, Michael Armacost, a wise veteran of the diplomatic corps (who went on to become president of the Brookings Institution in Washington). Although Armacost had surely heard it all before, the auto executives went through their whole litany. The reason that Japanese models had won a 30 percent share of the American auto market–while the U.S. share of Japan's market was less than 3 percent–was obvious, the Detroiters said: The Japanese were cheating. They had used all sorts of devious ploys to protect their domestic market from imported autos, but were meanwhile flooding foreign markets with their own cars at bargain prices. It was Pearl Harbor all over again. Nobody could be expected to compete against such sneaky Asian tactics.

These charges weren't true, and Armacost knew it. He knew that the Japanese had won their share of the U.S. market by taking advantage of Detroit's weaknesses in the 1980s–by producing smaller, more efficient, and higher-quality cars than the U.S. makers did. Detroit, in contrast, had never tried very hard in Japan; at the time, the American manufacturers didn't make a single model with the steering wheel on the right side, Japanese style. But Armacost was also a good enough diplomat to know he couldn't say that. An American ambassador would not enhance his career by insulting the top brass of American industry. But what would he say? I held my breath and waited for his reply.

"Well, I think we can compete against them," the ambassador began. "We can't criticize these people for working hard, saving a lot, investing in the future, educating rigorously. Those are the very things we've always called Yankee virtues. They helped us build the most successful nation in the world. So it shouldn't surprise us if the same values turn out to work for people here as well."

As a diplomatic ploy, it was a brilliant answer: the Asians had succeeded by applying our values. And it served neatly to get the ambassador out of a tight spot. But if you think about it for a minute, Armacost's answer implied a separate question, the very question we've been struggling with in this book. How come these traditional values seem to working better in Asia than in the West?

I would say it's because the East Asians, at least over the past half century or so, have done a better job of inculcating their cultural tradition, of bringing their basic moral values to bear on the events of daily life. A good deal of this book has dealt with the ways the Asians do it: in school, on the job, in the subways and streets and parks. They strive relentlessly to remind people that the basic moral values of their civilization really matter, right now. They put up banners on the viaduct ("Good manners behind the wheel are better than a fancy car"), posters on the wall of the train station ("Have a Safe and Pleasant Journey, in the Spirit of a Caring Society"), and those signs I used to love in the public parks ("To make the park a pleasant place for everybody, let's try not to do anything that might bother the other people who are here"). They hold big public ceremonies at regular intervals all year long to get the point across ("The privileges of adulthood come with serious responsibility—to obey the law, to protect the people and the environment of Shibuya Ward, to work hard to preserve the future of our country").

We ought to do the same thing. We ought to find excuses to hold big ceremonies—in the neighborhood, in the workplace, in school, or at the club—to set forth our values. We have the holidays already: Flag Day, Mother's Day, Thanksgiving. Instead of turning those special days into excuses for overeating or binge shopping, why not set them aside for civic ceremonies, reminding people of the values underlying our society?

For that matter, we could copy some of the Asian ceremonial days. My choice would be Japan's Coming-of-Age Day (described in Chapter 6), when all the twenty-year-olds-to-be in a given year are herded into the local city hall and lectured about their responsibilities as adult citizens. We wouldn't even have to change the date. Coming-of-Age Day is celebrated each year on January 15. That's the day we remember (well, we're supposed to remember) the values–equality, community, nonviolence–espoused by a great Confucian, Martin Luther King, Jr. What better day could there be for a hundred thousand local ceremonies, in every nook and cranny of the country, to emphasize that our success as a nation depends not so much on our huge GNP and our powerful army as it does on the content of our character?

The U.S. government is already looking around for ways to promote traditional values. In 1998, the president convened a White House Conference on Character Building for a Democratic, Civil Society–which sounds exactly like the kind of thing an Asian government would do. The conference summarized its conclusion in terms that would have been completely familiar to Confucius: "Individual rights presume personal and social responsibilities. We must defend our rights vigorously, but also live up to our responsibilities."

Americans love to talk about their commitment to family values. On the assumption that we mean it, we ought to put that commitment into practice the way the Asians do. We ought to make it harder for single people to start families; we ought to make it harder for married couples with children to break up. Some have suggested that this should be done by changes in the law–the elimination of no-fault divorce and similar steps. That might work. A much more powerful form of insurance for the family, though, would be a change in attitude. What would happen if Americans–like that Japanese woman on the Larry King show–actually felt ashamed about breaking up a family? What would happen if politicians who have walked out on their own families were portrayed as hypocrites when they started talking about "family values"?

Business people in the West, too, should try to learn something from East Asian business practices. I don't mean just-in-time delivery systems or quality circles, which were the hot lessons of the 1980s, when books on "Japanese management" were all the rage in the United States and Europe. The long economic boom in the United States and some European countries shows that Western companies can get along just fine, thank you, with their own systems of production and distribution. But business executives do have something to learn from their Asian counterparts about the cultural values that make for a stable and healthy society.

The Confucian executives who run East Asian businesses recognize that their companies don't exist in a vacuum. They know that they are part of a larger society—and that membership brings with it responsibility. In the West, a corporate executive who lays off thousands of workers is often treated as a hero, with a big cover story in *Fortune* or *Business Week* and a hefty bonus at the next salary review. But Western managers should realize that this kind of social disruption does not come free.

There are inevitably social costs associated with a single-minded emphasis on efficiency, with "creative destruction," with the vast gaps in earnings between corporate chieftains and their employees. Massive layoffs in any community are likely to produce a quick upward spike in crime, drug use, and family problems in the same community. Asian executives recognize this connection. In the West, we often ignore it.

With a confidence spawned by our decade of prosperity, we Westerners tend to scold the Asians if they refuse to do things our way. A colleague of mine at *The Washington Post* criticized Japanese executives for "going through severe contortions to keep midlevel workers in their jobs." *The New York Times* warns that "Japan is perhaps too civilized for the 1990's." Consultants from the World Bank and International Monetary Fund have been traveling through East Asia urging companies to cut more costs, to lay off more workers, to become "efficient" in the Western sense.

But efficiency can't be the only measure of success, for a business or a society. If a company enjoys big profits while the community around it grows desperate, neither company nor community really comes out ahead. At the same time we are teaching Asian societies about business efficiency, we might be learning a thing or two from them about loyalty, civility, and the value of a stable community.

To learn these lessons from Asia doesn't mean that Western societies have to "Go East," as my friend Mahbubani suggested. We don't have to turn Asian in order to move more toward the civil, harmonious sense of community that our family found in Asia. In recognizing the importance of individual responsibility, family stability, and a sense of loyalty to fellow members of our companies, clubs, and neighborhoods, we would be reaffirming traditional tenets of our own Western culture. We would be applying basic moral lessons that we learned long ago. We would be doing exactly what Confucius was talking about in that famous first line of the Analects: "Isn't it a pleasure when you can make practical use of the things you have studied?"

Appendix: Defining "East Asia"

A BASIC PROBLEM facing anybody who hopes to explain what is happening in Asia is deciding what is meant by "Asia."

The *National Geographic Atlas of the World* shows the continent of Asia running from the Arabian Peninsula at the eastern end of the Mediterranean Sea to the midpoint of the Bering Strait, where the eastern tip of Siberia and the westernmost point of the American mainland almost touch. It is easily the biggest of the seven continents, covering 30 percent of the land surface of the planet, containing both the highest (Mount Everest, 29,029 feet) and lowest (the Dead Sea, –1,339 feet) surface points on Earth. It is home to about 3.5 billion people, or 60 percent of the world's population.

But the "Asian miracle," and this book about Asia's social miracle, deal with a subset of the great Asian landmass. The phenomenon we're concerned with is taking place in East Asia, which is defined roughly as the area between Mount Fuji, in Japan, to Mount Everest, on the border of Nepal and Tibet. (This definition leaves out the area commonly known as South Asia–India, Pakistan, Bangladesh, Nepal, and Burma—a region which may soon have a renaissance of its own.) East Asia, so defined, is home to 2.5 billion people, or 40 percent of the world's population. Traditionally, it was one of the poorest areas on Earth, but today East Asia is as wealthy as North America and Western Europe. Thanks to two decades of stunning economic growth rates, it is the home of the largest middle class on Earth. It is the world's largest market—a gold mine for exporters in the industrial countries of the West.

East Asia is not just a region on the map, however; it's also a distinct cultural entity. There have been several attempts in recent years to provide a culture definition:

- The brilliant Japanese journalist Funabashi Yoichi refers to Asia's "chopstick culture"—that is, all the countries where chopsticks are used daily as eating utensils.

- That "chopstick culture" would be roughly equivalent to the "rice-bowl culture," which is to say, those countries where white rice grown in paddy fields has been the traditional staple food. As the Chinese discovered at the dawn of agriculture, rice is just right for East Asia, because "wet rice" cultivation—that is, rice grown in sunken fields flooded by the spring monsoon—produces a crop with more caloric value per acre than any other agricultural product.

- Some scholars talk about the "kanji culture," referring to all the nations that regularly use traditional Chinese characters (kanji) as the primary or supplemental alphabet.

- The slick new magazines catering to East Asia's newly rich Generation X tend to define their market as the "Star Channel culture," which is to say, all the countries that receive TV broadcasts from the Star Television Network in Hong Kong, with such daily features as Chinese historical dramas, Korean soap operas, Japanese cartoons, Sumo wrestling, and, of course, MTV Asia.

This is not quite as complicated as it sounds, because the various cultural definitions of what constitutes East Asia overlap fairly neatly. To take the broadest description possible, we could say that East Asia includes all the countries in the classical Chinese cultural sphere. It was China, after all, that taught the rest of East Asia how to grow rice and eat with chopsticks and write with the ancient characters (and it is China today, through its rather heavy-handed government controls, that dictates what is permitted to be broadcast over the Star cable network). And it was China, through the preservation and dissemination of the Confucian Classics, that created a Confucian ethic which serves as a value system for the whole of the East Asian world.

Confucius offered ethical principles for individuals and governments, but he was a teacher, not a preacher. There is no religion, there are no deities or sacred mysteries in the Confucian teachings, and there are no missionaries of a Confucian faith. But the ideas that Confucius and his successors taught were spread by missionaries. These were the Buddhist priests, who carried the teachings with them—plus the white rice culture, the chopsticks, and the kanji—as they set out to take their religion to every corner of the East Asian world. (The Philippines, Australia, New Zealand, and New Guinea, all of which call themselves East Asian countries today, were too far away to be washed by this cultural wave.) Today, this Confucian corner of Asia is the home of the HPAEs, the high-performing Asian economies, which is to say that the East Asian miracle has taken place in countries that fell under the sway of Confucius, to one degree or another.

In addition to these geographic and cultural descriptions, there is also a "political" East Asia—that is, the various countries that make up the region. Moving from East to West across the globe, the major nations of East Asia include:

Japan (population 126 million)

The Japanese archipelago is a long chain (superimposed on the United States, it would stretch from Maine to Miami) of mountainous, heavily forested islands, with just a few open patches of plain, where most of the Japanese people live in some of the most crowded cities on Earth. And yet this cramped, teeming country is polite, decorous, peaceful, and neat as a pin. Industrious, too. Japan led Asia into the industrial age a century ago, and its amazing financial success in the decades after World War II made it the prototype and the financier of the "East Asian miracle." Its long economic swoon in the 1990s was a prototype for the broader Asian economic flu that spread through much of the region in 1997–98.

A resolute determination to catch up with the West–to prove that the Orient can do anything the Occident can–has been a powerful motivator for Japan's achievements. Having caught up with the Western nations in wealth, Japan became the most Westernized of Asian countries; in diet, dress, music, architecture, urban design, etc., the Japanese often seem to be modeling their lifestyle on some suburb in southern California. Japan has a popularly elected democratic government, a free press, and strong protection of human rights.

But much of that Westernization is only skin deep. Japan's religions remain Asian–after more than a century of work, Christian missionaries have converted less than 1 percent of the population–and ancient China holds the same place in Japanese culture that Greece and Rome have in Western culture. Japan is a thoroughly Confucian country.

Japan's traditional name for itself was Yamato, or "Land of Great Harmony." Modern Japan calls itself Nihon, pronounced "Nippon," written with two characters meaning "Home of the Sun." That name came from the Chinese, who saw the sun rising in the east every morning and concluded it must be coming from the long chain of islands off to the east in the Pacific. The word "Japan" evidently comes from a French effort to emulate the Chinese pronunciation of "Nippon."

Taiwan (population 21 million)

This is a single mountainous island, roughly the size of a small U.S. state. Almost a quarter of the population live in the noisy, dirty, crowded, and incredibly lively capital, Taipei, and its sprawling middle-class suburbs. When the self-styled "Generalissimo" Chiang

Kai-shek and one million Nationalist followers arrived on the island in 1949 and declared it to be the "real" China, Taiwan was one of the poorest nations in the world. Taking full advantage of support from anticommunists in the United States, and following the Japanese model for industrialization, the Taiwanese built a successful high-tech economy—so successful that Taiwan is now lending money to nations that were much richer than Taiwan a quarter century ago. Taiwan is also one of the biggest foreign investors in mainland China.

The autocrats in Beijing still insist that Taiwan is just another Chinese province and will soon return to the fold. This is unlikely. Taiwan has turned itself into a free-market democracy; its free and honest national election in 1996 represented the first time in four thousand years that people of China were allowed to choose their own government. The island is gradually gaining recognition as an independent entity, as countries around the world conclude that doing business with democratic Taiwan is so lucrative it is worth enduring a few roars from the mainland tiger. Taiwan's stature was enhanced considerably in the late 1990s when it largely avoided the currency crisis and economic downturn that hit other East Asian economies.

Officially, at least, the Taiwanese still call their own country the Republic of China. But nowadays they say that with a knowing smile. More and more they use the name Taiwan, formed from two characters meaning "Great Harbor."

South Korea (population 41 million)
North Korea (population 23 million)

Korea is two countries at the moment, but it feels more like one big family. For centuries, Korea has had its own language, culture, and government. The national sense of kinship is so strong that the Koreans never felt much need to create a lot of different family names. More than half the Korean people bear the name Kim, Lee, or Park.

Given its precarious position—the Korean peninsula hangs off the far eastern edge of the Asian mainland, with Japan a few miles to the east and China a few miles to the west—it's not surprising that the kings of Korea have often been vassals of either Japan or China. So it was sad, but not unprecedented, when the United States and the Soviet Union decided to use Korea as a Cold War pawn in 1946 and split the country into two.

North Korea, which ranks with Cuba as one of the last desperate outposts of Communism, is a tragic case. Its people are probably the poorest and hungriest on Earth, and are totally devoid of political freedom. South Korea, in contrast, is one of the shining stars of the East Asian miracle, and its economic transformation triggered a dramatic political miracle as well. After four decades of military dictatorship, the people of South Korea went to the streets in 1987, demanded democratic government–and got it. Today there is a freely elected president and parliament in Seoul. The last two generals to run the government were both sentenced to life in prison for corruption, but the current president, Kim Dae Jung, an old adversary of the dictators, released them as a humanitarian gesture.

The name Korea comes from the Koryo dynasty that ruled the peninsula in the tenth century. The two Koreas currently refer to themselves as the Republic of Korea (south) and the People's Republic of Korea (north). Because the North has no resources and no allies, reunification is inevitable. A single Korea, with the South's industrial strength and the North's rich resource base, will be one of the richest countries in the world.

China (population 1.2 billion)

China is the colossus of East Asia, but that's only half the story. China is the colossus of the world, with a population about 30 percent bigger than that of India, the world's second-largest nation. Most international economists agree that China will become the world's richest country as well, sometime in the twenty-first century–a development that came all the closer in 1997, when China regained control of Hong Kong, the most successful of the Asian "NICs" (newly industrialized countries). The scary prospect is that this huge, rich country may also try to become the world's strongest nation; Beijing is already in the market for used bombers, submarines, and aircraft carriers, largely from the former Soviet Union.

These projections for a future of wealth and power all presume that there will continue to be one place called China. The Chinese point out that theirs is the world's oldest continuous civilization. But today's China is a somewhat fragmented collection of different races, religions, and civilizations forged into one country by Genghis Khan and other warlords over the centuries. Hundreds of millions of people officially counted as Chinese citizens–in Mongolia, Tibet, and the vast steppes of Central Asia–have little connection either with ancient Chinese culture or with the modern Chinese power structure in Beijing.

Since China now seems committed to free-market capitalism, Beijing will eventually face the demands for political freedom that always seem to accompany economic freedom (cf. Taiwan and South Korea, above). Can the regime find a way to hold on to power and keep its huge nation united? Or will mighty China split apart, the way the once mighty Soviet Union did? Looking at the heavy-handed clique of elderly autocrats running the country today, it is hard to imagine that they will be graceful or swift-footed enough to dance successfully around the demands for political freedom and local autonomy that now seem inevitable.

China's name for itself is Chung Kuo, formed from two characters meaning "Middle Kingdom." That reflects the ancient but still powerful Chinese conviction that their huge nation is the center of the universe. Our word "China" comes from the Chin dynasty (221–206 B.C.), the era when the Great Wall was built and China first became known to the West.

Vietnam (population 74 million)
Cambodia (population 11 million)
Laos (population 5 million)

These three countries constituted French Indochina during the colonial era, and each became an independent state following the revolutionary war against the French in the 1950s. The Vietnam War inflicted death and destruction on all three. But things didn't get much better after the United States pulled out. The Communist factions that took over–the Viet Cong, the Khmer Rouge, and the Pathet

Lao—carried out mass murders and purges, and the nations suffered economic stagnation. Taking a lesson from their more successful neighbors, these former French colonies are now hoping to use Japanese foreign aid and investment money to become the next wave of newly industrialized countries. But that may take several decades.

Thailand (population 60 million)

Besides its lush tropical environment of mountains and jungle, Thailand—known for seven centuries as Siam—seems proudest of the historical fact that it is the only East Asian country that was never conquered, occupied, or controlled by Western colonial powers.

Thailand held itself out as an "ally"—a better term might be "puppet"—of Japan during World War II, thus avoiding the utter destruction suffered by the East Asian nations that were first conquered by the Japanese army and then reconquered by the Allies. Since Japan's emergence as a financial power, the Thais have renewed their old friendships. With heavy Japanese investment and technical assistance, Thailand has moved toward an industrial economy, although with more ups and downs and fiscal crises than the other NICs have experienced.

Thailand is a democracy, but a struggling one beset by coups and failed governments. The country has also had more trouble with drug abuse than its East Asian neighbors (although the rates of crime and drug abuse are still lower than in most Western countries). A thriving prostitution industry, catering largely to Japanese salarymen traveling to Bangkok on "sex tours," spawned an AIDS crisis that is far worse in Thailand than in any other Asian nation. The problem was so severe that the Ministry of Health distributed free condoms to male tourists arriving at Bangkok's airport.

This is the place where Anna met the King of Siam. The country that now calls itself Thailand was the Kingdom of Siam from 1350 or so to 1939, when it switched to the current name. "Thailand" (Muang Thai in the Thai language) means "Land of the Free," reflecting the pride of a nation that was never anybody's colony.

Malaysia (population 22 million)

This green, green nation is one of the loveliest spots on Earth, dotted with ancient rain forests, rugged mountain peaks, caramel-brown rivers, and spectacular coral islands—the movie *South Pacific* was filmed not in the South Pacific but just off the Malayan coast, because the islands here look more like paradise than the real South Pacific paradises. Maybe that's why the Malay Peninsula was so attractive to colonial powers. Over the last four centuries it has been ruled in whole or part by Sumatra, Portugal, Holland, the Brooke family (the famous "White Rajahs," Englishmen who owned the north shore of Borneo), Great Britain, Japan, and Great Britain again. Britain's Malay Federation finally became independent in 1957, and the ensuing forty years have arguably been happier and more prosperous than any of the four hundred under foreign rule.

Malaysia is divided into two landmasses separated by four hundred miles of ocean. It includes the southernmost part of the Asian mainland, where the Malay Peninsula swells up like a sore thumb, plus the northern third of the massive island of Borneo, far to the east across the South China Sea. Until recently, Malaysia had a classic colonial economy, as the world's biggest supplier of commodities like rubber and tin. The rubber in the tires on your car probably came from Malaysia—but nowadays, the CD player on the dashboard and the microprocessor controlling the brakes probably came from Malaysia as well. Just twenty years since the first high-tech factory opened, Malaysia is the world's biggest exporter of microchips.

Malaysia is also divided racially, among Malays, Chinese, Indians, and indigenous tribes (particularly in North Borneo). The young nation had angry riots in the 1960s, but today the various peoples get along well. Malaysia has a democratic government, more or less, and respects human rights to some degree (although political opponents of the ruling party have been jailed when they criticized the thin-skinned leadership). The press has no political freedom; it is subject to government regulation and thus tends to praise just about everything the prime minister says or does.

The name Malaysia ("Mah-lay-see-ah") derives from the native name of the peninsula, Melayu.

Singapore (population 3.4 million)

Singapore is the Manhattan of Southeast Asia, a long, crowded island of soaring skyscrapers, lavish penthouses, and gridlocked streets. Like Manhattan, Singapore considers itself richer, trendier, more stylish, and all in all more important than any other place. The crown jewel of the Malayan Federation during the long colonial era, Singapore became part of the new nation of Malaysia when the British finally left. But it broke away in 1963 after the local politicians, mostly of Chinese descent, rather cynically decided that they didn't want to cope with the heavily Malay vote up on the peninsula (and the Malays who ran Malaysia's ruling party decided with equal cynicism that they could do without those two million Chinese voters on Singapore). The autocrats who rule Singapore have created a sort of nanny state—a neat, clean enclave where nobody dares to do anything that might offend the governing clique. The island has been aptly called Disneyland with the death penalty.

Singapore's economic achievements are mind-boggling; this minute city-state with less than half the population of New York City has made itself a global center of banking, finance, shipping, and high-tech manufacturing. It has surpassed the United States in per capita income, which is to say that the average resident of Singapore is richer than the average American. In the Asian economic setbacks of 1997–98, Singapore avoided a currency crisis of its own but suffered somewhat because of losses in its export markets to other Asian countries. Singapore is also a world capital of the Confucian ethic, with Confucius's sayings taught in all schools and even set into the tile on the walls of the subway stations.

But the small coterie of strong men who rule Singapore have appropriated Confucianism for their own purposes, arguing (preposterously) that the sage envisioned this sort of hyper-regulated regime where public order is considered the highest good. Police with binoculars watch from the rooftops to snare any citizen who dares to jaywalk, chew gum, or paste a sticker on a street post. But since almost everybody is doing well these days, the residents of this prosperous state don't seem to mind Big Brother watching all the time. Freedom of speech is allowed only for those who support the government unconditionally. If this paragraph were ever published in Singapore, I'd definitely be held liable in one of the regime's compliant courts.

The name Singapore comes from a Sanskrit word for "lion city." The natives call their island SingaPORE, with the accent on the third syllable; if you say "SINGapore," everybody knows you're a tourist.

Indonesia (population 199 million)

The Indonesian archipelago has everything–and arguably too much of some things. It is the world's fourth-most populous nation, with 200 million people scattered over 7,000 inhabited islands. It has oil, gas, coal, tin, copper, nickel, and millions of acres of rain forest that are being burned away so rapidly (to make room for farms, factories, and freeways) that the smoke has besmogged much of Southeast Asia. Indonesia has 130 active volcanoes and 40,000 species of flowers, including 5,000 orchids and the world's largest blossom, the rafflesia, a dark red flower the size of a hubcap that looks and smells like spoiled meat.

They still grow coffee on Java, but Indonesia's main island is now primarily sprouting industry and new cities. More than 100 million people live on Java, about a fifth of them in and around Jakarta, a capital city so crowded that they actually block off the streets leading downtown at six in the morning to keep cars out of the central city. (The result has been to make rush hour start two hours earlier.) As industrialization and public education expand, this well-endowed nation has strong prospects. It was hurt badly by the currency crises of 1997–98, and will take some years to recover fully. Racial animosity, fueled by resentment of the rich Chinese minority, is probably worse here than in any other East Asian country. But Indonesia at some point is probably going to be one of the world's richest countries.

Indonesia had only two heads of state for the first thirty-nine years after it achieved independence in 1949. And then, with the financial crisis, the old establishment was driven from power by rioting in the streets and a quiet rebellion engineered jointly by the army and corporate interests. The new "temporary government," backed by the military, promised quick elections and a movement toward democratic rule. Frankly, these promises are hard to believe. They would reverse the pattern of Indonesian government since the nation was born.

Of all East Asian countries, Indonesia is probably the one least influenced by the culture of China. Its culture comes more from the Arab traders of the Mideast–Indonesia is the world's biggest Islamic nation–and from those centuries of Dutch control. Perhaps for this reason, Indonesia is markedly less harmonious than its neighbors. Relations between the Muslim majority and the Christian and Chinese minorities are much less placid than in Malaysia to the north. Religious tension is a chief reason for the ongoing mutiny in East Timor.

This huge island chain was known for 350 years as the Dutch East Indies. The Dutch colonial governors switched to the more modern-sounding Indonesia in 1948 to play down the colonial taint of the old name. Indonesians still call their country "Een-do-nee-see-ah."

A Note on Sources

IF YOU'RE GOING to research and write a book about a place as vast and varied as East Asia, stern duty demands that you pack your bags and go traveling.

To meet this responsibility, my family and I trekked from the Golden Temple in Kyoto to the golden sands of Tioman, a Malaysian island paradise so idyllic that the movie *South Pacific* was filmed there, even though it's nowhere near the South Pacific. We climbed up to the top of Mount Kinabalu, the highest peak on Borneo, and rode down the Pearl River delta on an aging ferry with a Cantonese heavy metal band blasting away on the upper deck.

We loved every minute of it. And yet, some of the most enjoyable "travel" I did in research for this project involved nothing more exotic than a tour through the shelves of the library. There are wonderful books on many aspects of East Asia. A full bibliography would run on forever, so I'll just recommend a smattering of titles here for readers who want further information.

East Asia's economic miracle has spawned a flood of books in English. (Most of these came out before 1997, when recession and a chain of currency crises took some of the bloom off that particular rose.) The most famous is the World Bank study *The East Asian Miracle: Economic Growth and Public Policy* (Oxford University Press, 1993), an excellent and frequently quoted explanation of what Asian governments did right during the period 1960–90. Jim Rohwer's *Asia Rising* (Simon & Schuster, 1995) is a more accessible account of the same phenomenon. No doubt there will soon be a counterflood of books on how the economic miracle turned sour.

There are several thoughtful books explaining the concept of Confucian capitalism—the idea that Asia's economic emergence was the product of ancient cultural traditions. A good short treatment is Professor Ezra F. Vogel's *The Four Little Dragons* (Harvard University Press, 1991); in the last chapter of his book, "Toward an Explanation," Vogel looks at the parallel between the Protestant ethic that shaped Western civilization and the Confucian ethic that shaped East Asia. The great Japanese journalist Funabashi Yoichi offers an Asian viewpoint in *Asia-Pacific Fusion* (Institute for International Economics, 1995).

Several scholars have probed the contemporary vitality of Confucian ideas in areas other than business. Professor William Theodore De Bary has spent much of his academic career on this issue, and he offers some conclusions in *The Trouble with Confucianism* (Harvard University Press, 1991). I can report from personal experience that Professor Frederick W. Mote is a great teacher of things Chinese; he takes on the origins of Asian, or at least Chinese, culture in *Intellectual Foundations of China* (McGraw-Hill, 1988). A comprehensive and up-to-date collection of studies will be found in *Confucian Traditions in East Asian Modernity,* edited by Tu Wei-Ming (Harvard University Press, 1996). Among the papers in that collection is one by Professor Robert J. Smith of Cornell, citing the letter quoted in chapter 6 of this book.

There are fewer books on the East Asian social miracle, which is why I wrote this one. I found two good studies linking traditional cultural values to the minimal levels of crime in contemporary Japan: *Forces of Order,* by Professor David H. Bayley (University of California Press, 1991), and *Everyday Justice: Responsibility and the Individual in Japan and the United States,* by V. Lee Hamilton and Joseph Sanders (Yale University Press, 1992).

For a reader who wants to dig deeply into Confucius, his life and his ideas, I think the best source is still the great work of James Legge, *The Chinese Classics, with a Translation, Critical and Exegetical Notes, Prolegomena, and Copious Indexes, in Five Volumes.* This hundred-year-old epic has been reprinted, handsomely, by Hong Kong University Press and is available in many libraries.

I listed several other translations of the Confucian Analects in Chapter 4 of this book. As noted there, the best contemporary translation, with erudite notes and commentary, is by the Australian scholar

Pierre Ryckmans. But you won't find it under his name. The Norton paperback edition of this work (1997) says "Translation and Notes by Simon Leys." On the back cover, it tells you that "Simon Leys is the pseudonym of Pierre Ryckmans" (which makes you wonder why they bothered to use a pseudonym in the first place).

Westerners who are learning Chinese will find the original text of the *Lun Yü*, or Analects, to be tough going but not impossible. For a middle ground, I relied on an excellent comic-book edition, with the text in both Chinese and English, by the cartoonist Tsai Chih Chung. (Comic book? Well, comics are often used for more serious purposes in Asia than in the West.) It's called *The Sayings of Confucius: Fuller Discourses on the Lun Yü* (AsiaPac [Singapore], 1994).

There are many books in English about Asian education in general and Japanese schools in particular. Catherine S. Lewis's *Educating Hearts and Minds* (Cambridge University Press, 1995) is excellent. The author sent her children to a Japanese public school that appears to be–not surprisingly–a carbon copy of Yodobashi No. 6, described in Chapter 5 of this book. Most, but not all, of her children's experiences were similar to what my kids found at Yodobashi. Lewis uses her Western training in anthropology to interpret what happened to her children in an Asian school.

Perhaps the leading advocate of the notion that Western societies are "too free" is my friend Kishore Mahbubani, the un-diplomatic Singaporean diplomat who argues that Western societies should "Go East, young man." He sets forth his ideas in a book with the characteristically acerbic title *Can Asians Think?* (Times Editions [Singapore], 1998). So as not to keep you in suspense, I'll reveal that the thoughtful Mr. Mahbubani concludes that Asians can and do think, often more clearly than Westerners.

In some of my previous books I've included a bibliographic essay like this one, using the title "A Note on Books." That title is now technologically obsolete, because there's another key source today for readers who want to probe further into the issues raised in these pages. The Internet–in effect, the biggest library in history, with hundreds of thousands of information repositories all tied together–is a cornucopia of data on Confucius, Confucian values, and the various Asian countries where they hold sway.

All the Asian countries—except North Korea, the citadel of secrecy—maintain their own Web sites. There are also many sites, in many languages, dedicated to Confucius. I won't try to list the URLs (that is, the "Uniform Resource Locators," the technical term for an Internet address), because they change now and then. But you can easily find the ancient Chinese sage in this most modern of libraries by typing in "Confucius" or "Kung Fu-tzu" on any Internet search engine.

Thanks

AS THEY HAVE endured five centuries of conquest, condescension, and caricature ("the Inscrutable East," "the yellow peril") at the hands of Westerners, it's not surprising that East Asians turn a suspicious eye on the blue-eyed visitors who parachute in now and then declaring a fervid determination to understand the Orient. I have met my share of suspicion during my years in Asia. But I have also been lucky enough to meet wonderful people in every Asian country who were willing to help me try to understand.

The debt I owe to my wise and compassionate Confucius-next-door, Matsuda Tadao, and his wife, Chioko, will be obvious to readers of this book. I suppose it won't be obvious to Matsuda-san, though, since he felt he was simply doing what anybody ought to do for a fellow resident of Subsection 3.

Less obvious, but just as large, is my debt to Maruta Yasuko and Togo Shigehiko (the man who shouted "Huck you!"), dear friends who struggled day in and day out to help me figure out how Asia works.

My pal Tan Gee Chin assisted me all over the place. This was partly because she can chatter along effortlessly in Mandarin, Cantonese, Bahasa Malaysia, Japanese, or English, and partly because she never spared the truth. One day she and I went shopping at the Kota Bahru market near the Malaysia–Thailand border, a place famous throughout Asia for its rock-bottom prices. There I found a woman selling jambu fruit, a sweet Thai peach. After extended negotiations, she sold me 2 kilos of jambu–4½ pounds!–for just one ringgit, or 20 cents. I grabbed the sack and went racing back to Tan Gee Chin to brag about my bargaining skill. Ms. Tan was not impressed. "You crazy?" she snorted. "You pay a whole ringgit for just two kilo?"

I'd double the length of the book if I listed all the others who guided me along the Asian way. But I would particularly like to thank Chikushi Tetsuya, the Fukuda family, Han Sung-joo, the Koizumi family, the Kuraishi family, Dr. Ho Zhiqian, Hosokawa Morihito, Kashiwagi Akiko, Kim Dae Jung, Lee Keum-hyun, Mah Swee Kien, Kishore Mahbubani, Moon Chung-in, Nakayama Tomoko, Sakurai Yoshiko, Shibata Atsuko, Shibata Masatoshi, Tamaru Mizuzu, and my oldest (in both senses) Japanese friend, Yoshida-sensei. I'm grateful to the newspaper *Nikkan Spohtsu* and the magazine *Shukan Shincho*, which gave me the chance to try out some of the theories in this book on Japanese readers.

Many Americans helped as well, both at home and in Asia. I'd particularly like to thank Kyoko Altman, Paul Blustein, Kent Calder, Clay Chandler, Robert and Joanne Fallon, Ned Kriz, Urban Lehner, Joan and Walter F. Mondale, Fritz Mote, and David Sanger. Dean Ved Nanda at the University of Denver and Professor Hitomi Tonomura at the University of Michigan generously gave me the opportunity to teach—and to use the marvelous research facilities—at their institutions. The Foreign Editors of *The Washington Post*, Michael Getler, Jackson Diehl, and Gene Robinson, tolerated—indeed, encouraged—the unconventional view of Asia reflected in these pages. Bob Edwards and the staff of *Morning Edition* on National Public Radio gave me a chance to share my ideas with millions of Americans, and I'm grateful to the countless people in NPR-land who sent me their reactions. The Japan Society in New York has been helping me, one way or another, for the past quarter century.

I owe enormous thanks to my agent, Gail Ross, who saw what this book could be even before the author did. Not for the first time, the brilliant editor Ann Godoff figured out how to make a book of mine work, with priceless help from Enrica Gadler.

Last but foremost, Margaret M. McMahon, Homer Reid, Penelope Reid, and Willa Reid put up with me and this manuscript in cheery fashion for two and a half years, a task far more formidable than writing any book.

TOKYO   LONDON
1995   1998